THE THEORY AND SCHOLARSHIP
OF TALCOTT PARSONS TO 1951

D0847985

THE THEORY AND SCHOLARSHIP
OF TALCOTT PARSONS TO 1951
A critical commentary

BRUCE C. WEARNE

Chisholm Institute of Technology, Victoria

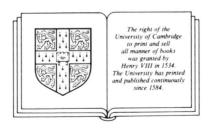

The right of the
University of Cambridge
to print and sell
all manner of books
was granted by
Henry VIII in 1534.
The University has printed
and published continuously
since 1584.

CAMBRIDGE UNIVERSITY PRESS

CAMBRIDGE
NEW YORK   PORT CHESTER
MELBOURNE   SYDNEY

Published by the Press Syndicate of the University of Cambridge
The Pitt Building, Trumpington Street, Cambridge CB2 1RP
40 West 20th Street, New York, NY 10011, USA
10 Stamford Road, Oakleigh, Melbourne 3166, Australia

First published 1989

Printed in Great Britain by
Redwood Burn Limited, Trowbridge, Wiltshire

British Library cataloguing in publication data
Wearne, Bruce C.
The theory and scholarship of Talcott
Parsons to 1951: a critical commentary
1. Sociology. Theories of Parsons, Talcott,
1902–1979
I. Title
301′.092′4

Library of Congress cataloguing in publication data
Wearne, Bruce C.
The theory and scholarship of Talcott Parsons to 1951: a critical
commentary / Bruce C. Wearne.
p.   cm.
Rev. version of thesis (Ph.D.) – La Trobe University, Melbourne,
1985
Bibliography.
Includes index.
ISBN 0 521 37003 5
1. Parsons, Talcott, 1902– . 2. Sociology – United States –
History. 3. Social systems. I. Title.
HM22.U6P3794   1989
301′.092 – dc20   89-1040   CIP

ISBN 0 521 37003 5

TP

Special thanks to Valerie. This book is for Oliver and Nicholas.

Contents

Preface

This book is the edited version of my doctoral thesis submitted in 1985 at La Trobe University, Melbourne. The research was begun back in 1974 with the impetus provided by the late Dr Bernard Zylstra of Toronto. Since that time there have been innumerable persons who have encouraged me along the way. David Bettison, at the University of Waikato, New Zealand, added his advice.

Since 1982, Alan Cubbon at La Trobe University has made a most important contribution to my evaluation of Talcott Parsons. My attempts to unravel the various strands of the argument in *The Social System* were greatly helped by the fruits of his long-term critical appraisal of Parsons' writings. I can now join the many others who can pay tribute to the busy and perceptive scholarship of teachers and mentors who have been so busy gleaning insights for their students that they have scarcely paused to compose journal articles and learned tomes.

I also thank Mrs Helen Parsons and Professor Charles Parsons for their warm and friendly encouragement. Victor Lidz, Clark Elliott, Bernard Barber, Harold Bershady, Jeffrey Alexander, Larry Nichols, Howard Brick, Ruth Barton, Keith Sewell and Charlotte Carr-Gregg are a few of the others who have made a contribution to the thinking that has gone into this book, and to these colleagues I am most grateful.

Thanks also to Tim Harland and Rita Jackson, willing helpers at various times when help was needed.

> Whenever we come upon these matters in secular writers, let that admirable light of truth shining in them teach us that the mind of man, though fallen and perverted from its wholeness, is nevertheless clothed and ornamented with God's excellent gifts. (J. Calvin (1559), *Institutio*, II.II.15)

PART 1
*Unravelling Talcott Parsons'
theoretical development*

1
Introduction

As the reader works through this book the going will get progressively more difficult. My aim, in this discussion of Talcott Parsons' contribution to sociology, has been to encourage the reader to experience something of the way Parsons' project developed, especially in the 1940s. By writing a critical commentary in this way, I wish to encourage a deepened and sympathetic critique of the theory of this 'incurable theorist'. Two central problems are addressed here: how did Parsons develop his theory over time? and how are we to interpret his theoretical statements, especially his major ones?

The method of presentation is chronological and comparative. I compare what Parsons wrote as a professional with what he wrote earlier in his intellectual odyssey. Consequently, I have limited myself very much to what he wrote and I have, in the main, refrained from comparing his evolving theory with what it became after 1951. This, I believe, constitutes the strength and the limitation of this critical commentary.

Parsons' theoretical development, as much as his theory itself, was a complex process. Here I try to outline some of the major lines of continuity manifest in his thought up to 1951. Some of the material I discuss is new, particularly the 'Amherst Papers' (T. Parsons 1922, 1923) – see Chapter 3 – as well as the unpublished paper 'Actor, Situation and Normative Pattern' (T. Parsons 1939/40), examined at length in Chapter 7.

This critical and textual examination of Parsons' writings gives special attention to his theoretical development between 1937 and 1951. These two dates represent the two major publications for which Parsons is famous: *The Structure of Social Action* (1937) and *The Social System* (1951).

These two imposing works have made their mark upon sociological theorizing world-wide for decades. The foundations of Parsons' theoretical approach were laid out in his 'first major synthesis' of 1937, and fourteen years later this perspective was fully developed into his 'major exposition'. Hence the focus of this study.

According to Jurgen Habermas 'any theoretical work in sociology today that failed to take account of Talcott Parsons could not be taken seriously' (Habermas 1981: 174). My aim is to produce a narrative which takes Parsons seriously. I have tried to present the student of social theory with a readable introduction and have concentrated upon showing the consistency and continuity of Parsons' theory *from his writings*. There are indeed many arguments about Parsons' contribution to sociology. I could have contributed to this controversy in novel ways. Perhaps a case can be made for asserting that over the years his theory progressively converged with his father's view of Christianity. How should we interpret Parsons' theoretical differences with Sorokin? How should we now unravel the reality of his theory from the image of 'incurable theorist', and what do we make of the controversial nature of his contribution? There are many questions like these which simply beg to be answered within the ambit of contemporary sociology. I have restricted myself to making a critical commentary on his theoretical development up to 1951. This may disappoint some readers, yet I am convinced that this kind of textual examination is most important.

Where I have broached controversy – namely in relation to Parsons' collegial relationship with his student Robert K. Merton – I have restricted myself to analysis of the public record, setting forth my conjectures in that context. There are other conjectures woven throughout the narrative, yet I would not have counted myself qualified to delve into Parsons' social setting if I had not first attempted to master his written and published statements.

In a previous publication (Wearne 1981) I argued that Parsons' appraisal of Alfred Marshall's economics gave critical leverage to his theoretical outlook, without which *The Structure* would not have been conceivable. Moreover, Parsons there adopted an experimental Paretian approach to the ongoing evaluation of his own theoretical writings and the long-term significance thereof. The incorporation of Pareto into Parsons' 'canon of classics' is indicative of a most important dimension of this theory; surprisingly, this has been neglected in the critical secondary literature.

Although Paretian logic is a most important part of the famous 'convergence' argument in *The Structure*, Pareto, along with Alfred Marshall, is all but ignored in Jeffrey Alexander's recent work, *Theoretical Logic in Sociology* (1982–4).

So this work is envisaged as a conventional secondary analysis of Parsons' theoretical perspective and how that emerged. I do not interpret Parsons solely in terms of Weber and Durkheim, but have expanded the secondary analysis to show, among other things, how Marshall and Pareto were *integral* components of Parsons' emerging project. Given the overwhelming concern in Alexander's work for divining the theoretical logic of sociology in the 1980s, his neglect of Pareto and Marshall is understandable. But this approach is not appropriate when we are trying to set forth Parsons' method in the terms in which he initially formulated it. Camic (1987), by seeking to reckon with the empirical importance of *all* the theorists considered by Parsons, has provided a very welcome addition here.

Moreover, my work not only tries to show the 'inner logic' of Parsons' convergence argument. It also seeks to delve into Parsons' intellectual *Umwelt*.

In the years before his arrival at Harvard in the late 1920s as a tutor in economics, Parsons had been nurtured into the intellectual culture of North American liberalism. As he developed his professional career in the 1930s he adopted his distinctive style of theory-writing. I shall try to outline how this style developed, how important factors from his background became manifest in his scholarship.

The Structure was the work of an aspiring professional. To develop a clear concept of this complex work I have tried to see its central argument in the North American context, in particular the Harvard (social science) academy. In addition I try to develop an argument about the manner in which Parsons continued European lines of theory in a typically American way.

To gain adequate understanding of *The Social System* it is important to analyse it as a product of a literary process. In my view the peculiar form of this famous document has everything to do with the way Parsons worked as a writer. I argue that Parsons-the-writer aimed to become Parsons-the-author.

Critical analysis has been combined with biographical material and other suggestive ideas about Parsons' background. Overall the focus is upon the development of Parsons' theory. Parsons wrote much about the term 'system', but, as he recognized, it is a matter of judgement whether he is to be viewed as a systematic thinker. New aspects of his project did not always emerge in a logical and sequential manner.

In 1951, when *The Social System* was published, another work appeared, the fruit of an inter-disciplinary co-operative effort in the 'theory of action'. This was *Towards a General Theory of Action* (T. Parsons and E. A. Shils (eds.) 1951). There is a slight puzzle here. It concerns Parsons' haste in having *The Social System* published alongside the book in 'general theory'. He says that a draft of *The Social System*, three-quarters completed, was in existence first, and was thoroughly revised in the light of the joint project. He then envisaged the need for further revision five years hence (T. Parsons 1951: ix–x). The three-quarter draft called 'The Social System: Structure and Function' (1949–50) was not published, and the anticipated revision never appeared either. (The 'empirical' chapter on 'Modern Medical Practice' in *The Social System* is the same as in the draft, with only minor amendments.) These facts point to an important aspect of Parsons' work. His theory was always subject to rapid development, with unevenness of progress on its various fronts. He saw a theoretical 'order' emerging out of the past to culminate with the fruits of theorizing in the present. Publication was a convenient sign-post. It indicates a provisional closure to the endless process of revision. Each particular publication dealt with a special problem. Upon its becoming available for professional consideration, Parsons was freed to 'revisit' more general problems. The process went on. Parsons was a writer and author of Theory. If this is kept in mind by the reader of his work then Parsons' writing, as human artifact, becomes that much more accessible.

Important theses about *The Social System*, included in Chapter 11 below, have been formulated on the basis of a close exegetical study of Chapters 1 and 2 of *The Social System*. The actual exegesis does not appear in this book. Such secondary work is somewhat at odds with contemporary academic publishing, and in any case it is perhaps better if the critic of *The Social System* reads it closely and painstakingly for himself. My view of Parsons' contribution has surely been sharpened by trying to follow the twists and turns of his difficult prose. Moreover, I found it very difficult to work out my own critical response to his argument until I began to write my own line-by-line commentary of the work, and I would expect that other critics will have to do the same if we are to contribute to an informed and truly critical debate about Parsons' contribution.

The Social System was chosen for my close exegetical scrutiny rather than the Parsons and Shils essay 'Values, Motives, and Systems of Action' (T. Parsons and E. A. Shils 1951) or the 'General Statement' (in T. Parsons and E. A. Shils (eds.) 1951: 13–29). *The Social System*, also published in 1951, was the culmination of his own project in theory-formulation which had begun in the 1930s. *Towards a General Theory* is important, but the internal logic of Parsons' theoretical development is adequately displayed in his own work. The organization of the material in *Towards a General Theory* gives a false impression about the logic of Parsons' theory. *The Social System* illustrates his 'emergent' logic much better. Furthermore his characteristic style, which also needs to be considered in any thorough examination of his approach to theory-building, is better exhibited in *The Social System*.

The material of this work falls into three phases: (1) the personal background which involves family, schooling and his 'conversion' from biology to social sciences; (2) the pre-1937 development in which he was busy searching for intellectual unity and a basis from which to launch his 'organon' – the theory of action (the Aristotelian term *organon* was the term he used to describe the 'extraordinarily complex' nucleus of Marshall's 'economic theory proper' (T. Parsons 1931: 102)); (3) the process by which he constructed his 'organon' – how he located his 'social system' within the structure of his own thought.

Throughout our concern is to identify major aspects of Parsons' view of the interdependence of the development of theory with the theory itself. This book is a conventional secondary study which takes a textual-critical point of view as its major focus. In other words the focus is upon what Parsons actually wrote, in the context of the theoretical problems he formulated.

There is a brief annotated bibliographical essay of some recent works on Parsons in the Appendix. The character of this work, concerned with how Parsons composed his own theoretical text, precludes exhaustive discussion on the other secondary literature.

The task has not been to demonstrate dogmatically that Parsons' theory was consistent or inconsistent; rather my aim has been to explore its internal consistency. What were the leading ideas of this single-minded project? My assertion that Parsons' theory manifests a consistent continuity of development does not mean, however, that his theory is taken to be internally consistent. Any definitive judgement c' ^that kind will have to be based upon a careful and thorough analysis of his major writings and the other things he wrote, in critical confrontation with his leading ideas.

PART 2
Talcott Parsons:
the roots of his thought

2
Talcott Parsons in relation to the thought of his time

Was this man a Calvinist?

Future biographers of Talcott Parsons might ponder the likelihood that his birth was not a 'meticulously planned' event. He was the sixth and youngest child in his family, considerably younger than the next youngest. His father, Edward Smith Parsons (1863–1943), was a 'Congregationalist' minister of 'calvinistic' orientation, who came from a long line of Yankee merchants. According to Martel he 'broke family tradition' by attending Yale Divinity School and becoming a Congregationalist minister (Martel 1979: 609–10). It is of note, however, that the 'Smith' in Talcott's father's name was given in remembrance of Edward Parmelee Smith (1827–76). Talcott's paternal grandmother was Smith's cousin. This man, also a Congregationalist minister, was general field agent for the US Christian Commission during the Civil War, general field agent for the American Missionary Association after the Civil War, later US Commissioner of Indian Affairs, and still later President of Howard University (Armstrong 1983).

Edward S. Parsons became an independent scholar of social gospel orientation, and specialized in the literary study of Milton (E. S. Parsons 1903). He wrote articles and books on various themes: religious, social and literary (E. S. Parsons 1889; 1904; 1912). Like E. P. Smith he became an academic administrator.

But E. S. Parsons was not a 'strict' Calvinist. Massachusetts Congregationalism, weakened through its controversy with Unitarianism, had dispensed with any 'calvinistic' formulae in the middle of the nineteenth century (Meyer 1964: 80). If Edward Parsons was 'calvinistic' it was in terms of an activistic predestinarianism. The doctrine was accepted as a motor for social action.

Father and son: the Christian-liberal orientation of Edward Smith Parsons

The words of Talcott Parsons can be used to justify this brief excursion into the thought-world of Edward S. Parsons.

> The specificities of significant change could not even be identified if there were no relative background of non-change to relate them to.   (Parsons 1961a: 220)

This principle is applicable to the analysis of intellectual change – the history of ideas. The 'relative background of non-change' – Parsons Snr's approach to society – suggests important themes of New England liberalism which were part of Talcott's world. Martel records what are, presumably, Parsons' own comments concerning his home life:

> Shortly before the outbreak of World War I, the family moved to New York City, where Talcott attended Horace Mann, the experimental boys' high school of Columbia University. He described his home environment as liberal for that era. His mother, Mary A. Ingersol Parsons, was a suffragist who also supported other progressive causes, and his father was a 'social gospel' Protestant of broad academic interests, who accepted the theories of Charles Darwin and viewed science as supplemental to religion. In the fall of 1920, Parsons entered Amherst College, which his father and two older brothers had attended.
> (Martel 1979: 610)

Just how does Parsons Snr's 'acceptance' of the theories of Charles Darwin throw light upon the son's intellectual development? This question can only be answered in general terms and should include some indication of how 'religion' and 'science' were related in Edward Parsons' thought. Talcott writes in the footnotes of his intellectual history that his father was an important personal influence in his switch from biology to economics.

> [In] my undergraduate days a ... basic decision was made, namely to go into social rather than biological science. My switch to social science – a qualified economics initially – was associated with my father, who, during my development, was a college teacher and administrator. When I was a student in college my father was President of Marietta College in Ohio. He had begun his career as a Congregational minister and was very much involved with the then important 'social gospel' movement, which, it is now clear, had much to do with the origins of sociology in this country.   (T. Parsons 1970: 877, n. 23.)

The exact nature of this advice is not clear, yet it seems likely that E. S. Parsons' liberalism was involved. Parsons Snr's approach to society in the late nineteenth and early twentieth centuries is outlined in 'A Christian Critique of Socialism' (1889), 'The Church and Education' (1904) and *The Social Message of Jesus* (1912).

Parsons Snr's critique of socialism, published in the *Andover Review* of 1889, involved an attempt to ascertain which, if any, of the possible relationships between Christianity and socialism was the correct one. Rather than put the case for Christian socialism in which the similarities between Christianity and socialism were the mutual basis for an historical synthesis, he put his case for a Christianized socialism. The great truths underlying socialism had been derived from Christianity in the first place. Socialism did not present them in their correct light. Certain facts had been omitted because socialism denied reality; it had no place for 'the facts of God and sin'. For Edward S. Parsons

Christianity, as the Church militant, should transform culture according to the mandate of its dynamic inner principle. For him 'culture' included systems of doctrine, religious and social, but it referred particularly, in the sense of 'cultivation', to the system of education.

> Christianity cannot yield the field to Socialism. The two cannot work together as colaborers. Christianity must be the teacher, and Socialism the pupil. Socialism must be Christianized, and it is a question whether Socialism could then exist, whether a Christian Socialism is possible. Can the Christian ideas of the worth of the individual and true cooperation be reconciled with the idea of the Socialistic state? One can readily believe that as society becomes more and more complex, there will be a great extension of the powers of the state; but that a Christian society will ever turn over into the hands of the state the control of those interests which are so powerful in the development of individual character is quite a different expectation. But however that may be, society has nothing to fear from a Christianized Socialism. (E. S. Parsons 1889: 611)

On the one hand, Edward Parsons was accepting the biblical doctrines in a personal sense. On the other hand he was using this Spencerian argument to secure a place for individual freedom *over against* State control.

Parsons Snr called upon the heirs of New England Puritanism to take up the Christian cultural task. The *Civitas Dei* will prevail and in the mean time a Christian transformation will only be possible on the basis of an *antithesis* in all social progress. In E. S. Parsons' view, Christians who join the socialist movement out of a desire to Christianize it are actually contributing to a way of life antithetical to Christianity.

Fifteen years later 'The Church and Education' appeared, in which the major issue was no longer socialism but the widespread perception of the irrelevance of the Christian Church. No doubt the 'retreat' of Christian faith involved the advance of evolutionism, yet Parsons admitted that the Church had been shackled by the inherent conservatism of human nature. It had been an obstructive force in the path of human progress.

Parsons Snr's response to this situation was three-fold. His historical argument focussed upon the central role of the Church in the development of education and scholarship. Then the discussion pinpointed the place of the Church in contemporary society. He then identified some important responses that the Church should make.

Historically, the Church had, like all human institutions, 'stood in the way', preventing the Truth coming to light, but on balance the historical record was favourable to the Church. 'He must be a blind man indeed, and woefully ignorant of the progress of human thought during the last twenty centuries, who does not realize the incalculable debt which education owes to the church' (E. S. Parsons 1904: 86). The Church emphasized the 'truth spirit'. The Church was 'one of the strongest influences in the development of the best scholarly type ... The highest type of scholarship is the product of the Christian character and the Christian Spirit' (ibid.: 88). The oft-despised monk in the Middle Ages prepared the way for post-Renaissance scholarly developments. In rather bold and Whiggish fashion Parsons Snr noted:

> The modern world, in a true sense begins with the Renaissance, that strange, bizarre, yet glorious time in the life of the world. And the Renaissance was made possible by the patient, self-effacing toil of the monk in his solitary cell. Of the Renaissance was born the Reformation, and to the Reformation we owe one of the priceless possessions of modern scholarship and modern manhood, freedom of thought, which is the foundation stone of our modern intellectual progress. It is therefore true that we owe to the oft-despised monk much of what has made our modern progress possible.   (ibid.: 89)

The Church had been a central, if not the central, influence within western civilization. Paradoxically the initiatives which the Church encouraged relativized the Church's place in society.

> In its early history Christian civilization needed the outward control which the church gave it; it needed the authority of a master; it needed the absolute monarchy in the church as well as in the state; it needed parental law as well as parental counsel and inspiration. But the world has grown out of the period of infancy and childhood and youth, and now the church sinks back to the place the parent should take after the child has come to years of maturity.   (ibid.: 91–2).

The contemporary Church confronted education in two ways. First, it stood opposed to sectarianism in all forms, including secularism. The secularization of education had occurred when the Church, at the Reformation, proclaimed freedom of thought, the cornerstone of modern scholarship and modern manhood. Second, the Church opposed, in principle, a social order in which any one social institution dominated all social spheres. The delimitation of the Church's task had encouraged other spheres to grow to maturity. The contemporary dominance of secularism was a bleak prospect. But the fact that religion had once been at the centre of historical development gave grounds for believing that 'the pendulum will without a doubt swing back' (ibid.: 93). Parsons Snr anticipated the rejection of sectarianism, believing the tide would turn against the sectarian approach of secularism.

The confessional diversity of the Christian churches does not figure prominently in his discussion. 'Religion', 'Christianity' and 'ethics' are equivalent terms for 'Church'. The emphasis is upon the achievements of the Church in promoting 'the truth spirit', the noblest form of scholarship. The Church has been the preserver of learning.

> To the Church therefore belongs the high honor of having set in motion and directed those influences which have developed to the highest degree of perfection the complex instrument of intellectual and moral discipline and adapted it to the needs of men.   (ibid.: 90)

When the Church becomes the 'inspirer of all of life' – rather than, as previously, the 'controller of all of life' (ibid.: 92) – it will be able to lead the school to a true transmission of ethical culture.

A non-self-centredness should manifest itself in the parent-church when it steps aside and allows the school to come into its own. This had its parallel in the teaching of non-self-centredness for personal ethics. That is the way the social world goes around – in non-self-centred circles. There may be a sense in which this view is an *extension* of a Congregationalist ecclesiology, whereby any central synodical authority is relativized by the principle of congregational autonomy. The principle of individual autonomy is extended into all spheres of social life. And these autonomous realms together relativize each other and are woven into an overall social fabric.

'The Church and Education' represents an interesting movement in the Christian perspective of Edward S. Parsons which is completed in *The Social Message of Jesus* (1912). The earlier approach is a critique of socialism from the standpoint of Christian individualism, whereas the 1904 article, whilst critical of contemporary trends, is an attempt to assess the co-ordinate relationship between church and public school, inspiration and education. The common element is the moral framework of society which Christianity, though now in decline, was instrumental in establishing. Christianity by definition is the central part of the institutional fabric of liberal society. The second article moves towards a 'corporate' view of society based upon an individualistic view of humanity.

Faith is synthesized with an evolutionary view of social history, and it is in these terms that Parsons Snr's 'acceptance' of the theories of Charles Darwin should be understood. In the earlier article a Christian individualism was the basis of Parsons' critique of socialism. The Miltonian torch of freedom was counterposed to State control. Socialism was evaluated as a regressive social movement which denies the moral progress which had been achieved in western society. The individualistic criterion is balanced by a corporate and public 'Christian ethic'.

In the earlier article Parsons Snr seems to have argued in terms of 'Christ the transformer of culture'. The later approach bears more affinity with the 'Christ of culture' standpoint (Neibuhr 1951). In the consideration of this transition, and the issues which he raised, a parallel with Ernst Troeltsch suggests itself:

> Little by little, for Troeltsch – a distant disciple of Melancthon – the problem of Protestantism's fate was widened to embrace the problem of the destiny of Western civilization. In him Christian and humanistic Europe posed the question of its own essence and drew up an inventory of its own values ... he hoped to derive from his analyses a clarification of the energies which had contributed to the rise of the West. He thought, moreover, that it was a duty and a vital necessity to proceed in the direction indicated by history.   (Antoni 1962: 41)

The period in which the young Talcott grew up falls into the later phase of his father's transition from contra-sectarian Christian individualism to a more secular, cultural form of Christian faith. *The Social Message of Jesus* (1912) begins in a most significant way for us concerned with the religious background against which Parsons Jnr developed his theoretical perspective:

> The lessons which follow do not aim to be a course in sociology, nor a discussion, except in an incidental way, of particular social problems. They aim to develop, from a study of His words and His deeds, the message of the great Teacher to His own generation and to every generation.   (E. S. Parsons 1912: 5)

There follows an exposition of New Testament teaching concerning human society. The Gospel is re-presented in terms of a social message; Edward Parsons covers the entire spectrum from the personal level, through family and social and economic groupings to the State. The work is in the tradition represented by Peabody, *Jesus Christ and the Social Question*, Shailer Mathews, *The Social Teaching of Jesus*, Rauschenbusch, *Christianity and the Social Crisis*, and others. Along with these writers he concludes that socialism is 'the completest modern expression' of Jesus' message.

> Jesus' message to the social life of His time and ours is . . . simply the application of the principle and motive of brotherhood . . .   (ibid.: 109)

This principle must come to expression personally, in the home, in industry in the relationship between employer and employee, in social circles, in education, throughout the nation and internationally. E. S. Parsons' view of the home is also spelled out:

> Oftentimes it is in the home that men and women find it most difficult to manifest the spirit of brotherliness; there an opportunity is too often found for a relief of the tension under which the restraints of good society put the individual, and a wife, or a child, or a brother, or a sister, is the object of an irritation which its subject would be ashamed to manifest toward any one outside the home. The spirit of the kingdom must change all this.   (ibid.: 110)

Students are needed, he concludes, who will use 'the organization of the Church and the untold power of the co-operation of those whom it has gathered into its membership to bring in the fullness of the promise of the kingdom' (ibid.: 114–15).

We recall that E. S. Parsons' saw his embracing of the theories of Charles Darwin as an intellectual decision in the faith that one day Christianity would again be publicly powerful. The resolving of the seeming irresolvable conflicts between religion and science must, he implied, be left in the hand of Providence. He had used a version of Spencer's rendering of human history, as the lawful development of 'individual freedom', to buttress his Christian hope. And we see here another side of E. S. Parsons' accommodative approach in which Christianity and socialism are brought together. By 1912, E. S. Parsons had concluded that the Christian transformation of socialism he had advocated in 1889 had been almost completed. Not only does he assert that socialism is 'the completest expression of Jesus' message' (ibid.: 5), but he also sees Christian socialism as the wave of the future. His work ends on a footnoted plea:

> Nothing is more significant socially and religiously, of better things to be than the drawing together of the labor unions and the churches. What can we do more than we are doing to complete this movement?   (ibid.: 115, n. 1)

So it is not only 'religion' and 'science' which were synthesized in E. S. Parsons' liberal Christian perspective, but also 'individualism' and 'socialism'.

In his intellectual autobiography Talcott Parsons refers to his father as having been 'very much involved with the then important "social gospel" movement, which, it is now clear, had much to do with the origins of sociology in this country' (T. Parsons 1970: 877, n. 23). The phrase 'it is now clear' indicates that the connections were not always clear even though the switch from biological to social science in the first place was 'associated' with his father. The fact that Parsons Jnr did not broach the 'social gospel connection' analytically in his writings, together with the fact that American writers do not figure at all prominently in his 'first major synthesis', indicates in fact that the young Talcott had a very strong sense of the derivative character of American society. Yet when he looked back to his roots he steered clear of making public any direct links with his familial context.

There seems to be an enduring ethic at work here, not unrelated to styles of thought characteristic of American liberalism. The first step is to make a break, assert an antithesis, make a declaration of independence. Then, in retrospect, 'it becomes clear' that the first step has its roots in the context from which independence had been asserted. In Talcott Parsons we are, I think, confronted with a certain cognitive style that has its basis in his response to the Christian liberalism espoused by his father. Talcott had grown up in an atmosphere in which one progressed on the basis of personal achievement rather than through inheritance. We can only surmise about E. S. Parsons' view of his application of the ethic of Christian brotherliness in his 'behind the scenes' fatherly support for his youngest son. But when we see Talcott in the context of the all-embracing Christian liberalism of his father, recurring themes in his thought take on a new importance. For instance, Parsons' earliest professional contributions in social theory involved his appropriation of the *inheritance* of recent European thought. Or another example can be found in relation to the famous 'pattern variables'. Crucial to this formulation is Parsons' understanding of the relationship between ascribed and achieved status, private and public spheres, family and public life. His search for personal achievement, mixed with his father's Christian liberal scholarship and his mother's suffragette progressivism seemingly also somewhere in the background, clearly encouraged him to look for the underlying patterns in social life. His theory would not interpret this order in a way which would draw attention to himself, yet he carried on the non-self-centred philosophy of Edward Smith Parsons, with the ethic of *public* accountability which that implied.

Parsons Snr had promoted an open interface between Christianity and the philosophies of the secular world. He had no sympathy for those who, building a fence around Christianity and the Bible, would try to keep intruders at bay.

Rather, welcome scientific investigation, higher criticism, rationalism, philosophical speculation – welcome every storm which beats upon the rock of faith. If it is rock it will stand; if it does not stand, our hearts tell us that God will provide for our feet some surer, safer resting place.   (E. S. Parsons 1904: 95)

This could well be indicative of the way the middle-aged Parsons encouraged his youngest child. Talcott did not see himself as a very religious person. Unlike his father he did not aim to integrate his learning with the Christian faith, but did follow the open, intellectual experimentalism which his father encouraged. The 'truth spirit' enabled E. S. Parsons to accept the theory of evolution in so far as it provided new answers. Evolutionism was kept within bounds by the basic question of consistency with Divine Will. Young Talcott, on the other hand, not only accepted evolutionary answers as legitimate, but came to view evolutionism as the basic tenet of his world-view; the question of evolution was the basic question. It highlighted the relative character of the evolutionary concept, and it inspired him to try to understand the evolution of theoretical knowledge.

Talcott Parsons followed the spirit of intellectual inquiry stressed by his father. Parsons Snr had linked the 'truth spirit' to the Renaissance via the Reformation. The son followed the Renaissance tradition, and kept a keen eye on the results of the Reformation. Whilst not appropriating the Reformational heritage for himself in a personal and confessional sense, as his father had done, Parsons Jnr came to accept an historiography of science which implicitly linked the this-worldly orientation of Protestantism to the development of modern science (Merton 1938/70). This was somewhat implicit in the liberal perspective of his father (E. S. Parsons 1904). In this way Calvinism and Puritanism, for Parsons, were important religious forms of humanistic consciousness. Together they represent the building-blocks of the modern scientific outlook.

Parsons' link with the Puritan world-view sets his theory apart from positivism. He was consciously oriented to a non-positivistic and liberal tradition of science.

3

The Amherst Papers

Classical schooling and Amherst liberalism

In 1920 the eighteen-year-old Talcott commenced his studies at Amherst College. He had graduated from Horace Mann School for Boys in New York, a 'highly unorthodox' education in preparation for college. Horace Mann, a unitarian educationalist from Massachussets, had founded a school which aimed to give 'the best possible preparation for college to boys intellectually and personally fit to profit by going to college'. The school was 'no place for weaklings or idlers'. The system was strict. 'Students who had been absent or had fallen behind in academic work had to study on weekends to make up their deficiencies and to pass special examinations. Demotion in individual subjects and the elimination of generally weak students were established principles of the institution.' The temperature of the classroom was kept at 55–60 degrees F, but 'it [was] found more satisfactory to let it fall below these limits than to rise above them'. In a word it was a school which was built upon the principle of the survival of the fittest. The aim of the school could be summed up in these terms: 'If a boy wishes to hold his place in the school, he must deserve it' (Prettyman 1915).

Staff–student camaraderie was facilitated by a sporting ethic. The young Talcott played soccer and was the manager of the only occasionally successful ice-hockey team. He was obviously a top-grade student. In his final year, 1919/20, his subjects were English, German, US History, Latin, Physics, Prose and Algebra (Horace Mann Records 1919/20).

In 1920 he entered Amherst College. This New England school was led by a President and academic staff who were wrestling with the same problems which had exercised his father. How was the relationship between Christianity and society to be understood? What was the link between personal faith and public morality? Where was a student to obtain his orientation for a useful life? The approach of Amherst stressed the importance of a practical Christianity. Horace Mann provided a neo-classical education with a heavy stress on Latin and German literature; Amherst also attempted to make some innovations, but it stressed an integrated liberal education. Amherst was trying to build a classical-liberal curriculum (Feuss 1935: 307–25, Chapter XXII: 'President Meiklejohn's Administration'; Gaus 1923: 7).

Parsons' discovery of intellectual unity

Parsons' commitment was to theorizing. This was the scholarly activity for which he would be known. What, then, were his deepest questions when, in his early years, he set out to discover intellectual unity?

Unlike some others (e.g. Freud 1963; Galbraith 1981; Skinner 1976), Parsons never wrote an autobiography exploring the personal sphere, and there have been no full biographies exploring the character, background and passions of this 'incurable theorist'. It is as if Parsons wanted to be simply known as a 'theorist'. This not only meant that he would seek to 'do theory' as his vocation; theory became the vehicle for expressing his 'large as life' response to liberalism. This would be his means of establishing himself in his own right. It is this desire to be known simply as a 'theorist' which is *the* central biographical datum which emerges from our examination of his writings.

Even his empirical studies come to function within his theoretical way of viewing things. His study on 'modern medical practice' came to light as a chapter of *The Social System*, illustrating the way in which such a study could contribute to such a comprehensive theoretical overview. In *The Structure* the results of his textual analysis are 'Empirically Verified Conclusions'. Thus, for him, 'general theory' was his specialization. Having become publicly known as a theorist, via his writings on 'general theory', Parsons responded to the academic public by continuing to present himself in these terms. His theory was instrumental in creating the 'theorist' stereotype by which he became known, and he stuck to it. This combined with what was, by all accounts, a 'very private' disposition. References in his writings to the personal sphere are always brief and anecdotal. It is not easy for us to know from his writings how he was nurtured or how he viewed his own parents. We never hear any reminiscences of his schoolboy adventures or of his experiences at the open-air biological laboratory at Wood's Hole. We cannot tell for certain whether he viewed his mother or his father as the greater influence upon his own cognitive orientation. From his own published comments we infer that his father was more important. Yet the few references are inconclusive. An indication of his personal uncertainty about how his thinking was formed is provided by his late-in-life *mea culpa* with respect to L. J. Henderson (T. Parsons 1977: 31–2 (new footnote 21)). He had *always* acknowledged Henderson as a central influence upon his reflections, underlining the fact at a most important time in his development (T. Parsons 1951: vii), but in the 1977 amendment he apologized for his failure to give Henderson his due. The personal uncertainty which this reveals could well be central to his intellectual orientation.

In the mid 1920s Talcott Parsons had become absorbed in the analysis, and interpretation, of Weber's *Die protestantische Ethik und der Geist des Kapitalismus*

(Weber 1904/5). His now famous translation appeared in 1930. Whether this absorption tended to resolve any intellectual problems created by his religious upbringing and scientific interests we do not know, but Talcott's fascination with Calvinism and evolutionism did mean that he followed in his father's footsteps – his father exemplified the fact that acceptance of evolutionism was not then precluded by a predestinarian theological outlook (see E. S. Parsons 1912).

Perhaps Talcott Parsons' most 'calvinistic' statement was his early assertion that 'Every theory of what is rational and economic, must be based upon some doctrine of "the chief end of man" ' (T. Parsons 1934b: 623–4). He defined himself as a Calvinist in an objective-cultural sense. In private correspondence with Eric Vogelin in the 1940s about his differences with Alfred Schutz, Parsons noted that he interpreted his own character as 'calvinistic in a cultural sense'; he added that being calvinistic in background had meant a personal aversion to philosophy – he was disposed instead to a scientific frame of reference.

(Possibly one of my troubles in my discussion with Schuetz lies in the fact that by cultural heritage I am a Calvinist. I do not want to be a philosopher – I shy away from the philosophical problems underlying my scientific work. By the same token I don't think he wants to be a scientist as I understand the term until he has settled all the underlying philosophical difficulties. If the physicists of the 17th century had been Schuetzes there might well have been no Newtonian system.)

(T. Parsons and E. Vogelin 1941, Parsons to Vogelin, 18 August 1941)

When the *innerweltliche* orientation of Calvinism is viewed as the autonomous cultural motor producing the modern scientific mentality, it is but a short step to a modern and secularized world-view. Such an outlook might well require a logical equivalent to 'Providence' or 'God's guidance in history', and in my view the concept of 'serendipity' functions in this way in the reflections of Talcott Parsons. Parsons was not a Calvinist in any strictly *intellectual* sense. But his style certainly gives evidence of his 'calvinistic' and liberal background. Let us look closer at that background to appreciate his American and 'calvinistic' roots.

The spirit of non-dogmatic inquiry

If Parsons had inherited anything from his father it was the bequest of a wide-ranging and exploring mind. Originally, the biological sciences with a future in medicine held his interest. Parsons Snr's influence seems to have changed that.

Talcott's theory was developed in the awareness of the secularization of western thought. Despite his calvinistic 'background' his basic questions were those of a humanist with an increasingly secularized view of knowledge. His theoretical advancement was propelled by an attempt to find those questions which were improperly put by preceding generations of thinkers. This was the manner of his advance, rather than seeking answers to the questions posed by the leading thinkers of the past (Bridgman 1955: 149–50).

The difference between son and father can be described in this way: for E. S. Parsons the experimental and cognitive investigation of the world in all of its modes is to be undertaken in the spirit of the Christian religion – his method was animated by a passion to be free from intellectual dogmatism in much the same way that Bacon had resisted Aristotelian scholasticism. Even so, 'openness' to the real world, even in Bacon's case, was based upon the belief that creation has been ordered by the Creator. Such a view is indicative of a 'frame of reference'. The claim of 'openness' implies an attempted non-reliance upon man-made interpretative systems, and in this sense Parsons Snr was 'open' to all kinds of new 'answers'; he was open to admitting that his basic question was a human question, but he also considered his 'basic orientation' to be a bequest of Divine Providence – the 'truth spirit'. That dimension of human activity stamps human faith as human *and* divine.

Parsons Jnr 'questioned the question'. His pre-1937 years can be interpreted as his search for his own 'basic question'. Whether he consciously abandoned the faith of his childhood or whether he just 'let things slide' (see T. Parsons 1951: 48) we do not know for sure. But his father's anti-dogmatism does contrast with his own perception that all people act on the basis of some or other 'frame of reference'.

Parsons Jnr accepted a modified form of apriorism. Talcott rejected the so-called open-minded approach of empiricism, which his father seems to have justified on Christian grounds. He took for granted that the empiricist 'letting the facts speak for themselves' was fallacious.

On another level, positivism had imposed its *faith* in the methods of natural science upon all the data of social action. It destroyed the validity of a scientific approach to human subjectivity. Instead, it directed attention to what could be stated in objective terms.

Parsons' approach to science was empiricist in the sense that science would demonstrate its utility in its own terms if left to do its own work. But how does it do this? In general it may be said that science is the construction of frames of reference for the analysis of facts. Facts, therefore, are *always* constructed in terms of a conceptual scheme. This view would avoid both *empiricism* and *positivism*. Parsons was committed to scientific open-mindedness, but he also tried to be open-minded about what this meant. In my estimation, his focus upon 'voluntarism' in social action coincided with his acceptance of the need for commitment in scientific theory-building. In this sense he followed Max Weber quite closely.

Eventually Parsons accepted that his own frame of reference derived from the god of Science: Evolution (T. Parsons 1937a: 41). But the young Talcott, convinced that everyone operated on the basis of some 'basic question', had first to decide which basic question his own search would be based upon. That puzzle intensified during his Amherst years.

The Constitution of Amherst College tied its policy 'so however, as not to deviate from the original object of civilizing and evangelizing the world, by the classical education of indigent young men of piety and talents' (Amherst College 1818: 2 (Art. 3)). Parsons was at Amherst some 100 years after the founding of the college, when the original aim of providing a classical education for future ministers had receded from its horizon.

The Meiklejohn 'awakening'

Parsons came to regard the Meiklejohn sacking as one of those serendipitous happenings which helped push him to the social sciences. The reasons for his move from biological to social science give an impression of uncertainty. His entire career perhaps was his attempt to clarify the reasons for, and implications of, this change. In his personal history he noted that the change 'is associated' with his father. The use of the present tense in his footnoted reflection (T. Parsons 1970: 877, n. 23) indicates this surfaced as an important factor only in his later reflective consciousness.

During 1920–4 Parsons developed a deep respect for Alexander Meiklejohn and the progressive thinkers on the faculty at Amherst. Meiklejohn and Parsons Snr shared an idealistic, liberal and public allegiance to Christianity.

The Meiklejohn sacking involved a severe community-wide disruption (Feuss 1935: 323–5). Thurman Arnold refers to the 'celebrated intra-faculty dispute over the resignation of the President of Amherst, . . . who was allegedly compelled to resign because the trustees of Amherst objected to his progressive educational views' (Arnold 1968: 315–16).

Meiklejohn had been 'at the helm' for ten years. Talcott's father and two older brothers were 'Amherst men', so it is not surprising that Talcott was active among the student body defending the President. After the sacking, when a new President had been installed, he with Addison Thayer Cutler publicly defended Meiklejohn in a national student newspaper – the *New Student*. Both were in the Senior Year and among the top seven students of their class, members of the select 'Bond Fifteen' (Amherst College 1924).

The Parsons–Cutler article, 'A Word From Amherst Students' (T. Parsons and A. T. Cutler 1923: 6–7), is a liberal and critical analysis of the polarities that had emerged. They attempted to convey their student understanding of the social processes at work in the disruption. Antagonism within society was drawn as a result of structural evolution in the progress of intelligence. The impression gained from this article is that it was Meiklejohn's reforming liberal perspective which had encouraged the Senior Year to return to Amherst for the 1923/4 commencement.

In his Junior Year, Parsons tells us, he was 'converted to social science under the influence of the unorthodox "institutional economist", Walton Hale Hamilton' (T. Parsons 1970: 826). Having been converted from biology to a new-found interest in social science, Parsons found his Senior Year disorganized as a result of the sacking. Hamilton went too. He was 'the leader of a group among the faculty that protested against what they considered interference by conservative businessmen in the educational policies of the college' (T. Arnold 1968: 315). This group, which included Clarence Edwin Ayres, Parsons' Junior Year philosophy teacher, resigned *en masse* in sympathy with Meiklejohn.

Parsons stressed that the conversion was to social science rather than to 'institutional economics'. Yet institutional economics was central in his change of course. A Junior Year philosophy class on 'The Moral Order' was his introduction to sociology, and this was taught by Ayres.

> We read Sumner's *Folkways* (1907) and a whole lot of things by people like Charles
> Horton Cooley and Emile Durkheim. We also read a lot of Thorstein Veblen, for
> Veblen was an important mutual hero of both Hamilton and Ayres. So institutio-
> nal economics was really my jumping off place.   (T. Parsons 1959: 4)

But it was also more than that. 'Institutional economics' had an impact which was to last beyond his Amherst years.

This kind of liberal education encouraged a method of critical self-reflection. An Amherst professor had discussed this course in the *New Student* early in 1923, only months before the dismissal. It was, he said, congruent with the entire educational programme. The course was perspectival. It was intended to unify the student's entire college experience into a meaningful whole. Intelligence, according to the Meiklejohn version of liberalism, was to discover the relationships which hold things together. These were not simply abstract and theoretical. The long-term aim of such discovery was the building of a liberal and humanistic culture.

> We may define a liberal culture as one which gives a unified interpretation of the
> human situation, and a knowledge of the means whereby that interpretation has
> been made possible. Such a culture, then, includes both content and method. Its
> basis is not a mere collection or confederation of any courses a college may offer,
> but rather a synthesis.   (Gaus 1923: 7)

The aim was that the student would construct his own scheme of values. In this way the college would help build a truly humanistic culture. The course had three basic foci: the first two, the physical world and the social heritage of institutions, codes and ideas, were studied as the two basic aspects of the world. The third was the study of the constitution of the dual world by mankind in literature, art and religion. Via this third aspect, the course stressed intelligence, participation and action.

In Meiklejohn's ten years he had tried to 'de-professionalize' sporting contests. The Student Association and the 'intellectuals', amongst whom Parsons was numbered, backed this initiative, and won the 'more sports-minded' over to their point of view. Parsons and Cutler tell us that an 'awakening' amongst their third-year cohort meant that the majority of the 107 students supported Meiklejohn as a matter of principle.

The Junior year saw a great intellectual change in most members of the class of

1924. It is often said that the Sophomore year is one of breaking down the illusions and prejudices and that the rebuilding must come in the later years. During the last year [i.e. 1922/3] after having many of our old ideas very completely shattered, we had a chance to see what the Amherst of President Meiklejohn had to offer in their place.   (T. Parsons and A. T. Cutler 1923: 6–7)

Was Parsons referring to himself here? Perhaps. Not only was one's nurturing placed in a new perspective, but one's inherited familial viewpoint was replaced by one's own perspective. Parsons, already very much at home in the Amherst environment, interpreted the ambivalence of his fellows as one who understood the tension.

Meiklejohn and Hamilton were supporters of Christianized public morality. The liberalism of Meiklejohn had close affinity with the approach of Parsons Snr holding high the Miltonian torch of freedom. Yet there were also important differences.

For Meiklejohn learning is criticism (Meiklejohn 1923b: 50). Edward S. Parsons held to the 'non-negotiables' of a faith upon which basic questions were to be framed. For Alexander Meiklejohn there was a faith to question. Parsons Snr saw the Church as the institution which inspired the entire community; to serve, it had to heed developments in modern scholarship. But for Meiklejohn liberalism led on to another phase in developing the critical spirit.

For E. S. Parsons, an individual has a personal need for 'truth'. With Meiklejohn the emphasis is upon 'intelligence' as something a person *does*. Parsons Jnr would later refer to intelligence in these terms: '*not* primarily as a trait of the individual but as a generalized symbolic medium of interchange'. His focus was upon the level of the general system of action (T. Parsons 1973: 70). He continued:

Intelligence is a generalized *capacity* controlled by any acting unit to contribute to the implementation of cognitive values through knowledge, through the process of cognitive learning, through the acquisition and use of competence, and through the pattern of rationality.   (ibid.: 70–7)

For Alexander Meiklejohn, Christianity expressed society's deepest values and as such was the means of mounting an intelligent criticism of society. In this way an *intelligent civilization* was promoted. The Christian idealism of Edward S. Parsons was oriented by its links with the past. Alexander Meiklejohn's idealism was oriented to the future. Action in terms of a (traditional) norm, for E. S. Parsons, corresponds to action oriented by intelligent choice for Meiklejohn. Talcott Parsons seems to have incorporated elements from both his father and Meiklejohn into his alternative theoretical perspective.

Committed to the Meiklejohn approach, Parsons and Cutler wrote as 'loyal Amherst men'; in spite of the fact that the Meiklejohn dismissal seemed to have been a victory for the forces of reaction, the two students wrote as Amherst liberals.

Meiklejohn had lost the battle, but he had not lost the war. Front-line command was now passed on to his students. Parsons and Cutler in taking up the Meiklejohn cause promoted 'true loyalty' to Amherst. Meiklejohn had shown them what Amherst really stood for, and they now applied his insights to analysing why he had been dismissed. Meiklejohn explicitly announced that their place was at Amherst (Meiklejohn 1923b: 51–5).

As if continuing that analysis, Parsons gave his graduation speech a year later. His topic was 'Secret Diplomacy'. Record of the speech is lost, but perhaps it was foreshadowed in the *New Student* article. Parsons' support for Meiklejohn's ideals clearly did him no harm at Amherst. He was appointed instructor in economics for the year 1926/7, even though he had gone on public record with Cutler as being willing 'to stake a great deal' on their support for Meiklejohn ideals. Parsons, from the evidence we have of him, was mature in his loyalty to Meiklejohn. He would honour this teacher because of his ideals. Parsons learned from this man that he had to take responsibility for developing his own frame of reference, and this kind of personal responsibility remained an inherent part of his view of intelligence (T. Parsons 1973: 70–1).

Parsons also imbibed something of the institutionalist understanding of institutional constraints. The critique he (with Cutler) mounted is from *within* the institutional setting. He sought insight from within the intellectual pattern of his time. This ethic of intellectual independence and personal exploration characterized his life-long contribution to sociological theory. He was a reforming liberal and *not* a sectarian.

Clarence Ayres at one stage worked at systematizing the institutional economics which Hamilton had left unfinished (Breit and Culbertson 1976:7). Ayres and Hamilton, inspired by Veblen, taught an alternative way to promote liberalism from within liberal society. Two essays that remain in Parsons' papers are from the Junior Year Philosophy III Course taught by Ayres. These papers are very early attempts by Parsons to develop a systematic theory of human society, his liberal intellectual response to the institutionalist challenge.

Parsons' initial response to critical liberalism

Parsons' two term papers are: 'The Theory of Human Behavior in its Individual and Social Aspects' (19 December 1922) (T. Parsons 1922) and 'A Behavioristic Conception of the Nature of Morals' (27 March, 1923) (T. Parsons 1923). They were written *before* the Meiklejohn dismissal and were envisaged as part of an ongoing study programme. He hoped to develop the theory of 'intelligent behavior' at a 'later more enlightened time'. They are at the beginning of our analysis of Parsons' development. Parsons refused to be identified as a philosopher, but his developing theory cannot be fully understood if the connection with Meiklejohn's philosophy of education is overlooked. The papers present a maturing approach to the analysis of the human condition. The style is similar to that of his later essays. His method is synthetic, summing up overall trends; in addition he comments upon the course in general terms. The essays are reports of 'thinking in progress'. They were the experimental part of the course. Quotes were few. Parsons' method of essay-writing did not involve close and detailed exegesis. He aimed for an 'overall viewpoint' of all the issues involved.

These experimental documents aim to derive approximate and provisory principles for explaining social forces. In these two papers Parsons seems to be won over to the 'education is an adventure' point of view. In the very process of writing his response to the course his own innovative ideas emerged in the context of the conventional wisdom. In this way he saw himself progressing.

> May I say, in closing, that although the paper itself may be rather incoherent, the writing of it has done more to bring out the important issues of the course than any other thing in connection with it.   (T. Parsons 1922: 23)

In the second paper Parsons concluded by anticipating 'a closer and more detailed study' of the nature and the function of 'intelligent behavior'. Presumably the final-year course was in view. It was cancelled when the Meiklejohn supporters quit.

> But that must be reserved for a much later and more enlightened time in the progress of this study of the moral order.   (T. Parsons 1923: 24).

Hamilton had outlined this approach to study in the following terms:

> Its concern is that a student should get interested in a problem and follow that problem wherever it may lead him. Its appeal is to the student, not to the docile pupil. It holds that no one can teach, that the teacher can only help the student to learn for himself. It is too conscious of the complexity of the world to believe that absolute truth can ever be surprised and is content with modest statements ... Its methods are those of honest and joyful inquiry, from tentative statement through many hazards to tentative statement.   (Hamilton 1923: 9)

This is also the perspective Parsons developed in these essays. Without such a framework the intent of the essays will be misread. There is a humanistic evangel involved in this educational orientation.

> In brief, education as an adventure aims to lead students to think by allowing them to think, to acquaint them with themselves by allowing them to see their living selves, to show them the world by allowing them to discover the world, to make them free by helping them to master themselves.   (ibid.: 10)

To this evangel Parsons had been won. Now he accepted that the first place in the curriculum should be given to helping students see how they had been shaped in their social and intellectual environment. The intellectual adventure involves a search for clarity about this process. These essays involve his appraisal of the changing socio-cultural milieu. The problem is followed wherever it leads; 'the problem becomes clearer as we go along'.

'The Theory of Human Behavior in its Individual and Social Aspects'

Parsons' experimental method in social science did not require a statement of procedure at the outset. It was half-way through 'The Theory of Human Behavior' that he formulated his procedure:

> In developing this argument we have taken the individual as our starting point and are trying to build up our theory of social organization on that basis. It is evident, however, that at no stage can we completely separate the individual from the society of which he is a part.   (T. Parsons 1922: 9)

Near the end he wrote:

> In this paper I have attempted to develop, however inadequately, the idea of human society as a product of cumulative change with its essential motive force the creative force of each individual contributor, small though that may be.
>
> (ibid.: 22)

Here the young student was somewhat perplexed about where he was to start. Once started he could order his thoughts by reflecting upon them. This order of narrative construction was a characteristic of his essay-writing throughout his long career. It is also the reason why the sympathetic reader is faced with a hermeneutical 'uncertainty principle' in his writings.

The difficulties involved in reading Parsons' essays are reminiscent of the conflict between Bohr and Heisenberg. The development of quantum mechanics by Bohr and Heisenberg had meant that the theory of atomic reality, and the sub-atomic structure, had become confused by a conceptual conflict between *particles* and *waves* (Weisskopf 1984). Parsons' writings are his *theory*, however much they contain reflections on work in progress and intimations of a more complete theory. They are the finished formulation of his conceptual scheme (particle), *as well as* his unfinished 'thinking in progress' (wave). His Amherst essays illustrate this duality. And Parsons' writings have always evinced both 'wave' and 'particle'; process and concept.

The wide-ranging first essay examines the philosophy of behaviourism, which views the universe as one continuous mechanism. Parsons illustrated its approach by reference to the dynamics of gas molecules. The action of any one molecule is determined by all the other molecules with which it comes into contact. In addition all the molecules together are largely controlled, in their movement, by the size, shape and temperature of the container. This analogy illustrates the relation of the individual to his environment. The movement of the molecules is congruent with human action, and any differences are due to the degree of complexity rather than of kind. The fact that the human body is composed of chemical molecules proves this point. But then Parsons wants to consider the mental or moral side of the individual. This, he wrote, is expressed by various social relationships. Behaviourism in psychology rejects the psychophysical parallelism of MacDougall and instead of speculation about psychic entities and instincts gives the prominent place to the concept of habit by focussing on the behaviour of the organism as a whole. Parsons opted for a behaviouristic wholism, a behaviourism which is changed from within by a rejection of any reductionism. He proceeded to apply the concept in a variety of contexts.

Psychoanalysis is viewed as a recent theory in which behaviour is considered to be organized into interrelated groups of ideas or complexes. It is referred to with approval.

> The conception, however, of behavior organized into complexes, which are really complexes of habit, habits of thought and of action, is most significant and does much to illumine our conception of human behavior. It brings out the immense significance of habit in our lives and the fact that it is really the hard, resisting fabric, which when it is once formed is so hard to break or even greatly modify.
>
> (ibid.: 6)

With the idea of complexes Parsons could analyse the development of the individual from birth to adulthood. Habit-forming influences are the most important factors determining a person's specific modes of action. But his emphasis is upon what has shaped the individual.

> The effect of the individual upon the institutions in which he finds himself bound up, is almost negligible compared with the effect which these institutions have upon him.   (ibid.: 7)

The discussion returns to analogy. People in 'the great organism of society' are likened to food being taken into the body via the digestive system. The influence of any one individual is very small, but when individuals are seen *en masse*, it is clear that society is subject to a constant state of change. The integration mechanism of institutions or individuals is counterbalanced by the differentiating action of separate individuals or groups of them.

> It seems that the two forces are always seeking to reach an equilibrium but never quite get there. Perhaps they will reach it by the time that the earth is as cold as the moon is now supposed to be.   (ibid.: 8)

Parsons here follows his father into Spencer's concepts of equilibrium and structural differentiation. Forty years after reading Sumner's *Folkways*, he would write an introduction to Spencer's *The Study of Society* (T. Parsons 1961c). Sumner's reading of this work had formed 'the decisive event of his life' (Persons 1963: 2). There is a restless search for balance on the micro-cosmic level, and meanwhile the great universal forces of the physical macro-cosmos overarch all minor events and give them their ultimate, yet infinitesimal, meanings. The 'great scheme of things' has thrown up 'life', for an instant, as it were; what seems of great significance to people is but a pin-prick of light in the ever-expanding void.

Parsons redefined his direction by appearing to take issue with a dichotomy in Cooley's theory:

> Our discussion of individuals is for the purpose of analysis purely. It must not be supposed, as Mr Cooley so strongly asserts, that when we discuss persons and when we discuss society we are talking about different things. We are merely looking at

the same thing from different points of view. The same actual materials, the biological individuals, make up both and hence it is reasonable that both are the same thing.   (ibid.: 9 (see also T. Parsons 1951: 18))

I note that this dissension from Cooley is almost identical with what Cooley actually wrote:

> A separate individual is an abstraction unknown to experience, and so likewise is society when regarded as something apart from individuals. The real thing is Human Life, which may be considered either in an individual aspect or in a social, that is to say, a general aspect; but is always, as a matter of fact, both individual and general.   (Cooley 1902: 36–7)

Almost identical, but not quite. Perhaps he was trapped by his own clumsy syntax, but just before this famous passage on the 'abstraction unknown to experience', Cooley had written:

> If we accept the evolutionary point of view we are led to see the relation between society and the individual as an organic relation. That is, we see that the individual is not separable from the human whole, but a living member of it, deriving his life from the whole through social and hereditary transmission as truly as if men were literally one body.   (ibid.: 35)

Hence for Cooley individual and society are two things constituting reality, whereas for Parsons it is a matter of viewing biological individuals from differing points of view. At Amherst, Parsons appears to have been a biologist challenged to become a scientist of society. Hence also his taking issue with Cooley.

Parsons next considers the relationship between psychology and culture. A knowledge of innate psychological traits of a people can only give a very general outline of a cultural pattern. Following Lowie, Parsons opted for the view that the most important factor determining a culture is the culture which preceded it. *Omnis cultura ex cultura.* In seeking a scientific explanation of cultural phenomena the historical method will prove to be the most fruitful, even though the psychologist will be of more help than the chemist in uncovering cultural factors. Culture bears much more on applications of psychology than of chemistry, but the difference is one of degree only.

> The psychology acts as a sort of set of boundaries which limit the operation of our causes, but is not in itself the primary active determinant.
>   (T. Parsons 1922: 10)

When Parsons moved from biological to social sciences it provided a perspective which cut across the various specialisms on either side of the natural science/humanities division. The essay moves on to the anthropologists whose business it is to study 'the evolution of culture' and 'to get at its organization from the historical point of view' (ibid.: 12).

In the *New Student* article Parsons and Cutler had referred to the unorthodox history course in the sophomore year, the net result of which was 'a considerably changed notion of historical process' (T. Parsons and A. T. Cutler 1923: 7). Presumably this means that human agency has to be identified amongst 'dates and famous people'. The general picture of a culture and its people derived from the psychological point of view has to be supplemented by an anthropological understanding of culture from the historical point of view. Parsons aimed for a general overview. Psychology and history have to be synthesized.

The theory of 'convergence' and the theory of 'diffusion' were the two current opposing anthropological theories of the evolution of culture. According to Parsons, both seem to have elements of truth. Convergence was 'very closely related to what is called the Biogenetic Law in biological evolution' (T. Parsons 1922: 12, 13). All cultures pass through the same phase of evolution. Diffusion, on the other hand, involved the view that there has been one world culture from the beginning. Parsons opted instead for a broad psychological homogeneity of human civilization in which both convergence and diffusion 'are of tremendous concrete importance'. The details which distinguish one culture from another, and which make one culture comparable with another, cannot be explained in psychological terms only. Parsons' conception of cultural anthropology included the cumulative effect of culture, psychological differences, the effects of cultural isolation and cultural fusion; he also recognized conquest as an important factor. All these factors contribute to civilization. Growth by internal necessity (convergence) was the internal force of development within the 'human group'. This was balanced by the other great influence – diffusion. Diffusion was the cultural effect which different civilizations exerted over each other when they came into contact (ibid.: 15). Following Sapir, Parsons included a discussion of both forces in the development of language. Before he concluded his discussion he made some observations about 'physical environment' and 'race, genetics and heredity'. These too were part of the analysis of human behaviour. He summed up his approach in these terms:

> I have attempted to bring out the tremendous conservative force of habits in determining the conduct of the individual, and of the habits of society or its institutions in shaping the habits of the individual.   (ibid.: 22)

The use of the term 'conservative' was not meant in political terms. It focusses attention upon social control of the creativity of each individual. Parsons considered that this conservative force is integral to the human organism – habits of thought and technology go together. There were three basic modal aspects of this organism – the physico-chemical, the psychological-mental and the social-moral. Likewise society is a whole. In conclusion he asserts:

> Our conception of society is as an organization of complexes of behavior into which the activities of each individual are inextricably interwoven.
> (ibid.: 22–3)

'A Behavioristic Conception of the Nature of Morals'

The second essay, 'A Behavioristic Conception of the Nature of Morals', developed a conception of moral order in which the 'moral factor' is identified with the 'social whole'.

> So we will consider 'the moral order' to denote the whole organization of social behavior ... and in particular show how the portion of it which might in the narrow sense be called moral or ethical fits in with the rest.
>
> (T. Parsons 1923:1)

Here biological analogies prove useful. In the human body the structures concerned with circulation, digestion and sensation are interwoven. These three 'inextricably interwoven' systems make up the human body. Parallel to this there are three principal phases of social structure: technology, institutions and ritual. Intelligence had emerged as a prime integrative factor in culture.

Durkheim's views of the sacred and the profane were here introduced in relation to ritual. In primitive life the distinction between the sacred and the profane was fundamental. The sacred is always expressed in ritual with the corresponding mystery and lack of understanding which that implies. Religion includes an intellectual element, the content of which depends upon the science of the time. The sacred, pre-eminent in all societies, contrasts with the profane, and the knowledge of this realm must always exist. Here Parsons, qua scientist, showed a bias towards the profane. For support he referred to Durkheim's *The Elementary Forms of Religious Life*.

Parsons has always referred to Durkheim in terms of his 'unlearning' the interpretation given at the London School of Economics some years later. But in this 1923 essay we do not detect any fallacious 'group mind' conception, which he was to learn from Ginsberg and Malinowski (T. Parsons 1970: 828; 1959: 7–8). Parsons' undergraduate essay implies that Durkheim's theory contributes to a better understanding of the *psychological* aspects of experience.

Apart from the three phases of social structure, Parsons isolated two other independent variables of cultural development – 'knowledge' and 'taste'. Knowledge is the intellectual side of mores whilst taste is the emotional dimension. They both 'cut through' the three phases of social structure.

What follows is an extended discussion of art explaining how taste functions in all aspects of the social order (T. Parsons 1923: 7–12). Parsons' argument opposes the common notion of art as a result of some divine gift. In his view art is a matter of technical perfection. This requires a long and arduous process of mastery.

> The modern workman, no matter how humble his occupation, practises an art. He does some specific technical job and does it well. In this sense the term represents the consummation of what Veblen calls 'the instinct of workmanship'. To make something with the hands and brain, whether it be for practical purposes or not, that is intrinsic art in its most general sense.   (ibid.: 7)

It is a sophisticated discussion about art and technique. Parsons discussed the ceremonial origin of all contemporary fine art. Art and religion have a common origin, something the modern secular mind is apt to overlook.

> Even now, however, this detachment is not by any means complete, and it is evident from a thorough analysis of the problem that the two represent essentially the same attitudes of mind.   (ibid.: 8–9)

The art critic is compared with the 'art connoisseur' – in a discussion of Veblen's concept of 'leisure class' motives. Both have an interest in art. The critic's appreciation has to be refined through a long association and usually a great deal of painstaking study. The 'connoisseur' aims to give an ostentatious display of wealth. Both types of art 'appreciation' are usually resisted by the masses, who think there must be 'more' to it than technical competence or mere exploitation for personal aggrandisement. Parsons, contrary to these popular views, emphasized 'cultural effort' – work in its full context. Such effort is not merely physical; it is motivational.

> It seems to be an almost universal fact that things worth while in the best and widest sense are by no means easy of attainment. Any old person cannot go out and off-hand, without training excell [sic!] in any field of endeavour he wishes. Practically all excellence in any field requires hard work and steady application. Is it strange, then, that both great attainments as an artist and worthy appreciation of the artist's work should be in the same category; that it should require long association with or submersion in the cultural influences that have produced said work?   (ibid.: 12)

For Parsons the cultural equivalence of 'art critic' with 'artist' is quite logical. The mores governing art govern various kinds of human effort which is expended in relation to this sphere. Thus the conservative character of the mores is displayed. The mores are a conservative factor, constraining the behaviour of people; art 'work', of whatever character, has to operate in relation to the mores. The mores can only be refined in exceptional circumstances. Developing Sumner's views at this point (Sumner 1906), Parsons continued:

> Only a few can get far enough out of the mores to be able to intelligently criticize them and to direct their own actions to some extent by rational, highly utilitarian motives; to do things not because others do them, but because there is some reasonable ground on which to think them worth doing.   (ibid.: 13–14)

Rational and enlightened thinking might, on occasion, run counter to the institutional complex of mores in society, but it is the mores which shape intelligence rather than rational action shaping the mores. Modification to the mores is slow, incremental and only achieved after a long continuous effort, usually over many generations. But how, asks Parsons, do mores develop? 'In the middle ages . . . the "mores" were accepted without question as of more or less absolute origin' (ibid.: 14). But for modern times things had changed. Parsons found it helpful to move on to an examination of post-Darwinian intellectual culture and developments in the evolutionary theory in biology.

He directed his attention to the central intellectual problem – *the evolution of evolution.*

Early evolutionary theory had argued for the effect of mores upon the growth of intelligence. The theoretical character of the concept was acknowledged. But with the acceptance of the theory came the widespread assumption that humanity is the inevitable result of the process; in these ways a dogmatic twist was introduced into this creative way of thinking, leading to the notion of a super-race.

> Hence we have the general statement of biological evolution that it is the process of change from simple to complex, from amoeba to man, etc. This statement seems to err by over-simplifying the problem very greatly.   (ibid.: 15)

Those who followed Darwin have caused his name to be associated with a dogmatic unilinear concept of evolution. After the work of Mendel on inheritance (the modern theory of mutations), and other careful scientific work, a view different from the unilinear conception of evolution had emerged:

> the present attitude is a great deal less of a dogmatic assertion and more of a tentative hypothesis. It is in short this: Organic evolution is carried on by the mechanism of inheritance.   (ibid.: 15)

Evolution itself had become an element in the process of development from one generation to the next.

> At more or less irregular intervals and in a manner not very clearly understood, rather abrupt changes or mutations tend to appear which from then on breed true to the type thus established. Whether or not any specific mutation will survive or not depends upon its relation to the environment in which it finds itself.
> (ibid.: 15–16)

Parsons perceived that some other factor enclosed within the mores of the time had hindered intellectual progress by twisting Darwin's theory into a dogmatic system. Early-twentieth-century sociology and anthropology had taken on the unilinear evolutionary concept. The historical schemes of Morgan and Maine were indicative of this aspect of the intellectual mores of the time. Morgan's formula of three principal stages (savagery, barbarism and civilization) was probably the most naive example that could be found. In the light of contemporary knowledge it was 'utterly ridiculous'. Maine's work on the development of legal systems showed the hand of nineteenth-century British individualism. Similarly Dewey and Tufts in their *Ethics* showed a similar mode of thinking. Hobhouse's history of reason, giving the various stages in the evolution of reason 'from the beginnings of amoebid behavior through the whole gamit of tropisms, reflexes, instincts, habits and intelligence', is also found wanting (ibid.: 19). Parsons recalled his earlier essay and the part played by internal growth and diffusion in cultural evolution. Most of these a priori theories had given an inordinate emphasis to 'convergence' without giving due regard to 'diffusion'.

Thus no one individual, and in like manner, no one culture, develops all its own cultural features from within as a biological race does through a variation of the germ plasm. It acquires such a large proportion as to make this acquirement the ruling factor in the lives of all but a very few individuals, and an important one in all except completely isolated societies, that is it is that fact which forms the basis of the mores.   (ibid.: 19–20)

Mores were developed through diffusion – cultural interchange. In the final pages Parsons addressed himself to the problems raised by theory's embeddedness within time and in particular to theory's relation to the mores of his time.

Will not our theories be as much colored by science and relativism as Maine's was with individualism? This is of course ultimately an unanswerable objection, but we have to act on some sort of preconceptions, and this by no means makes it inevitable that one set of preconceptions is no better than another.   (ibid.: 22)

To test this argument, we could ask whether this statement (i.e. 'we all have to act upon some kind of preconception') is itself a formulation of the communal mos. But though the question appears to relativize the meaning of the statement radically, we should not conclude that Parsons refrained from believing that his theory was right. He considered that his theory corresponded to the facts. In science the truth is always a matter of the degree of correspondence between the always-tentative formulations of theory and the facts. He was working at increasing the degree of correspondence.

The only real justification of any theory is whether it works or not, whether it fits the facts.   (ibid.: 22)

Parsons' argument focusses upon the 'evolution of evolution'. This is an early formulation of an analytical 'uncertainty principle' in his social theory (T. Parsons 1937a: 41). It is not just any theory that is subjected to Parsons' relentless analysis; it is also his own theory and his own theorizing, his non-unilinear theory of the evolution of morals. With the unilinear theory of evolution superseded, the task of science remains unchanged.

As Lowie so aptly says, about the only thing we can do is to get all the facts we can possibly dig out and make such generalizations as we can piece out of them.
                                                            (T. Parsons 1923: 21)

The method of science is related to the progressive development of knowledge by scientific investigation. A scientific explanation of mores will play an important part in this evolution of knowledge.

We have to get at the causes of this change (i.e. in civilization) by careful analysis of an endless mass of evidence, and draw conclusions when we can, and only when we are reasonably justified in doing so. We have to recognize the irrational origin of many of the mores, and make sufficient allowance for it in our theories.
                                                            (ibid.: 22)

Mores, Parsons concluded, are dependent upon the past; there is very little one person can do to change them, and they are in a state of constant change. What can be achieved in social change can never negate the fact *that* social change is dependent upon what has been handed down from the past. This fact cannot be changed.

From these two essays we detect the influence of Veblen and Sumner. But did he then acquiesce in their views? There is sufficient reason to suggest that even in these early essays Parsons was attempting to *diverge* from their patterns of thought. Sumner had described the 'mores' thus:

> They coerce and restrict the newborn generation. They do not stimulate to thought, but the contrary. The thinking is already done and is embodied in the mores. They never contain any provision for their own amendment. They are not questions, but answers, to the problem of life. They present themselves as final and unchangeable, because they present answers which are offered as 'the truth'.
>
> (Sumner 1906: 1038b)

Parsons perceived in Evolution a means, a hypothesis, by which the mores of evolutionism could be significantly modified. In this way he began to 'question the question'. Rather than simply taking his place within the 'mores' and working out answers to pre-determined questions, he began to ask: how adequate is the theory of mores for explaining how human agency shapes mores? It was via this route that he chose to 'get far enough out of the mores to be able to intelligently criticize them' (T. Parsons 1923: 13).

Parsons' theoretical orientation around 1923/4

In the past few pages I have summarized two of Parsons' junior-year term papers. They show the method of a maturing and self-critical scholar. An aversion to dogmatic affiliation with any theory or school can be detected, but there is a bold assertion that science needs to be developed past its current stage of accomplishment. We see the early stages of an interdisciplinary approach, a liberal orientation to learning which anticipates 'further research' into the nature and function of 'intelligent behavior'. Ironically the project he had begun in Philosophy III was not to be brought to any provisional culmination in his senior year. Maybe he interpreted the disruption as confirmation of Sumner's view of the mores and social change. Maybe also he was tempted to concentrate upon philosophical speculation rather than scientific theory.

> I made do with more courses in biology, some in philosophy, including one on Kant's 'Critique of Pure Reason', and some in English literature.
>
> (T. Parsons 1970: 826)

Parsons' liberalism and his emergent theory of society stamp his contribution as that of a non-conservative. But his analysis of society was an attempt to expose and to clarify the conservative aspects of liberal social structure; he outlined the potential for individual creativity within the social context. The person, or the group, can do very little to change the institutional complex of mores within which social life, though still developing, is constrained. Thus for

Parsons, like Durkheim, education, as an ongoing intellectual process, had a particularly important role.

Parsons' training does not seem to have been shaped by a devotion to secondary literature. His knowledge of the intellectual mores provided the framework for his projected theoretical contribution. The institutionalist critique of the conservative structuring of social institutions gave Parsons room to develop his own social perspective. Whilst further refinement would be required, this critical standpoint also suggested a method for analysing the current phase of the history of social theory as a basis for his own social theory work later on. An appreciation of theoretical 'diffusion' would be one step towards discovering any analytical 'convergence' in recent social thought.

Intellectual adventure

Parsons was encouraged to go to the London School of Economics for a year without registering for a degree. Presumably, after the year at LSE (1924/5) he would be in a better position to attempt graduate study at an American university. His Amherst AB, together with his acquaintance with the developing institutionalist school, made graduate study in economics a possibility. American sociology of the time did not attract him. Probably the LSE trip was part of a 'general education'. He was exercised by economics, the philosophy of history and the intellectual opportunities raised by the 'evolution of evolution'. He had moved away from biology and medicine. The trip seems to have become Parsons' attempt to find his feet in study. He was now making his own way on an uncharted path.

> After graduation from Amherst I went to the London School of Economics, which was another rather unorthodox move. Formal sociology was taught there, and I got a great deal from T. L. Hobhouse [sic] (whom he had earlier criticized in his class papers, T. Parson 1923: 19) who was still teaching, and his successor, Morris Ginsberg. But the formal sociology was not the most important influence on me. Without any question the most important influence on me there was a man I had never heard of before I arrived, Bronislaw Malinowski. He introduced me to an area of borderline considerations between sociology and psychology, and started out my interest in problems of kinship, family structure and socialization. All these were things about which I had certainly never had any real inkling in the Amherst phase.   (T. Parsons 1959: 4)

What did Parsons mean by 'no real inkling'? After all, these matters *were* dealt with, after a fashion, in his Philosophy III papers. Parsons' ambivalence about the pre-Malinowski phase of his odyssey involves his uncertainty about the extent to which institutional economics shaped his sociological frame of reference. It is most likely that any specialist 'sociological' frame of reference had not then firmed in his mind. Any claim to be a specialist in sociology could only be made after further training. His own theory of social expertise, as expounded in his discussion of the artist and the art critic, indicates that even had he then aspired to a specifically sociological career, it would require more training. His Eurocentrism indicates, as well, a desire to break away from the intellectual mores of North American sociology, at least for a time.

The approach of Hobhouse and Ginsberg did not make any lasting impact upon his theorizing. Though Hobhouse was the most important social evolutionist in the English-speaking world after Spencer (T. Parsons 1973: 77–81), his metaphysically based sociology was not attractive to Parsons. Instead the problem of the 'evolution of evolution' seems to have turned him in an analytical direction.

Before he went on to Heidelberg from London he had accepted an instructorship in economics at Amherst. His correspondence with Manthey-Zorn was, it seems, rather important. Then came the offer of a German exchange fellowship. By January 1926 Parsons had decided on his thesis topic and the preparations for his teaching at Amherst for the 1926/7 academic year were well in hand (T. Parsons and O. Manthey-Zorn 1925/6). The 1925/6 academic year had been a particularly important one. If sociology was to be his speciality, and his Amherst teaching post included responsibilities for an 'advanced course in sociology', then he would have to come to terms with both the 'evolution of evolution' and also the changing form of the philosophy of history and historicism he had found in Germany.

Parsons' task was set out for him. He would immerse himself in the institutionalized mores of the social sciences. But like the art critic he needed to establish an easy familiarity with the field. He had to acquaint himself thoroughly and systematically with all the technical dimensions of theory production. Parsons set himself very high standards. He aimed for a high quality in his work. Only with hard work towards such a goal could he hope for the exceptional circumstances which could lead to a change in the predominant 'mores' in the theoretical field. If his long-term contribution to the discipline was to be effective, it would need to be via a distinctively new direction in sociological theory.

PART 3
The development of theory

4
Max Weber and the vision of a unified social science

Taking bearings

When Parsons was 'converted' from biological to social science in Walton Hamilton's economics course, the problem of capitalism and the structure of western society were the central issues. Within the modern world some societies had greater links with their past than others, and at the back of the institutional critique of economics was the way in which American scholars appropriated European intellectual developments. This is a most important dimension of our attempt to appraise Parsons' reasons for neglecting the American theoretical developments which had emerged prior to his own discovery of Max Weber.

Seckler points out that the institutionalist critique emerged against the background of *Historismus* and *Methodenstreit*, and the appropriation of the legacy of the German historical scholarship in the American context. Seckler goes on to point out that the misidentification of institutionalism with *Historismus* has meant that much of the criticism of Veblen simply missed the mark.

> The importance of the historical school (i.e. the German Historical School and its American followers) lies not in its real but rather in its imputed influence. When Veblen published his attack on mainstream economics, ... [he] seemed to be advocating an even more pernicious doctrine than the specific *Historismus* in economics. It sounded like Hegel and the philosophy of history ... Veblen had utter contempt both for the historical school of economics and for the philosophy of history. Indeed, he was one of their most formidable critics. Yet the conjuncture of his writings with these controversies caused him to be indelibly identified with both. (Seckler 1975: 19–20)

We shall note here in passing that in *The Structure* Parsons goes close to identifying Hegel with the German Historical School, and moreover institutionalism and the Historical School are bracketed as essentially 'anti-theoretical orientations' (T. Parsons 1937a: 125, n. 1; 477).

At this point in our discussion we need to consider the United States in its relation with Europe. Was the United States a separate culture or simply a variant of European civilization? How was a young American scholar to conceptualize this? Parsons discovered in Weber's *global* perspective a way to move towards his own answer. It may have provided him with a means of side-stepping any feelings of cultural inferiority. It may suggest that at this stage Parsons began to see himself as a member of global society, by refusing to circumscribe his role purely by reference to his American background. Parsons began to reflect theoretically about the common institutional basis of European society and its derivatives.

The interpretation of recent German social theory

There were two steps Parsons had taken before his own theory emerged. The first concerned Max Weber, whose thought was representative of the mores of recent German social theory. The second involved the history of economics and Weber's place within that.

Parsons' consideration of Max Weber in his *Journal of Political Economy* articles established his scholarly standing. During the years 1928–30 Parsons translated Weber's 'Die protestantische Ethik'. The *JPE* articles, alongside 'The Protestant Ethic', were the initial public expressions of his intellectual independence.

For Parsons the material–spiritual dichotomy was but one way of developing understanding of the human spirit. In this sense Parsons' thought showed an affinity with that of his teacher Karl Jaspers (Jaspers 1961; T. Parsons 1979). Parsons saw Weber's theory in close proximity to Oswald Spengler's *Der Untergang des Abendlandes* (Spengler 1920; T. Parsons 1928: 658; 1929: 46–7). The philosophic and pessimistic dimensions, he knew, required philosophical clarification. But Parsons, looking for *scientific advance*, focussed upon Weber's method. Spengler had anticipated the decline of the West; Parsons saw a scientific offensive in the social sciences. For Parsons social science was a part of a renewal in western society; the frontiers of Europe had shifted as the New World began to assert its maturity. The relentless genius of western freedom idealism was beginning to reassert itself creatively in the realms of social science. The USA was related to Europe just as the early Roman Empire was related to Ancient Greece (T. Parsons 1933: 5–6). And it is this historical world-view which should be kept in mind when we consider Parsons' earliest response to Max Weber's thought.

Parsons' Heidelberg research involved him in the writings of Max Weber, which for all their insight did not present a systematic theory. These writings provided Parsons with analytical *problems* – a unique theoretical task. Whereas Ayres had begun to systematize the writings of Veblen, the youthful Parsons threw himself into the task of coherently representing Weber's theory.

Unlike Sombart, Weber never developed a unified theory of capitalism. In spite of the fact that a very large proportion of his sociological work was devoted to this problem, he left only a number of fragments which from our point of view are to be regarded as special investigations. It is thus unavoidable that in piecing these together a certain element of construction should enter in.

(T. Parsons 1929: 34)

He resolved this problematic with a hermeneutic reminiscent of Bohr and Heisenberg's resolution of the conceptual difficulties encountered in quantum mechanics. The assumption is that a fixed core of theory can be found in Weber's writings (particle). But his theory also operated on various levels in its own historical context (wave) (see Weisskopf 1984: 587–90). This same problematic can be seen in his second Philosophy III essay (T. Parsons 1923: 21–2) (see Chapter 3, pp. 26, 35 above). Despite the obvious bias in favour of a scientific mind-set and the uncertainty of epistemological relativism, Parsons went ahead and 'constructed' his response to Weber's theory.

Yet Parsons could not 'place' Weber in his historical context without also redefining the initial phases of his professional career. Parsons turned from the restrictive dogmatism of 'institutional economics' to fashion his own cosmopolitan approach. His intellectual style was an implicit challenge to the mores. He did not direct his attention to the institutionalist appropriation of *Methodenstreit*. Instead he presented a new account of the history of western social thought. If American social theory was to incorporate European developments in terms spelled out by Sumner's history of theory, then no innovation could get very far. But Parsons wanted a frame of reference which would transcend the various conflicting utilizations of European social thought on the American frontier. He would then return to New England promoting an American sociology with an immediate sense of its European origins. It is worth repeating that, in this view, Parsons was not the 'connoisseur' of European social theory in any Veblenian sense. Instead he saw himself as the 'critic'. He 'apprenticed' himself to the technicalities and details of the European social theory, in a painstaking search for overall patterns and new insight. By rejecting institutionalism as anti-theoretical he avoided the previous attempts to appropriate the insights of the *Methodenstreit* debate in the American context. His 'construction' of Max Weber's thought becomes the beginning of his contribution to theory. Max Weber became the personification of the mores for Parsons' social scientific enterprise.

Alfred Marshall's economics was a 'fulcrum' for Parsons' development in the early 1930s. Pareto's theory of residues was much more important in his method than has been recognized (Wearne 1978; 1981). The utilization of Durkheim's theory in Parsons' reflections was a later development (1935 onwards), despite the brief Amherst encounter. So, Parsons' response to Max Weber and the intellectual milieu of social science at Heidelberg in the mid 1920s constitutes the initial turning point. His Heidelberg teacher, Karl Jaspers, had observed that the way to honour a great man like Weber was by endeavouring to make his labours one's own and to develop further the lines of his ideas (Jaspers, quoted by Fischoff 1963: xvii). Parsons interpreted Weber's theory of capitalism in this way. It was this general orientation which guided his 1930 translation of Weber's 'Die Protestantische Ethik und der Geist des Kapitalismus' (Weber 1904/5/1930).

The ten-year period from Parsons' Heidelberg studies until his 'first major synthesis' was an enriching time in his theoretical development. His marked copy of the 1925/6 *Heidelberg Catalogue* (T. Parsons 1925) indicates his interest in political and legal philosophy, the history of theology, and the philosophy of religion. He took classes with Rickert, Jaspers, Salin and Lederer among others. Of note is the coincidence that, like his Amherst teachers, his liberal and social democratic mentors had, only a few years before, taken a very strong national stand against undue outside involvement by business and government in university affairs (Ringer 1969: 202–3, 497). The Amherst controversy could too easily be read as the disruption of a provincial town when compared with the sophisticated *Realpolitik* of the Heidelberg group, but Parsons' development occurred as the maturation of a new world-view, in which socialism found a new accommodation to the liberal tradition. His courses with Heinrich Rickert were in *Weltanschauungslehre*, whilst with Jaspers he studied the philosophy of religion. These teachers were important shapers of twentieth-century philosophy.

The climate was neo-Kantian. Was this the time when a 'Copernican revolution' occurred? Undoubtedly Parsons' ethic of intellectual independence was extended by the neo-Kantian climate of Heidelberg. It was in this environment that he immersed himself in the ancient traditions of European thought.

Finding classical roots

For Parsons' actual writings at that time we consult 'Capitalism in Recent German Literature' (T. Parsons 1928; 1929). The English-language articles were eventually accepted by his examiners as his 'definitive dissertation' (Schluchter 1979: 13–15); here we will keep to those. Although they were written for examination in Germany, Parsons set forth his views with an English-speaking, predominantly American, audience in mind. It is of note that his examiners, Edgar Salin, Karl Jaspers and Alfred Weber, considered the two-part discussion as the best re-presentation of Weber's work that was then in existence (Salin, quoted ibid.: 14–15).

In my view there are still important aspects of Parsons' theoretical development which remain to be disclosed by a close and comparative analysis of the German *Kapitalismus* manuscript with the English 'Capitalism' articles. Such careful and critical work will provide most important insight concerning Parsons' theoretical orientation in the late 1920s.

How did Parsons see the relationship between Europe and America? In his Harvard lectures in the early 1930s he commented upon this relationship in terms of the historical connection he perceived between Ancient Greece and the Roman Empire.

There seems to be a possibility that the United States stands to Europe somewhat as Rome stood to Greece. It is a very large unit, rather heterogeneous within. Culturally, like the Romans, we are not creative, our genius is 'practical'; that of the Romans having been predominantly political and legal, ours is mainly economic. We, like the Romans, are fairly receptive to art and taste, and to ideas, tho we do not create them. There seems a fair possibility we may help create a social framework within which European culture can have a fairly long life of peace and enjoyment, but not development, a predominantly hedonistic era. The parallel seems to apply in science. America has been prolific in invention, but hardly in basic scientific ideas in the sense in which either Greece or Europe has been. The unity of our culture is rather that of economic–legal institutions, than the type of basic 'consensus' which always seems to be involved in a creative culture; though the most brilliant culture often appears during the breakdown of such a 'consensus'.   (T. Parsons 1933: 5–6)

Parsons' 'Capitalism' articles were his initial attempt to introduce into his own context a recent development in the German scholarly tradition, which, he wrote, was little known outside its own milieu (T. Parsons 1928: 641–2). Parsons was convinced that he had been given something to say, through his contact with German continental scholarship.

An American contribution might help create a long-lasting equilibrium now that Europe had reached a kind of plateau, but 'great breakthroughs' were *not* to be expected. In the early 1930s 'stability' was to overshadow 'plasticity' in cultural development (to use the concepts of Cooley). Yet those engaged in theoretical and intellectual labour need not rule out advance a priori.

The 'consensus' Parsons divined in 'recent European social thought' has a futuristic implication, but in the late twenties and early thirties we see Parsons intent upon confirming himself in the role of 'steady worker' – one who painstakingly laboured in terms of a longer-term view of things. His later discovery of 'convergence' might in fact be the completion of his attempt to overthrow Weber's pessimism. But if there is a tension between 'optimism' and 'pessimism' in Parsons' thought, then this is held in place by his optimism concerning the future. The future role of social theory is never in doubt. Parsons' view of America's relation to Europe provides us with an idea of how he saw his own contribution on the world stage.

'Capitalism' confronted in a new context

Let us look at what Parsons wrote in his doctoral articles. The 'Capitalism' articles are neither rhetorical nor polemical. The overall effect is somewhat ambiguous. Weber is presented as having transcended the dialectical relation between Marx and Sombart in the history of social theory. But Parsons' relation to Marx was problematic, and it may have then had something to do with his rejection of Veblenian economics. Sombart and Weber had suggested solutions to general problems for social theory. Parsons' discussion of their contribution generalizes about their historically oriented work. They, in turn, had based their generalizations upon a massive tradition of cumulative research.

Parsons' aim was to introduce 'another major strain in modern thought' (T. Parsons 1928: 641). From its individualistic and rationalistic roots, orthodox economics had developed abstract theoretical systems to analyse economic behaviour. It had failed to account for the historical evolution of economic systems. But it had not been the only approach.

> It has been pre-eminently occupied with the problems of history, and among its most important accomplishments is the formulation of various philosophies of history, in Germany notably those of Hegel and Karl Marx. It forms the background of the theories which this paper is to discuss.   (ibid.: 641)

Capitalism, no longer only a system of mores which defines a person's position in society, is a great epoch in social and economic development. It defines the meaning and significance of individual action. Parsons aimed to explore this concept. The theories of Sombart and Weber were his way in.

> In both Sombart and Weber there are views of history which are largely to be understood as answers to the questions raised by the economic interpretation, and in each there is a further development of the idea of capitalism as an epoch of history, tinged with the views of Marx, but at the same time showing important divergences from him and from each other.   (ibid.: 642)

Sombart and Weber in their scrutiny of global economic developments went beyond any national and provincial interest. And Parsons would continue the transformation they had begun in economics by deriving further analytical insight from their work.

The ideal-type and coherent analysis

Parsons did not totally go along with the then current American view of the anti-theoretical character of the German Historical tradition (Iggers 1968: 63–5). Explaining the approach of Sombart, as this was manifest in his 1902 six-volume *Der moderne Kapitalismus*, he had this to say:

> He is certainly not alone concerned or satisfied with working out an ideal type of capitalism which has for him only abstract interest, but his theory is a means of illuminating and understanding the concrete historical development. But he is not a 'mere' historian. He is interested, not in working out the particular circumstances of the economic history of any single country for its own sake, but in presenting European economic life as a whole, in its great common trend, and in getting at the laws of its development. His aim is thus definitely theoretical, and his work should be judged as a whole from that point of view. The term 'theory', however, is here used in a different and more general sense than that common in economic science, to mean, not merely a system of equilibrium, but any consistent and unified system of concepts to be used in the analysis of social phenomena.
> (T. Parsons 1928: 643–4)

Parsons' deep dissatisfaction with the divide between history and theory led him to consider how theoretical analysis operated in orthodox economics. Theory should not be non-, un- or anti-historical. But then history should not be subordinated a priori to the requirements of some abstract system. Historical science has its own theoretical character. Sombart's analysis was theoretical because he attempted to construct an 'economic system'. An economic system, as an attempt to capture the concrete reality of an 'economic epoch' analytically, was Sombart's version of the *ideal-type* (ibid.: 644).

It is difficult to represent the logic of Parsons' view if his argument is only analysed sequentially. The *ideal-type* concept is not explicitly discussed until the second instalment, where Weber's analysis of capitalism was considered (T. Parsons 1929: 31–2). Then another dimension of Parsons' consideration of Sombart emerges. The reader can be forgiven not just a little confusion. The implication is that the *ideal-type* is also a device for injecting *literary*, and not simply *analytical*, unity into theoretical discussion.

According to Parsons the *ideal-type* was Weber's special instrument of sociological analysis by which he sought interpretative understanding in investigations of cultural phenomena.

> It is a special *construction* in the mind of the investigator of what social action would be if it were directed with perfect rationality toward a given end.
> (ibid.: 31–2).

The *ideal-type*, a special instrument for the analysis of the infinite array of facts which confront the historical and interpretative social sciences, requires that a meaningful selection must be made. It must be a purposely fictitious construction which can never occur in reality; it must be a picture of what things would be like under ideal, not actual, conditions (ibid.: 32).

Parsons used this instrument himself in his investigation of Weber's thought. But he also applied the *ideal-type* in his discussion of Sombart's 'economic system'; the difference in its application emerged in his comparison of the respective theories of these two thinkers.

> Unlike Sombart, Weber never developed a unified theory of capitalism. In spite of the fact that a very large proportion of his sociological work was devoted to this problem, he left only a number of fragments which from our point of view are to be regarded as special investigations. It is thus unavoidable that in piecing these together a certain element of construction should enter in.   (ibid.: 34)

For Parsons, Weber's writings were the 'infinite variety of facts from which a selection for purposes of analysis must be made'. To make this selection and reach 'understanding' about Weber's theoretical orientation, Parsons required an *ideal-type* to enable him to reconstruct Weber's overall approach. He interpreted Weber as one who attempted to construct his theory by means of cumulative historical research – historical analysis provided the 'raw data', the analytical building-blocks, for his kind of systematic theoretical reflection. Parsons came to see Weber's Author's Introduction to the 1922 *Gesammelte Aufsatze zur Religionssoziologie* (Weber 1922) as a most, if not *the* most, pregnant statement of Weber's sociological method (Nelson 1974). The Author's

Introduction was a kind of ideal-typical representation of Weber's sociology as a whole.

But Sombart's theory is Parsons' fictitious picture of what Weber's theory would have looked like if he had lived long enough to formulate it comprehensively. Sombart's theory of capitalism functioned as an *ideal-type* for Parsons' reconstruction of Weber's theory. This is a surprising conclusion. Whereas Weber was later to become the personification of the analytical mores for contemporary sociological theory, Sombart's theory was used to illustrate the mores within which Weber laboured.

How did Parsons reconstruct the basic thrust of Sombart's theory? What *ideal-type* did he utilize in the analysis of his writings? Parsons was less than consistent, indicating a desire for theoretically relevant and practical conclusions rather than the scholarly desire for intellectual consistency. His critical attitude derived from a scientifically trained mind; his workmanship was 'practical' rather than 'elegant'. He was the 'theorist' rather than the historian or the philosopher of history.

In the background of Parsons' analysis of Sombart was Karl Marx, the central figure for the theory of capitalism. The major point of reference for Parsons' analysis of Sombart's theory was Marx's belief in the creative power of capitalism. Marx was a cultural optimist, but Sombart believed that salvation could only be found by a departure from capitalism (ibid.: 660–1). Marx had launched an economic interpretation of history in which social evolution was viewed as *one* process. Sombart, however, held to the concept of 'historical epoch', discarding the dialectical and evolutionary connections between systems, leaving them, in principle, quite discrete (ibid.: 659). Marx and Sombart, therefore, represented dialectical opposites in Parsons' representation of recent German social thought. Parsons clearly aligns himself with Marx's optimism, if not his theory.

An *ideal-type* had something to do with 'an infinite array of facts' from which selection must be made and 'construction' attempted. Parsons, having argued that Sombart developed a *unified* theory of capitalism, required some other thinker, or ideal, to represent, and give a sense of *unity*, against which the *unity* of his theory could be evaluated. This 'unity' was present in Parsons' definition of theory: 'a consistent and unified system of concepts . . . used in the analysis of social phenomena' (T. Parsons 1928: 643–4; the reference is to Edgar Salin, Parsons' doctoral promoter). And there was also the unified background of the western intellectual tradition.

Applying these concepts Parsons could have explained 'Capitalism' in the recent German literature by reference to the one single process in the evolution of social theory. But he could also have analysed the various thinkers as setting forth discrete and separate analytical systems as if there were no historical links between them! Building on the method he had developed in his undergraduate days, and refining that approach via Weber's *ideal-type* concept, we note that he took a third approach, something of an amalgam of the methods of institutionalism and neo-Kantianism. This is seen most clearly when Parsons placed Sombart in the 'pendulum swing' of German thought since Kant.

> In Hegel the pendulum swung far over to the 'spiritual' side; then with Feuerbach and some of the young Hegelians it swung just as far the other way. At this point began the application to the analysis of capitalism, starting at the left, so to speak, with the historical materialism of Marx. It was in terms of the Marxian view that the problem was presented to Sombart, and in a sense he represents the extreme of the swing back again toward Hegel. There is, however, the important difference that while retaining in essentials the matter–spirit alternative, Sombart has discarded the peculiar evolutionary form, the dialectic, in which the doctrine appeared in both Hegel and Marx (though in different senses), and has substituted his own type of 'cultural morphology'. This he derived from conceptions long existing in various forms in historical thought, especially its more romantic aspects.   (ibid.: 645–6)

From this we might conclude that the 'dialectic' between Marx and Sombart was also an 'ideal-type' of the 'pendulum swing' of German thought since Kant! Parsons' method may be complex, but his consideration of Sombart and Weber was sufficient for his purpose – to 'understand' the entire German idealistic tradition since Kant. There is a sense in which, having successfully analysed the internal 'strains' of Weber and Sombart's theories, he had for his purposes accounted for this tradition of western thought. In my view this explains, in part, why the subsequent treatment of Marx and Kant has always been shrouded with ambiguities. It is the ambiguity of a pragmatist who picks up insights, the results of rational inquiry, whilst steering clear of the historical debate about the meaning and validity of the insights. We will return to these matters below. But let us look closer at Parsons' approach to the theory of Karl Marx.

Interlude: Parsons' brief excursion into Marxian theory

Despite Parsons' repeated assertions that the lost chapter of his doctoral dissertation contained his treatment of Marx, the draft located in the Harvard Archives (T. Parsons 1927) is self-contained and does not consider Marx directly at all. Rather it is the work of Richard Passows, Georg von Below and Lujo Brentano which provided Parsons with his initial orientation to the Marxist definition of *Kapitalismus*. In the dissertation draft the question of the ideal-type is raised, but it is firmly connected with a lexical discussion of the problem of coming to an adequate definition of the historical concept.

Yet in his *JPE* articles his pragmatic style is focussed quite specifically. In Parsons' intellectual frame of reference Marx's theory is present as a useful benchmark against which subsequent developments can be measured. Whether he wrote anything significant in the chapter lost by Bergstraesser is almost beside the point. Parsons is at his most utilitarian when referring to Marx. This is not to say that this style is absent in Parsons' references to other writers. Rather the utilitarian motif comes most clearly into view with his pragmatic use of Marx's theory.

Parsons accepted the view of Benedetto Croce, who maintained that historical materialism should be considered as a heuristic principle rather than as a theory of the forces of evolution (T. Parsons 1928: 645, n. 9). 'Dialectic', whether historical or analytical, was interpreted in terms of the 'ideal-type' concept. 'Historical materialism' is an instrument of sociological analysis, an ideal-type, by which the investigator injects order into the analysis. This, wrote Parsons, was the way in which Sombart (and Weber) viewed the concept. The Marxian theory of value was an *ideal-type* of a hypothetical capitalist society to be used in comparison with the real economic system of capitalism.

> The latter view is much more favorable to Marx and the unity of his system, and brings him into much closer relations with Sombart and the general currents of thought dealt with in this paper. Of course this interpretation would admit that the content of Marx's theory was largely taken over from Ricardo, but would maintain that the logical use to which it was put was much different.
>
> (ibid.: 658, n. 23)

For Parsons Marxist theory is a form of historicism *and* a heuristic device (ibid.: 645, 658). 'Ideal types' are attempts to understand the evolution of society and as such contribute to the evolution of social theory. Sombart's thought, as the culmination of Marx's work, would be incorporated within the higher synthesis when it eventually emerged (ibid.: 654).

For Parsons, Marx was the initiator of the theory of capitalism. Though completed by Sombart, the theoretical development begun by Marx had some fundamental flaws. But these flaws had only became apparent in the light of Weber's contribution. So how did Parsons view Marx's place in the history of western thought?

Parsons located Marx in a two-fold way. He was part of the pendulum swing of German idealism since Kant and Hegel, and the content of Marx's theory of value comes from Ricardo (ibid.: 654). Marx was part of the German historical tradition *as well as* the Anglo-Saxon individualistic and rationalistic tradition. Marx is presented as an important intersection-point in the recent history of social-economic thought. Whether there could be other possible 'intersections' in western thought is not broached explicitly. This again illustrates Parsons' pragmatic style. Sombart is placed in the history of German thought since Kant, but then Parsons focusses upon the 'relationship' between Marx and Sombart. He gave his attention to Sombart's theory of capitalism, and in so doing turned to Marx's theory of value as 'an "ideal-type" of a hypothetical capitalist society to be used for purposes of comparison with the real capitalistic and other economic systems' (ibid.: 658, n. 23; Croce 1914/66). The Marx–Sombart relation changed considerably in the course of Sombart's theoretical development, but Parsons took his point of departure from Sombart's *later* works. Sombart was taken to be the inheritor and the one who completed the theory of Marx; Parsons explicitly underlined the fact that he did not treat Marx separately because Sombart had done the kind of analysis he would have done anyway (T. Parsons 1928: 661).

Here is strong internal evidence that Parsons excluded close textual examination of Marx's writings from his investigations. But does this mean he gave no attention to Marx at all? Parsons' treatment of Marx has always seemed ambiguous. Marx's writings were never subjected to the kind of analysis which he gave to those of Weber.

It would seem that Parsons would 'understand' Marx simply as the originator of the Sombart–Weber dialectic. His 'understanding' of Marx seems to have emerged when he placed him in the 'pendulum swing' of German thought. His method of 'understanding' Sombart was more a matter of confronting the logic of what Sombart had written. With Weber it was a matter of 'constructing' and translating the actual text.

Hermeneutically there is a move from the *abstract* (dialectic: Marx) to the *construction* (ideal-type, logic: Sombart) to the *concrete* (theory, text: Weber).

In his attempt to formulate his own view of capitalism Parsons took one step which he considered to be the culmination of the movement from Marx to Sombart to Weber. An account of the concept of *Kapitalismus* in *recent* German literature, he implied, was sufficient for his purpose. If he was to understand Sombart's theory totally, he then had to understand Marx. If Marx was to be understood, then Hegel, the physiocrats, Ricardo and Adam Smith; if Hegel, then Kant; if Kant then Hume and so on all the way back into antiquity to the pre-Socratics. Comprehensive knowledge of the history of thought was not his aim. In his one step he sought a practical and analytical understanding of capitalism in its latest phase.

These articles are indicative of an attempt to explain and summarize universal global developments in terms of recent European theoretical insights. He was formulating the ideas which he considered to be *central* to western society.

Sombart's view of capitalism

Parsons had difficulty with Sombart's denial of the 'existence of economic laws which transcend history' (T. Parsons 1928: 643). Such laws had been acknowledged by the entire history of economic science. Such laws make a unified system of concepts possible. The discovery of these laws is the historical task of theory. Parsons pointed to ambiguity in Sombart's theory: he had denied the existence of such laws, yet he developed a consistent and unified system of concepts. If a theory is unified then it illustrates the coherence of reality *even if the theory is antinomological*. On this basis Sombart's consistent and unified system of concepts is at odds with his explicit denial of laws which transcend history.

It is not clear from these articles whether Parsons accepted 'laws which transcend history', or whether the coherence of reality derives from within itself, or is imposed from 'outside'. How were such laws to be related to the 'ideal-type' and 'pendulum swings'?

Parsons respected Sombart's theory as an *attempt to strike a balance between two extremes*. He did not criticize his theory in any comprehensive manner, but he did criticize Sombart's failure to achieve a balance. It was Sombart's historicist approach which reduced economic laws to merely immanent historical phenomena.

Sombart's historical analysis asserted that the suppression of human creativity had not always been a characteristic of capitalism. He pointed to the development of 'inventive activity that swept Europe' in the Industrial Revolution. According to Parsons Sombart had recognized the historical increase of true freedom like any other liberal historian in western countries (ibid.: 653–4; 658; see also Croce 1941). Parsons sided with liberal historiography; and by doing so provided himself with critical distance over against Sombart's pessimistic view of the direction of history – 'economic historians of liberal leanings would strongly disagree with him' (T. Parsons 1928: 646).

Sombart's view was that in the early capitalist era, the *traditional* principle gave way to the principle of *rationality*. Modern science, based upon objective scientific reasoning, could then come into its own. It had made a start with exceptional men like Leonardo da Vinci, yet only later did 'the rational way' *converge* with the wave of inventive activity to give birth to Modern Science (ibid.: 655).

How is Sombart's view of the development of science related to his 'completion' of Marx's view? Marx had interpreted changes in class interests in terms of an economic interpretation of history, a theory of social evolution in terms of one single process. But Sombart held to a different view.

> It is a fundamental contention of this work [i.e. *Der Moderne Kapitalismus*] that at different times different attitudes toward economic life have prevailed, and that it is the spirit which has created a suitable form for itself and has thus created economic organization.　　　　　　　　　　(quoted in T. Parsons 1928: 644)

Parsons' commentary on this stated:

> Each spirit is for him a thoroughly unique phenomenon, occurring only once in history. There is no line of development leading from spirit to spirit, and thus from system to system, and each is, therefore to be considered by and for itself.
>
> 　　　　　　　　　　　　　　　　　　　　　　　　　　　　　　　　(ibid.: 644)

Sombart had organized his argument in *Der moderne Kapitalismus* to emphasize the variety of unique and economically qualified epochs in history. Each epoch was qualified by its own 'spirit', and this concept was central to his analysis. The 'spirit of capitalism' was Sombart's leading concept (ibid.: 651). But it had led him to develop his theory without due regard to the relationships that link economic systems with each other. Parsons related this failure to the Hegelian concept of discontinuous evolution inherited through the influence of Marx. Sombart's method was thus opposed to the more acceptable concept of 'continuous evolution'. Parsons' emphasis was upon the unity of culture in its evolutionary development.

> There seems to be little reason to believe that it is not possible on the basis which we now have to build by a continuous process something more nearly approaching an ideal society. In any case the process of social change is certainly neither so radically discontinuous nor so radically determined by any 'principles' as Sombart would have us believe. In the transition from capitalism to a different social system surely many elements of the present would be built into the new order.
>
> (ibid.: 653)

Sombart saw socialism as a system pertaining to the capitalist epoch. It retained capitalism's shortcomings. Marx's theory of capitalism was completed by Sombart's concept of the spirit of capitalism (T. Parsons 1928: 661), yet it could only do so with a new pessimism overtaking Marx's optimism. Whilst Marx had emphasized one side – the 'material' – and Sombart had focussed upon the other – the 'spiritual' – it would be Weber's contribution which combined this spiritualist interpretation of capitalism within the materialist orientation of Marx. In Weber the Marx–Sombart dialectic could be transcended. Marx and Sombart had diverged quite fundamentally in their ethical judgements upon capitalism. But they had not said all there was to be said on the issue. Weber provided a third way of looking at it.

Max Weber – on the wave of the future

Weber penetrated to the ethical framework in which both Sombart and Marx had launched their criticisms of capitalism.

> Weber's attempt to explain capitalism in terms of a particular set of ethical values at once brings out his attitude to the problems of the economic interpretation of history. The essay in which this view was presented was intended to be a refutation of the Marxian thesis in a particular historical case by proving that capitalism could only be understood in terms of an ethics which preceded it in time. The interesting thing is that Weber puts the question in this way: that either a materialistic or a spiritualistic interpretation or a compromise between them must be accepted. There is no other way of looking at the problem. Here he is on common ground with Sombart.   (ibid.: 40)

Max Weber was the culmination of *recent* developments in German social thought. 'There is no other way of looking at the problem' (ibid.: 40) which Weber had formulated in definitive form. Weber provided the synthesis and Parsons followed in this direction.

Weber had developed an alternative by identifying the ethical preconditions which undergirded the growth of free enterprise in 'the west'. He distanced himself from the ethical systems which had been at the basis of previous social theories and pointed the way to avoiding undue pessimism or undue optimism even though he lapsed into a form of pessimism himself. His rational approach was a *scientific* concern for the problems of modern society. Weber's research extended over the whole of human history. Parsons interpreted Weber as one, like Sombart, who sought for a 'consistent and unified system of concepts to be used in the analysis of social phenomena' (T. Parsons 1928: 644). But unlike Sombart his analytical concentration was not fixed upon a single line of development.

> His researches extend over the whole of human history. He investigates the classic world, China, India, ancient Judea and others. But it always remains his purpose to throw light upon the problems of modern society, and especially upon modern capitalism.   (T. Parsons 1929: 31)

Weber's comparative method avoided the European bias evident in Sombart's view of social evolution (ibid.: 31). Sombart restricted himself to European civilization. Weber's approach was global-historical, locating capitalism as a primary characteristic of Western society comparable to the leading aspects of other cultures at other times, in other places.

For Weber modern capitalism was based on the bourgeois ethical system which had preceded it. It was in this way that he emphasized and explained the world-wide power of European capitalism. Weber's all-embracing perspective sought to include *all* world-historical systems, occidental and oriental, ancient and modern.

For Parsons Weber's key concepts were: ideal-type, interpretative understanding (*Verstehen*), rational inquiry. Key sociological themes included: 'the capitalistic order of society as a whole' (ibid.: 36), the growth of bourgeois business enterprises (ibid.: 37), rational organization and bureaucracy (ibid.: 37–8), the modern State (ibid.: 38), modern science, the rise of Protestantism (ibid.: 41ff.) and the place of religion in modern society (ibid.: 43ff.). The polemical aspects of Weber's work – his pessimism and his critical alternative to Marxian historiography – were also noted.

Parsons was not here putting himself forward as a Weberian. He concentrated upon how Sombart and Weber developed their views against the background of Marxian analysis. He sought to formulate general problems for the development of sociological theory (ibid.: 50–1). His approach was critical.

Parsons viewed Weber's method as contradictory. The theory of ideal-types, Weber's most suggestive contribution to the sociological study of capitalism, was ambiguous (ibid.: 51). Modern social thought should seek to overcome this ambiguity, yet he did not then rule out the route suggested by Sombart. He did not follow Sombart's lead, yet in following Weber he also rejected Weber's cultural pessimism. In aiming towards the 'ideal society' he left Weber's pessimism behind.

> Capitalistic development has meant by and large the destruction of the charismatic elements of social life. The whole of it has come to be dominated by settled routine, and predominantly of the rational, bureaucratic, rather than the traditional, type. It is this which is the ground of Weber's pessimism. He holds that the really vital human forces appear only in charismatic forms, and that the very

nature of social development progressively eliminates the possibility of the further
appearance of such forms.   (ibid.: 47)

Weber, in Parsons' view, had allowed the creative element of society, the
realm of human freedom, to become subject to an externalized rationality.
Objective freedom and capitalism were incompatible in Weber's view.

> Capitalism presents a dead, mechanized condition of society in which there is no
> room left for these truly creative forces because all human activity is forced to
> follow the 'system'.   (ibid.: 47)

Parsons argued against Weber's pessimistic rendering of historical reality.
Weber's pessimistic sociology did not accord with the factual possibilities
inherent in history. Parsons, a professional realist, was led by his optimism. He
explained his rejection of Weber's pessimism in these terms:

> Surely Weber puts the question in a false form when he denies any possibilities
> other than that either the spiritual forces (charisma) or the material conditions (in
> this case the rational bureaucratic machine) must dominate society.
>   (T. Parsons 1929: 47)

Like Sombart Weber was a child of his scholarly traditions. He had accepted
options that were presented to him; the realism of his attempt to synthesize the
material and spiritual was blocked by his pessimistic evolutionism. Modern
capitalism, through its bureaucratic mechanisms, opposes 'spiritual freedom'.

> But is it not possible . . . that the present-day power of the bureaucratic mechanism
> is due to a very special set of circumstances which do not involve the necessity for
> its continued dominance over life, but leave the possibility open that it may again
> be made to serve 'spiritual' aims? Weber does not admit this possibility, but to him
> it would be the only hope for Western society, for no one was more insistent than
> he on the impossibility of returning to pre-capitalistic conditions.
>   (ibid.: 47–8)

Parsons here discusses Weber's theory in personal rather than logical terms.
Weber's failure to admit this 'spiritual option' is emphasized by reference to
'him' rather than a criticism of the implication of 'his theory'. He thus
demonstrated a sympathetic understanding for Weber, the human actor and
theorist. But in so criticizing Weber's view of capitalism, Parsons linked it to
the transcending personal factor of his *pessimism*. This is most important for
understanding Parsons' theoretical development at this time. It shows him
interpreting the theory as Weber's 'system of action'. Parsons would consider
Weber's theory once it had been abstracted from the context of the pessimistic
world-view within which it was set forth. Parsons' unbiassed approach could
not admit such wholesale pessimism.

Parsons tried to understand the personal difficulties which Weber had faced
in completing his work. The fragmented character of his work may have
presented problems, but it was the *dual* usage of the *ideal-type* concept which
Parsons diagnosed as the crucial factor. The ideal-type was an instrument of
analysis. But, for Weber, it also had historical connotations.

They are directed toward *one particular* historical individual and are applicable only to it, are thus *historical* and not general concepts like the others.

(T. Parsons 1929: 33)

The *ideal-type* promoted interpretative understanding; the researcher compared the actual record of events in various milieux. Used historically, the 'ideal-type' referred to *one particular historical individual* and was an attempt to grasp 'the whole "essence" of the thing, not just one side of it' (ibid.: 33). It was not simply a means, but was the final product of investigative research.

That Weber calls both ideal types without distinguishing them leads to serious confusion, a confusion which is especially marked in his analysis of capitalism . . .

(ibid.: 33)

At the end of the discussion in the second article he observed that Weber's concepts of 'capitalism in general' and 'modern capitalism' ran parallel with his 'bureaucracy in general' and 'modern bureaucracy' concepts. Each set of concepts illustrated the dualistic usage of Weber's 'ideal-type'.

The one deals with generalized 'aspects' of phenomena for comparative purposes, the other with unique historical epochs, cultures, etc, as wholes and by and for themselves.   (ibid.: 49)

Weber constantly wavered between them, Parsons implied. Even the distinction was not followed through consistently. The historical picture tended to become a 'useful fiction'. Parsons explored the immanent logic of Weber's historical sociology, and located the source of the error in Weber's inability to distinguish clearly between the historical and methodological forms of the concept. Weber's 'engine of analysis' – his 'system' (T. Parsons 1928: 643–4; 1929: 32–3) – had been confused with his analysis of the 'iron-bound' character of rationalization (T. Parsons 1929: 49). This was the root of Weber's theoretical difficulties. He had identified theory as a 'useful fiction' but lived by the reality he derived from his *ideal-type*. Parsons seems to interpret Weber's theory as Weber's 'iron cage' (Weber 1930: 181–2). In this way the reality of theoretical analysis was confused in Weber's research. In other words Weber's pessimism is indicative of a failure to reckon with the *creative* possibilities inherent in the theoretical frame of reference. Parsons interprets Weber as the genius who has imprisoned himself in his own theory. The only way to avoid such confusion is to become *optimistic* again about the creative power of theoretical reflection.

I think there is no doubt that the logical basis of Weber's iron-bound process of rationalization lies in the isolation of one aspect of social development and the attribution of historical reality to an ideal type which was never meant to represent it. If this error is corrected the absolute domination of the process of rationalization over the whole social process falls to the ground.

(T. Parsons 1929: 49)

Parsons could now take the next step in his theoretical inquiries. A comparative analysis of Weber's 'ideal-type' with other social theories suggested itself. The 'means–end' schema, which has been identified as a dominant factor of

Parsons' thinking in its earliest stages, is implicit in these articles on 'capitalism'. It shows itself in Parsons' self-critical reflection and his method. For Weber the 'ideal-type' functioned as a means and as an end. For Parsons, Weber's 'ideal-type' construction functioned as a means to his (i.e. Parsons') all-inclusive *theoretical* end – a general theoretical account of human action. This Weber had forfeited through his pessimism.

How did Parsons interpret his study of Weber? He accepted his task which was to piece the various fragments of Weber's *theory of capitalism* together – 'a certain element of construction is unavoidable' (ibid.: 34). The word 'construction' was also used in discussing the ideal-typical representation of the 'historical individual'. He noted 'such a concept cannot be purely a means, but its construction must be in some measure the end of the investigation in question' (ibid.: 33). Parsons' articles, then, are not only an historical investigation, in the realm of ideas. They continue the style found in his Amherst philosophy essays. The search for an equivalent to Newton (and perhaps quantum physics) in social-theory writing was being maintained. He was attempting to develop his own theory. The impetus towards theory-building was enclosed within his interpretation of Weber's theoretical perspective. And his own acceptance of the relative and provisional character of this interpretation is to be seen in his repeated 're-visiting' of Weber's works along with other 'classics' (T. Parsons 1981).

Introducing Weber's theory to the North American academy

The Structure of Social Action (1937) found its unity in Parsons' consideration of neo-classical economics alongside of his incorporation of important insights from the philosophy of science. 'The book' could easily have been a collection of critical studies on various theorists with his own methodological and theoretical conclusions. But it was not. Instead Parsons sought to demonstrate a 'convergence'. And some initial hints of 'convergence' are to be found in his 'construction' of the fragments Weber left behind.

Parsons' 'construction' was his attempt to formulate the basic frame of reference. He insisted that the *Vorbemerkung* (the Author's Introduction to Weber's collected essays in the sociology of religion) was a very crucial document in understanding Weber's sociology. Its importance for the proper understanding of Weber's perspective should not be missed. Moreover Paul Siebeck, the German publisher, had made it very difficult to get Weber's *Religionssoziologie* published in English. Since 'Die protestantische Ethik' was the only essay to be published at this time Weber's own 1920 interpretation of its significance also had to be included. Parsons explained its significance in the Translator's Preface to 'The Protestant Ethic' in these terms:

[Its inclusion] has seemed particularly desirable since, in the voluminous discussion which has grown up in Germany around Weber's essay, a great deal of misplaced criticism has been due to the failure properly to appreciate the scope and limitations of the study. While it is impossible to appreciate that fully without a thorough study of Weber's sociological work as a whole, this brief introduction should suffice to prevent a great deal of misunderstanding.

(T. Parsons 1930: x)

The publication of 'The Protestant Ethic' meant that a section of Weber's oeuvre was now available in a new context. Its significance, like Weber's historical 'ideal-type', could become obscured in the process of theoretical elaboration, if it was not read in the context of Weber's overall intention. Weber's sociology in Parsons' view was a unified act; this fragment was illustrative of Weber's sociological intention. His work must be considered as a partially fulfilled project in rational social scientific analysis.

Parsons' articles presented a 'more condensed and systematic form than that in which [Weber's theory is] available in German' (T. Parsons 1928: 642). But Parsons' interpretative involvement in the writings qua translator, secondary analyst and critical theorist led him to conclude that 'The Protestant Ethic' 'is in many ways of central significance for Weber's philosophy of history' (T. Parsons 1930: xi).

For Parsons 'The Protestant Ethic' became an *ideal-type* of sociological analysis – a classic document of sociological research. 'The Protestant Ethic' was a sociological work, and Weber was a sociologist. Let us note that Parsons' 'ideal-type' of Weber's theory (in *The Structure*) admitted no internal theoretical development. In *The Structure* Parsons did not examine the development of Weber's sociological theory, even though Marshall, Durkheim and Pareto were discussed in such terms. This anomaly is also illustrated by Parsons' fundamental divergence on the matter with his Heidelberg teacher, Edgar Salin. Salin had written in these terms:

> A first study, as a valuable supplement to Sombart's work, had proved in exemplary lucidity what Puritanism had meant for the rise of capitalism. But in the later work the basic problem is methodically replaced by that of the influence of economic and social conditions on the religious sytems.
>
> (Salin 1932: 41, quoted in translation in Dooyeweerd 1953: 292–3)

By itself 'Die Protestantische Ethik' was one thing. Placed alongside Sombart it meant something else; seen in the context of the debate it helped to generate it becomes a dynamic theory with a life of its own; alongside other of Weber's works in the sociology of religion it can be 'read' to imply something else again. The essay 'The Protestant Sects and the Spirit of Capitalism' (Weber 1946: 302–22), with the other essays, are later works and supplemental to the earlier work. When the 1904/5 essay is read as a historical study in the terms spelled out for it in the 1920 Author's Introduction, a new picture emerges. But Parsons' interpretation was his attempt to transcend this flux by placing 'Die Protestantische Ethik' at the fulcrum of Weber's 'turn' to sociology. Weber's 'move' from historical economics to analytical and encyclopaedic sociology bore this out. 'The Protestant Ethic' captured the methodological direction of Weber's enterprise.

A few years later Parsons reviewed Robertson's critique of 'Max Weber and his School' (Robertson 1933). In a concluding footnote Parsons observed:

> Of course, it is too much to expect that Dr. Robertson should have gone beyond the one essay to try to see its significance in terms of Weber's sociological thought as a whole – that would be resorting to the 'sociological method' and be unworthy of a historian. But nevertheless a final assessment of Weber's work cannot omit this.   (T. Parsons 1935b: 696)

The historian, Parsons implied here, focusses attention upon particulars – in this case Roberston was viewed as confining himself, qua historian, to the 'Protestant Ethic' essay. Parsons, the sociologist, attempted to 'go beyond' the one essay, yet he saw in that same essay the best example of Weber's sociological frame of reference. Sociological method, in Parsons' view, had a power of generalization alien to the historical method.

Given that Parsons accepted Weber's sociology as the end point of a transition *from* history *to* sociology, and that Weber's original economic interpretation of the history of Protestantism was part of that transition, how did Parsons view the relationship between the historian and the sociologist? How was the historical dimension of the sociologist's task to be construed? There seems to be no methodological connection – there is just an external relationship of two university disciplines competing for alternative interpretations of the same socio-historical phenomena. Even if Parsons was here adopting a rhetorical style the question remains: where does historical scholarship go now that the transition has been made? Is it simply out of date?

In Parsons' view Weber was a sociologist, *not* a historian. His sociology allowed the social scientist to interpret the passing of a kind of historical research, and thus place contemporary social theory in its historical context. But is there any place left for the historian? Parsons' subsequent view that history 'may be regarded primarily as the general historical science concerned with human action' (T. Parsons 1937a: 771) is even less convincing unless we take the view that Parsons here advocated the subordination of historical scholarship to sociological method. In that sense he was promoting a new form of historical research, as Bershady (1973) and Müller (1969) have observed.

It is known that Parsons was an appreciative reader of Arthur Darby Nock, the social historian of early Christianity, and Perry Miller, the historian of American Puritanism. But he did not view his 'system' as a guide for the study of history and the construction of historiographical narratives, at least not at this stage of his development.

Weber's Author's Introduction was very important. It was a 'master key' for unlocking the meaning of Weber's transition. It gave Weber's own interpretation of the meaning of his investigations. It explained the sociological framework which was emergent in the work of an economic historian (Nelson 1974).

Parsons' ideal-type construction of Weber's systematic sociological theory was presented in *The Structure*. The only way to interpret Weber, he implied, is to read him as one trying to make sense of his own historical research by utilizing a sociological framework – that is a theory concerned with the institutionalization of patterns of value orientation (T. Parsons 1937a: 768). Parsons' Weber was also formulating the transcending laws of social evolution via the construction of 'ideal-types'. If Sombart's theory became a kind of 'ideal-type' of the more fruitful contributions of *Historismus*, Weber is an 'ideal-type' of a scientific attempt from within Idealism to develop a unified social science.

Parsons' theoretical development between 1925 and 1937 was an amazing achievement. His empathic criticism of Weber's pessimism seems to have become woven into an interpretation of why Weber could not complete his work. Weber was 'on the verge' of accepting the full implications of the 'personal factor' (or as Parsons came to term it, 'the subjective frame of reference') in science, but his pessimism had been an obstacle. The attempt to 'go beyond' Weber into such a voluntarist theory had been foreshadowed in his 'Capitalism' articles on Sombart and Weber.

Return to America – Parsons at Harvard

This final section of Chapter 4 is very short. Parsons' return to America in a cultural and geographical sense is possibly one of the most formative moments of his entire odyssey. In this exposition I have directed my attention to Weber, and in the next chapter I will consider Parsons' response to economics at Harvard. Via his work on Weber, Parsons established himself as a scholar of standing. Early in the 1930s, with the demise of institutionalism, Paul T. Homan encouraged him to make Weber *and* Vilfredo Pareto known to American social scientists (T. Parsons and P. T. Homan 1932; Homan to Parsons, 10 March 1932). Stimulated by the Henderson/Pareto influence, Parsons developed a social scientific contribution to the Harvard tradition.

In his Amherst essays a knowledge of scientific method had provided him with critical distance in the study of society. His *non-empiricist* position was further developed by his 'construction' of Weber's theory. The 'ideal-type' concept was central, but Parsons discerned ambiguity in Weber's use of it. He aimed to 'iron out' the conceptual confusion.

5
The position and prospects of sociology at Harvard in the 1930s

Parsons' scholarly engagement at Harvard during the 1930s

How did Parsons 'fit in' with the Harvard of the 1930s? We can answer this question by looking at the collection of journal articles which were published at this time. They represent the progressive refinement of an argument which came to culmination in *The Structure of Social Action*. In that work he achieved his 'quantum leap' from 'theories' to 'theory'. He had also established himself at Harvard.

We must now consider how Parsons came to view himself as a *theorist*. Harvard required original work of its faculty (Morison 1936: 53ff.). It sought out 'first raters'. In this competitive atmosphere Parsons finally produced 'the book'. There was more than just institutional pressure from 'without'; Parsons laboured to produce an original response to the intellectual environment of the American university, from within the discipline of economics.

Parsons acknowledged that he was a 'maverick'. He fought a running battle against rigid lines of division between disciplines (T. Parsons 1959: 5–6, n. 3).

> For there is absolutely no reason to suppose that concrete action is divided up into water-tight compartments, each dominated by radically different principles. Only the relatively high degree of differentiation of modern western society has enabled this illusion to stand up as long as it has, and now it has definitely broken down. Human life is essentially one and no concretely possible degree of functional differentiation can destroy its unity. (T. Parsons 1935a: 660)

The question which emerges here is: how could a 'general theory' contribute to the reorganization of the university faculty? Parsons understated the critical and rhetorical potential of his theory in its immediate institutional setting – at least in his publications. His focus was upon the creative potential of the theorist in the context of the tradition in which he worked. In this way Parsons accommodated his theorizing to the traditions of the Academy. The new 'division of labour' among the social sciences which he envisaged did not have to imply the radical reorganization of the university faculty in line with his concepts (ibid.: 660 n. 4). That he so positively *denied* this would seem to suggest a desire to keep the discussion on a 'purely abstract' level.

But his disavowal of critical intent needs to be contrasted with his reorganization of the Harvard social science faculty in the 1940s – after he had gained tenure and a professorship. Parsons, though a theorist, was not an idealist. He seems to have been a *pragmatic* realist, in political terms. His 'present position and prospects' were always an important factor on his horizon whatever the sphere.

From economics to sociology

In 1930 Parsons was taken on as a founding member of the Sociology Department at Harvard. Sorokin had been brought to Harvard to be its Chairman. For the previous four years Parsons had taught economics under an 'unsympathetic' Chairman, H. H. Burbank. Sorokin suggested that Parsons could thank him for being retained on the Harvard circuit (Sorokin 1963: 241–68, especially pp. 243–4). Parsons' important contacts in economics at Harvard and elsewhere had helped him obtain an instructorship first at Amherst, and later at Harvard (T. Parsons 1970: 827–8); he wanted to master economic theory, especially orthodox economics. He did not enrol for a Harvard Ph.D. programme; Parsons chose his own route. The debate between institutionalists and the classical economists was raging; he would resolve the issue by developing a 'third' position.

> Meriam was quite right in maintaining that the knowledge of economic theory I could acquire at Harvard was far superior to that I had learned at Heidelberg. It gradually became clear to me that economic theory should be conceived as standing within some sort of theoretical matrix in which sociological theory also was included ... The results, published in 1931–32, crystallized the first stage of a theoretical orientation that seemed to me to go beyond the levels attained by my teachers in articulating the theoretical structures of the two disciplines.
>
> (ibid.: 827–8)

Economics was subordinated to his own theoretical project (T. Parsons 1931, 1932), as he sought to understand the relationship *between* economics and the science of society in all its aspects. Parsons' *immanent* critique of neo-classical economics examined the internal logic of Marshall's theory. It had the critical style of the Dr. phil. articles on Weber and Sombart, documenting Parsons' response to the entire history of economic theory. Marshall's theory was an *ideal-type* of the economics at the time.

> To analyze the whole history of orthodox economic thought ... would be a fruitful tho a heavy task. The present study sets itself a much more limited aim; to examine the work of one leading orthodox economist as a sample, with a view to seeing what basic elements make up his thought. For such a study Marshall presents an excellent opportunity. On the one hand he is overwhelmingly the most eminent representative in his generation of the orthodox school, so that their case may almost be said to stand or fall with his work. On the other hand he went to far greater pains than most economists of his tradition to avoid the charge of abstractness and unreality ... In short, he was in a sense an example of what the 'unorthodox' are striving for; yet he failed to satisfy them.   (T. Parsons 1931: 101–2)

Parsons' initial critique of Marshall is a conventional secondary work. This initial discussion of Marshall stands unchanged as Chapter 3 of *The Structure*. The conceptual linking of 'wants' with 'activities' was developed by a second article. Marshall's 'problems' were then related comparatively to the perspectives of Weber and Pareto. Chapter 4 to the end of *The Structure* should therefore be interpreted as expansion and development of this second Marshall article, 'Economics and Sociology: Marshall in Relation to the Thought of his Time' (T. Parsons 1932; see also Wearne 1981).

Parsons' emerging career faced peculiar difficulties. What did it mean to be a 'theorist'? Did not a calling in 'theory' lead to obscurantism? Who needed that kind of work? He launched into an extensive and critical investigation of the important theorists of the previous generation: Marshall, Pareto, Hobhouse, Tonnies, Simmel, Weber and Durkheim were the theorists dealt with in his teaching work during this period (Harvard University 1930–) (N.B. *not* Karl Marx!).

Although Weber was being championed as an 'institutionalist' in America (Homan 1933: 395), he had given careful and respectful attention to the theory of orthodox economics. In economics Parsons' sympathies lay with the unorthodox. But via Weber's example and Meriam's encouragement, he became willing, even while teaching, to *learn* from a theoretical position, such as classical economics, which was, *in principle*, on the periphery of his *theoretical* interest. If sociological analysis was to contribute to the reform of economics then his theory had to include an understanding of the prevailing mores of economic thought. That also had been Weber's approach.

During Parsons' pre-1937 development he came to de-emphasize the 'right or wrong' aspects of theory. In the unpublished manuscript, Chapter XVIII of *The Structure*, he wrote in relation to Tonnies and Simmel:

> Let us hope that some day we will get over feeling the necessity to dub a writer as either 'right' or 'wrong' ... The progress of science consists in the continual amendment and restatement of conceptual schemes, not in deciding they are 'right' or 'wrong'.   (T. Parsons 1937d: 12)

Parsons' method was transformational. He turned his attention to fruitful lines he discerned in any theoretical movement. But logically this is a very difficult position to maintain, especially if one believes it to be 'right'. It is possible to argue on this basis that Parsons' rejection of Marx's theory was on the basis of Marx's failure to understand the character of progress in science. But what are we to make of the assertion that 'the utility theory of economic motivation is correct and not the hedonistic theory' (T. Parsons 1937a: 122)? Or that 'Hobbes' interpretation of an individualistic order was right, that of Locke and his successors wrong ... Hobbes was theoretically right, but factually wrong' (ibid.: 362)? Parsons was trying to highlight the historical and conceptual relativity of 'right' and 'wrong' in relation to theories –

conceptual schemes. Yet in his view some theories had *proved to be right* by the processes of intellectual evolution, thus rendering other schemes 'wrong'. He identified long-term structural tendencies in theoretical evolution. Any theorist was a potential contributor to the history of social thought. The Darwinian principle of 'selection' provided an explanation for why some theorists were 'in vogue'. Their theories had 'survived' because of their usefulness and 'success' in scientific explanation (T. Parsons 1935a: 661). L. J. Henderson's reference to sociology as that which sociologists study (T. Parsons and L. J. Henderson 1939; Henderson to Parsons, 17 July 1939) echoes such 'survival'. Such relativism is illustrative of Parsons' approach to truth. Bridgman made a similar point about scientists in general:

> In his attack on his specific problem he suffers no inhibitions of precedent or authority, but is completely free to adopt any course that his ingenuity is capable of suggesting to him. No one standing on the outside can predict what the individual scientist will do or what method he will follow. In short, science is what scientists do, and there are as many scientific methods as there are individual scientists. (Bridgman 1955: 83)

Parsons defined himself as a scientist. Therefore he viewed his work as scientific. It is in this sense that the 'right' and 'wrong' aspects of any theory are relativized.

Institutionalism and the theory of institutions

Parsons' critical investigation of Marshall, Pareto and Weber led to published results. Durkheim was given extensive treatment in *The Structure*. Tonnies and Simmel were considered in a draft chapter which was not included in the final version. But there is only a nine-page analysis of Veblen, found in the first instalment of 'Sociological Elements in Economic Thought' (T. Parsons 1934c: 435–44). The failure to write a full-length article 'Veblen in Relation to the Thought of his Time' is quite remarkable. Clearly Parsons was convinced that the unorthodox institutional economics had failed. The 'debacle of institutionalism' meant that social science would be receptive to a new impetus (T. Parsons and P. T. Homan 1932; Homan to Parsons, 10 March 1932), but presumably it did not need to be enlightened about the fact of the demise.

Parsons 'stood above the battle' as he made Weberian sociology available to Americans. His *transcendent* critique of the debate between neo-classical orthodox economics and institutionalist unorthodox economics included an implied rejection of the 'intellectual technology' of institutionalism. Parsons' stance towards institutionalism seems to imply a critique of it in its own terms. He identified the anti-intellectual 'institution' upon which the institutionalists had launched their critique. Let us attempt to outline Parsons' critique of institutionalism in more systematic terms than he did.

Walton Hamilton wrote:

> Institutions fix the confines of and impose form upon the activities of human

beings. The world of use and wont, to which imperfectly we accommodate our lives, is a tangled and unbroken web of institutions.   (Hamilton 1932: 84)

This statement implies an explanation of the progress of science. Hamilton did not address this issue directly, and Parsons detected in institutionalism an even greater scientific evasiveness than he found in Marshall (T. Parsons 1932: 335–6). Institutionalism may have created various possible openings in the social sciences, but it effectively denied the necessity of a theoretical core for *scientific* analysis. Hamilton said as much explicitly:

> The institutional method had to wait until the idea of development was incorporated into academic thought and the mind of the inquirer became resigned to the inconsistency which attends growth.   (Hamilton 1932: 89)

The idea of social evolution, for Hamilton and the institutionalists, was the result of a maturation in science. It could be applied effectively in economics, history, philosophy, law and politics. Parsons would have countered with the critique of institutionalism's anti-intellectual idea of evolution (inconsistent growth). Thus they had denied the *theoretical* character of their critique. In this sense Parsons would have quoted Marshall *against* any anti-theoretical empiricism:

> The most reckless and treacherous of all theorists is he who professes to let facts and figures speak for themselves.   (quoted in T. Parsons 1932: 346–7)

Without a conscious and explicit identification of the analytical categories which were being employed in their critique, the institutionalists must become one-sided.

> It must suffice to say here that the institutionalists are even more open than Marshall to the charge of failing to consider the basic implications of their position. In so far as they do not repudiate theory altogether, which is fatal, they tend to fall back into the 'psychologism' and 'survivalism' which Marshall successfully avoided. It is clear that a *sine qua non* of a position satisfactory from the present viewpoint is immunity from such tendencies. This does not mean, of course, that many of the institutionalists' criticisms of the orthodox, especially the more dogmatic of the latter, are not well taken.   (ibid.: 339, n. 6)

Parsons would not consign institutionalism to the scrap-heap. He would try to locate the reason for the one-sidedness of their approach. Hamilton had got hold of a perspective which was self-critical and reflexive, which Parsons admired. But, in Parsons' terms, Hamilton would not have gone far enough. Institutionalism had become satisfied with showing the institutional character of all aspects of the human world.

> An inquiry into institutions may supply the analytical knowledge essential to a program of social control or it may do no more than set adventures for idle curiosity. In either event the study of institutions rests itself upon an institution.   (Hamilton 1932: 89)

Here Hamilton appears to have come very close to Durkheim, on the non-contractual elements of contract, and to Weber, on the concept of value-relevance. Parsons had described Durkheim's view of contract in these terms:

> There is ... present in all *concrete* contractual relations a qualitatively different element which may be called the *institution* of contract, a body of rules and norms, both legal and informal, determining the conditions according to which contracts are and may be entered into.   (T. Parsons 1935a: 648)

A *system* of contractual relations presupposes this 'non-contractual' element. But Parsons seems to have diverged from institutionalism because of its imputed negative valuation of theoretical knowledge, and he did not try to extract the analytical elements for a reconstruction of the institutionalist critique.

Hamilton's institutionalism does not seem to have applied to 'analytical knowledge'. Parsons assumed that any inquiry presupposes 'analytical knowledge'. Rather than stopping short with Hamilton's either/or (knowledge for some end or knowledge as an end in itself), Parsons accepted the independent and dependent character of theoretical knowledge in the progress of science. Though still firmly committed to an inductive and scientific approach, Parsons would maintain that a study of institutions, whilst presupposing an institutional context, *also* rested upon a *theory* of institutional behaviour. Thus in his turning away from institutional economics Parsons attempted to work out the basic *analytical* categories for a theory of institutional behaviour. In contrast to Hamilton's relativism, Parsons accepted a theory of the institutional character of scientific theory in which a selected group of recent theorists were analysed to derive the current position and prospects of theory. His was relativism within bounds. The various *theories* were analysed comparatively in terms of their contribution to *theory*.

A further discussion of Veblen's theory appeared in Parsons' discussion of the sociological elements in economic thought (T. Parsons 1934c: 435–41). By this time Parsons viewed institutionalism as one of the *various* unorthodoxies which, since the beginning of the nineteenth century, had modified orthodox economics. But *The Structure* is Parsons' most fully developed critique of institutionalism and of the anti-theoretical posture it shared with the German Historical School (T. Parsons 1937a: 125, n. 1, 477). What are we to make of the fact that no attempt was made to include the institutionalist tradition in 'convergence'? Parsons was bypassing the American traditions of utilizing European thought for the purpose of carrying on the American tradition of operating as Europe's frontier. A fresh look at the 'sources' would be the best way forward, after the 'underbrush' of secondary American and other interpretations have been cleared away. Parsons' aim was to make a contribution to western social theory. He aimed to be an American source for sociological theory.

For Parsons, a new perspective had emerged with the important thinkers of the previous generation. Marshall's thought had moved in this direction even though he had not been cognizant of the fact. Pareto, a mathematical economist, formulated his system for sociology late in life. Weber, an economic historian, had also made the transition. Parsons followed Weber and searched for a 'far more comprehensive' frame of reference which would allow him to respond theoretically to the economic debates which confronted him.

The context of Parsons' contribution to Harvard social sciences in the 1930s

Marshall and Marshall's Harvard follower, F. W. Taussig, represented the 'ruling paradigm' in economics. Parsons' articles on Marshall (T. Parsons 1931; 1932) and his contribution to the Taussig Festschrift (T. Parsons 1936a) are indicative of a deeply respectful scholarship. Taussig, then in his mid seventies, was according to J. K. Galbraith an 'old-fashioned liberal', 'the acknowledged centre of the economics constellation' (Galbraith 1981: 44). Galbraith pictured Taussig in these terms:

> Taussig was the American counterpart of Alfred Marshall. The world he described was also one of many firms competing in each and every market, the flawing exception of monopoly aside. Production provided the income to buy what was produced. There were cyclical rhythms that brought occasional bad times, but these were self-corrective. Trade was best when free, although measures to arrest the exploitation of consumers or workers commended themselves to men of good will.   (Galbraith 1981: 44–5)

Parsons viewed Taussig's theory in a different light. His approach was shaped by general-analytical, rather than specifically economic, criteria. He believed that the sociology enclosed within the current economic theory could be made better. His procedure was reformist – he took one step at a time. In terms of his own goals his was a bold attempt to reconstruct the economic tradition, even though in the context of the Harvard academy he writes as one trying to avoid the ethos of intense competitiveness (T. Parsons 1935a: 660, n. 4). Parsons' contribution involves his attempt to ensure that 'theory' is possessed by a corporate and professional body, rather than by individuals competing in the academic market place.

The 'completion' of Weber's sociology was his intellectual 'goal'. The consideration of Marshall was a means to that end. Marshall's theory was a 'condition' shaping his project. But how was he to analyse Marshall? The notion of 'pure theory', gleaned from Pareto (T. Parsons 1935d; 1936b; 1936c), gave Parsons room to discuss the sociology inherent in Marshall's economics. Parsons' *ideal-type* hermeneutic was being replaced with, or supplemented by, an approach which would derive the analytical system inherent in a thinker's doctrines. Marshall's sociology was a 'non-logical residue', and in this Parsons modified Weber's ideal-type method. But the 'second Marshall article' had contained an inner problem which had to be resolved. Who was to receive the priority in Parsons' post-Marshallian sociology? One of Pareto's major contributions was his 'correction' of the 'rationalistic bias' in Weber's account (T. Parsons 1937a: 533–8). The 'competition' between Pareto and Weber (T. Parsons 1932: 345ff.) was, however, only resolved when Emile Durkheim was included in Parsons' evolving agenda. Durkheim's concepts 'reality sui generis' and 'conscience collective' were crucial. Parsons assumed that theory itself is a reality sui generis; he sought to identify the 'conscience collective' of his group of writers. Durkheim's concepts allowed Parsons to identify the analytical 'institution' predominant in current sociological theory. Durkheim's transition from positivism to idealism confirmed the 'convergence' (T. Parsons 1935e). It also represented the transformation from one form of secondary analysis to a new form. With Durkheim included in his evolving analytical horizon 'convergence' could be specified as a *sociological* account of the latter-day emergence of a common frame of reference for sociology.

Durkheim was the writer located exclusively within sociology. Parsons interpreted Durkheim's sociology as a shift from radical positivism to a viewpoint aligned with 'analytical realism' (T. Parsons 1937a: 708–14). In 'Sociological Elements in Economic Thought' (1934c, 1935a) he argued that Durkheim's approach resolved the problems highlighted in his critical investigation of economics. Durkheim appeared towards the end of Parsons' attempt to reform economics from within; his theory became part of Parsons' attempt to specify 'the division of labour' (N.B.) within the 'society of the social sciences' (T. Parsons 1934a: 535; 1935a: 646–7).

With Durkheim's theory included, *sociology* emerged as a discipline in its own right. Parsons' consideration of Durkheim marks the end of his departure from economics proper. From this point on he set forth his 'general theory of action' from *within* a sociological frame of reference with a modified 'sociologistic' position (T. Parsons 1937a: 671; Sorokin 1928: 433–4).

Parsons' proposals to reform economics did not make headway in economic thought, especially after the publication of Keynes' *General Theory of Employment, Interest and Money* in 1936. Parsons' dynamic utilitarianism set him on a non-economic path. In fact it was not until the 1950s that he read the *General Theory* of Keynes (T. Parsons 1970: 845). Such an omission seems inconceivable during the period when Keynesian economics came into prominence. Yet this was the time when clearly Parsons was picking up the implications of his broadening extension of an Anglo-centric view of the world. Taussig had derived his intellectual stimulus from Marshall in Cambridge (England). In moving out of the ambit of *economics* at Harvard, Parsons was also moving in terms of an alternative way of reforming and drawing upon the American intellectual tradition. His was a Eurocentric, rather than Anglo-centric, view of the history of ideas. In the early 1930s Parsons had commenced his transformative critique of theory in economics. But by 1937 he had found his own theoretical standpoint as he turned right away from making any special contribution to economics.

Analytical realism and the reconstruction of history

Parsons attempted an anti-dogmatic theory. Commenting upon his 'outline' of a conceptual scheme in *The Structure*, he observed:

> Above all I wish to avoid one misunderstanding of my attitude toward the outline – that I regard it as definitively solving the theoretical problems of contemporary social science and hence to be accepted as a matter of dogmatic faith. That would make of its adherents just one more among the many warring schools.
>
> On the contrary, such a scheme is to be accepted if at all, as a tentative set of working tools. In the course of working with them it is inevitable that they should be re-shaped and new ones invented. Moreover there should be complete open-mindedness on the possible usefulness of other tools not part of this system. Dogmatic faith is the death of science.   (T. Parsons 1937b: 13)

Rejecting dogmatic systematizing, Parsons advocated a new way of thinking for sociology. The doxological fulcrum of his theory was expressed in these terms:

> The god of science is, indeed, Evolution. But for those who pay their obeisance in a true scientific spirit, the fact that science evolves beyond the points they have themselves attained is not to be interpreted as a betrayal of them. It is the fulfillment of their own highest hopes.   (T. Parsons 1937a: 41)

This was Parsons' 'theory of (the development of) theory'. *The Structure* was not a 'history of social theory'. It called for a new utilization of historical understanding in building social theory. 'Convergence' had its roots in the 'bio-genetic law of evolution' (T. Parsons 1922: 12, 13), and was also the central concept of Parsons' analytical philosophy of the history of social theory (Wearne 1981: 835). He aimed to synthesize positivist and idealist elements in a third posture, which had emerged in the previous generation of social thought.

> Thus, as long as social thought has remained divided between the positivistic and the idealistic systems there has been no place for an analytical sociological theory in the sense in which it has just been defined. The possibility of giving it a place is, perhaps, the deepest symptom of the great change in social thinking the process of convergence here traced has brought about.   (T. Parsons 1937a: 774)

What began as an attempt to introduce Weber's thought involved the critique of positivism from the standpoint of idealism, the critique of idealism from the standpoint of positivism, and *a critical overview of both traditions* from a third standpoint which Parsons called *analytical realism* (ibid.: 730). This promoted the scientific reformation of the history of social science in all its modes.

Parsons' history of economic thought was recorded in the first of the 'Sociological Elements' articles (T. Parsons 1934c). This duo developed the second 'critical' article on Marshall. Sections II and III ('The Main Lines of English Social Thought' and 'Marshall's Relation to the English Tradition') of that article (T. Parsons 1932: 321–36) were now expanded to comprise the bulk of the analysis in 'Sociological Elements in Economic Thought: I –

Historical' (T. Parsons 1934c). Marshall initially was the *ideal-type* of the orthodox tradition: the validity of this position 'stands and falls' with his work (T. Parsons 1931: 101). But later the orthodox tradition is his starting-point for transformational theory-building.

> Taking what may be called the orthodox tradition as its starting point, it will attempt to trace some of the principal elements which have modified it, which have been put forward under the rubric of economic theory in the course of the last century, trying above all to determine their logical relations to the initial orthodox core.   (T. Parsons 1934c: 414)

This indicates a change in his approach to history. This does not mean that the method used in the 'Capitalism' articles is totally invalid. But now the *entire* development of economic theory since Adam Smith and Ricardo comes into view. Previously he had identified Marshall's thought with orthodox economics, but now this is compared with other trends. Parsons formulated a series of 'ideal-types' for his history of economic thought. And Marshall 'the very ideal-type of orthodoxy' (ibid.: 442) was placed also in the category of 'romantic empiricism' (ibid.). Marshall was the very end point of the history of orthodox economics since Adam Smith, and dealt with those general problems which Weber and Sombart had confronted in German historical economics (ibid.: 442–53).

It is not usual for Parsons to be considered as an economist. Nor is he recognized as a historian. He had made a contribution to economics and he also adopted a historical approach. In these articles he assumed the presidential style of one who saw things in their full context.

> The methodological battle between 'orthodox' forms of economics and 'institutionalist' or other unorthodox forms has been raging now for a good many years without much sign of a peace. The contestants are so deeply absorbed in pressing their own case that perhaps they do not often stop to try and see the issues in the perspective of the history of social thought. The present study is an attempt to appraise the question of the status of 'orthodox' economic theory in terms of the history of economic thought since roughly the beginning of the nineteenth century.   (ibid.: 414)

This was not a slip of the pen. 'The history of social thought' was not being made synonymous with 'the history of economic thought'. If there was any equation then the latter had to be seen as a function of the former. In Part II of 'Economics and Sociology – Marshall in Relation to the Thought of his Time' (T. Parsons 1932) – Parsons discussed the 'main lines of English thought'. There developments since the seventeenth century were considered – 'Hobbes and Locke may be regarded as initiating the trends which are of primary interest' (ibid.: 321). Parsons charted the *later* developments in economic orthodoxy from Adam Smith, Ricardo and Mill down to Alfred Marshall to show how orthodox economics had generated, within its ambit, various problems that could only be resolved via a fundamental theoretical analysis of economic behaviour. 'The problem of social order' and 'the problem of the place of the individual in social life' required articulation with a 'general theory of action'. Weber, Pareto and Marshall reasserted 'strains' in the tradition of social thought which went back to Hobbes and Locke. Just as the seventeenth century saw great advances in mechanics via Newton's theories, so the twentieth century would see great scientific advances in the social sciences via Weber, Pareto and Durkheim. These three were, in essence, re-establishing the Hobbes–Locke tradition of social theory.

In this sense Parsons anticipated that the insights of sociology would outlast, out-run and generally replace those of the economists. From this angle Parsons' theoretical development after 1937 can also be interpreted as his progressive adjustment to the endurance of disciplines which he had implicitly. concluded were 'on the wane'.

Parsons always referred to the early 1930s as the 'start' of his theoretical labour in sociology (T. Parsons 1937a; T. Parsons 1949a; T. Parsons 1959; T. Parsons 1970; T. Parsons 1981). His independent *theoretical* adventure was severely tried and tested in the Harvard milieu. Originality was not enough – one had to *show* how one's theoretical perspective had potential for the further development of science.

The underdevelopment of Parsons' impact in economics

Mark Blaug refers to Parsons' analysis of Marshall as 'the pathbreaking study of Marshall's *philosophical* preconceptions and their influence on his economic views' (Blaug 1968: 68; my italics). Parsons would *not* consider his study of Marshall to be a philosophical one. Blaug seems here to represent a typical economics view of sociology: sociological theory is the economist's philosophy. By a Paretian method Parsons had derived the *residue* of Marshall's sociological concern. But Parsons did not consider this method to be philosophical. He was more prosaic. For his methodological flexibility was part of the professional *theorist's* tools of trade. Philosophy may direct its attention to the ontological prerequisites of such self-consciousness, and try to explain the 'ultimate reality' thereof. But for Parsons 'knowing what you are doing' is a necessary part of all theorizing.

In contrast with his preferred theoretical orientation, economics was involved in the scientific evasiveness of Marshall, who '[took] a position of the highest importance on the fundamental questions he professes to ignore' (T. Parsons 1932: 335–6). A radical change of theoretical attitude was required. Nothing less than a 'thoro reconstruction of the intellectual tradition of which Marshall formed a part' (ibid.: 346) was required.

Parsons' 'thoro reconstruction' anticipates the revival of concepts which had somehow fallen into disrepute. A first step towards this reconstruction had already been taken in the second Marshall article. He pointed out, years later, that this was his initial attempt to work out 'convergence' (T. Parsons 1970: 828). The two Marshall articles did not go together like the later duo,

'Sociological Elements in Economic Thought'. The second Marshall article
was a first attempt to present an analytical 'cross-matching' between Marshall, Pareto and Weber, based upon logical analysis. But in the second set of
articles the elements were reversed in their order of presentation. Then the
discussion was organized with the *historical* material 'setting the stage' for the
'analytical factor view' (T. Parsons 1935a). With this historical/analytical
distinction central to his theory-building, Parsons surveyed the history of
economic thought in terms of its particular problems and ongoing debates. In
the 'Marshall articles' the distinction between 'secondary analysis' and
analysis of the recent history of social thought was primary. Marshall was
placed in relation to 'the thought of his time'. They were two distinct forms of
scholarly inquiry. The 'Sociological Elements' essays provided a historical
background for an 'analytical factor' view of recent economic theory, and
hence represented a most important change in method.

Parsons diagnosed the problems faced by economics in terms of 'the fallacy
of misplaced concreteness', derived from Whitehead (Whitehead 1925). There
was, he maintained, a tendency for the economic element to be completely lost
in contemporary economic thought.

> The most conspicuous result is the tendency to submerge what we have started out
> to call the economic element altogether, so that we have the curious spectacle of
> the science of economics being derived from the principles governing every other
> element of human action except the economic.   (T. Parsons 1935a: 646)

The attempt to construct a science of economics on an empiricist basis had
failed. Either you ended up with water-tight compartments and no interrelation between economics and the other social sciences (sociology, political
science, psychology), or one of them became the encyclopaedic synthesis of all
of our social knowledge. There was a way to avoid this. The 'water-tight'
compartments myth was powerful only because it corresponded with the high
degree of differentiation in modern society. But the credibility of this myth had
broken down, with the emerging recognition that societies are basically
interdependent.

> Human life is essentially one and no concretely possible degree of functional
> differentiation can destroy its unity.   (ibid.: 660)

The unity of the theory enterprise could be established by holding to the unity
of the many-sided social reality. It is in this sense that Parsons broke
fundamentally with the *scientistic* approach of positivism to rebuild society
according to the demands of Science, respecifying the essence of science.

> The essence of science, the *understanding* as distinct from the mere photographic
> reception of concrete phenomena, is theory and the essence of theory is analytical
> abstraction. Whatever its dangers, there is no other way.   (ibid.: 661)

Parsons began to outline his alternative position. In a review article on the
nature and significance of economic theory (T. Parsons 1934a), he suggested
alternative arrangements among the various socially related disciplines, as

they were presented in the modern university. This was a call to economics to engage in a 'thoro reconstruction'.

But what tradition in economics has *ever* subsequently followed his call? Parsons' pre-1937 contributions, which he came to interpret as those of a sociologist (ibid.: 511), were not peripheral to economics. He may have been moving, intellectually and professionally, *from* economics *to* sociology, but in the transition period, before Harvard sociology had gained any great reputation, he did make a creative contribution to economics. The work of Clarence Ayres and the institutionalists has lived on in a recognizable form (Breit and Culbertson Jnr 1976; Coats 1976), yet Parsons' influence has remained negligible.

Parsons' response to economics was one factor shaping his pre-1937 theoretical development. There was also his critique of Weber, von Schelting and Rickert (T. Parsons 1936d), his implied response to Sorokin's *Contemporary Sociological Theories* (1928) by opting for 'theory' rather than theories, and his attitude to sociology at Harvard as it had been under the rubric of 'social ethics' (Buck 1965).

But in what sense is this a shift *from* economics *to* sociology? He resisted being confined too rigidly to one or other specialism (T. Parsons 1959: 5–6). He sought to understand the *relationship* between economics and sociology, and would later occasionally 'revisit' economics (e.g. T. Parsons 1949b). But his approach, even in these early years, was led by a vision of a 'general theory'.

General theory

Early in his time at Harvard, Parsons began to see economic theory standing in some kind of theoretical matrix within which sociological theory should also be located (T. Parsons 1970: 828). He viewed the rigorous formulation of laws as an integral part of theory in science. Mathematical laws in mechanics exemplified this most clearly. But he did *not* formally address himself to the mathematical side of economics. The mathematical economics of Marshall, Pareto and Schumpeter were taken as read *for economics*, illustrative of the great steps taken by that discipline towards scientific maturity.

Now, if science is of one piece, and the theory of systems is equally applicable to all social sciences, then it follows that it should be possible to derive the contemporary 'sociological theory' by concentrating upon the sociological elements of contemporary economic theory. This he had begun to do with Marshall. Thus in one sense sociological theory is a function of theory in economics. But if sociology can be derived from the 'sociological side' of mathematical economics, what about the 'mathematical side' of sociology? Parsons seems to have avoided that side of the equation. He assumed its underdevelopment. The underdevelopment of theory and the primitive stage of sociometrics in sociology were closely aligned in his vision for the building of 'general theory'.

If sociological theory could be derived from an analysis of economic thought, then what is there to prevent the derivation of economic theory from sociological thought? Here Parsons seems close to contradiction. The 'sociology' he found in Weber, Pareto and Marshall appeared as the culmination of a logical development within the discipline of economics. But he also implied that the development was caused by a breakdown in the utilitarian paradigm due to the uncontested tradition of reification within classical economics (T. Parsons 1937a: 757). In this sense Parsons *was* encyclopaedic; he was convinced that a new approach to social science in its many modes was imminent. But did he push for a new economics? It seems that he may have anticipated that sociology would replace economics as the major social science.

Parsons derived his concept of 'system' from Henderson, but the concept itself was present in his Dr. phil. articles. There it had mechanistic overtones identified with what Parsons saw in English thought as an 'engine of analysis' (T. Parsons 1929: 33). But it was Durkheim's concept of 'reality sui generis' which proved crucial in the years immediately prior to the publication of *The Structure*. He had had an acquaintance with Durkheim's writings on religion since his Amherst days, but it was only as his *theory* of society (as well as *society itself*) was explicitly accepted as a reality sui generis that the principle of organic self-regulation and self-generation became the fundamental cornerstone of 'theory'.

It was from Schumpeter and his exposition of Pareto's mathematical economics that Parsons derived his concept of 'pure theory' (T. Parsons 1959: 6). The contrasting concept for 'pure theory' is 'applied theory'. It seems likely that it was from Pareto's sociology that Parsons began his search for a statement of 'general theory'. 'General theory' is of equal applicability in the realms of 'pure' and 'applied' theory.

Parsons wrote at that time that an understanding of Pareto's 'central analytical scheme' would show how he was the first to transcend the dilemmas of positivism in a thoroughgoing way. Though he had not developed a satisfactory 'general theory' of human action, he had pointed in the direction in which it could be achieved. A 'clear grasp' of this scheme was essential, Parsons concluded, if the rest of his work was to contribute to the further development of the theory of action (T. Parsons 1936c: 261–2). Again, problems in the interpretation of recent theories were overcome by a hermeneutic which pinpointed their 'central theoretical core' and their contribution to the emergence of the general conceptual scheme. Thus Parsons' 'uncertainty principle' in the development of a 'general theory of social action' was maintained.

With his turn to Durkheim, Parsons identified himself as a sociologist. Previous to that his articles were those of a *theorist* concerned with the integration of economics and sociology. With Durkheim's theory established as a prime pillar of his thought, Parsons accepted his role as a *sociological theorist* (T. Parsons 1935c).

Confronted with the transition in Durkheim's thought, *from* positivism *to* idealism (T. Parsons 1935e), Parsons now had a 'matching pair' for Weber, whose development had been in the other direction. Weber and Durkheim represented the two most prominent 'classical writers' who pointed the way to the kind of multi-dimensional analytical realism he was looking for.

6
Convergence and its construction

Convergence

Parsons' intellectual search culminated in the discovery of 'convergence'. The 'convergence' argument has to be understood in terms of the debate about the future of a general theory of society within economic thought. Parsons analysed the various moves afoot to relativize the encyclopaedic tendency of economics (T. Parsons 1934c: 414). Another *analytical* possibility had emerged within the social sciences. The Hobbes–Locke tradition of social thought was being rediscovered.

'Convergence' in *The Structure* was set forth as an analytical movement in the writings of four thinkers against the background of apparent disorder in the interpretation of modern society.

[A] basic revolution in empirical interpretations of some of the most important social problems has been going on. Linear evolutionism has been slipping and cyclical theories have been appearing on the horizon. Various kinds of individualism have been under increasingly heavy fire. In their place have been appearing socialistic, collectivistic, organic theories of all sorts. The role of reason and the status of scientific knowledge as an element of action have been attacked again and again. We have been overwhelmed by a flood of anti-intellectualistic theories of human nature and behavior, again of many different varieties. A revolution of such magnitude in the prevailing empirical interpretations of human society is hardly to be found occurring within the short space of a generation, unless one goes back to about the sixteenth century. (T. Parsons 1937a: 5)

The convergence he had discovered was the corrective to intellectual disorder. It was a synthesis of the great western traditions of positivism and idealism (T. Parsons 1935c: 282–3, n. 1; T. Parsons 1937a: 774). He had discovered the reunification of western rationality. Sociology, a relative newcomer on the frontiers of science, was finding its task in a new systematic theory of social action. The revolutionary movement was not simply a change from one theory to another. It was not a shift in the theoretical frame of reference as much as a change in the very idea of theory. It was an objective change in the details of theories and it involved the subjective interpretation of theorists. And Parsons positioned himself at the centre of these changes.

Theory not only formulates what we know but also tells us what we want to know, that is, the questions to which an answer is needed. (T. Parsons 1937a: 9)

It is this 'theory of theory' which had made the recent development in social theory possible. Of *The Structure* Parsons wrote the following:

In one of its main aspects the present study may be regarded as an attempt to verify empirically this view of the nature of science and its development in the social field. It takes the form of the thesis that intimately associated with the revolution in empirical interpretations of society sketched above there has in fact occurred an equally radical change in the structure of theoretical systems. The hypothesis may be put forward, to be tested by the subsequent investigation, that this development has been in large part a matter of the reciprocal interaction of new factual insights and knowledge on the one hand with changes in the theoretical system on the other. Neither is the 'cause' of the other. Both are in a state of close mutual interdependence. (ibid.: 11)

Thus, in Parsons' work, 'convergence' has, at least, a *three-fold* reference. There is the historical merging of idealism and positivism. Second, there is a new theory of theory in relation to the theory of society. Third, there is the empirical–analytic discovery of 'convergence' in the writings of Parsons' four principal authors. The 'voluntaristic theory of action' is related to the recent breakdown in positivism and utilitarianism. In this sense, 'convergence' is a contribution to the history of modern science and the sociology of knowledge.

The textual-critical analysis of Pareto, Weber and Durkheim would, henceforth, have to deal with Parsons' 'construction'. After *The Structure of Social Action* twentieth-century sociology would not be able to theorize without Parsons. He covered the entire field. Systematic theory was brought together with secondary studies and the history of theory.

Parsons' method was empirical. 'The basis on which the four writers were brought together for study was rather empirical', he asserted (ibid.: vi). *The Structure* was *not* a history, or a congeries of theories, but theory. It is a work 'in' theory, in the sense that it was an empirical demonstration of a theoretical point of view. The work was framed in empirical terms seeking to chart its emergence. The aim was 'to verify empirically' (ibid.: 11), to present 'an *empirical* monograph' (ibid.: 697), to formulate 'empirical conclusions', claiming 'empirical demonstration' (ibid.: 698). He had, in his terms, provided 'proof' which was 'adequate' (ibid.: 719), 'empirical' (ibid.: 721) and valid (ibid.: 725, n. 3). The voluntaristic theory emphasized empirical verification.

one major factor in the emergence of the voluntaristic theory of action lies in correct observation of the empirical facts of social life, especially corrections of and additions to the observations made by proponents of the theories against which these writers stood in polemical opposition. (ibid.: 721)

'Convergence' depended upon the acceptance of empirical standards of proof for building a theory of action. 'Eliminating observation of the facts amounts to eliminating action itself' (ibid.: 723). The fact that the theory had been empirically validated helped explain its emergence (ibid.: 725, n. 3). The observation and verification of fact is integral to the structure of theoretical systems. The voluntaristic theory of action converged with this new understanding of the place of empirical validation in scientific thought. Parsons was pushing on beyond Whitehead's 'fallacy of misplaced concreteness' to a new formulation of the relation between science and its conceptual scheme (Whitehead, he later observed, had in some respects 'not gone far enough' (T. Parsons 1974: 126)).

Parsons derived his confidence within this act of theorizing; the fact of abstraction was his taken-for-granted reality. Scientific open-mindedness was the corollary of a theoretical system of observation and verification of fact.

But what of Parsons' *second* great project? After *The Structure*, how did he conceptualize the theory of its own terms? His intentions were already well formulated in *The Structure*. His vision of theory-building was derived from his confrontation with Pareto in the transition from economics to sociology, involving Schumpeter's concept of 'pure theory'. Parsons' goal was to formulate a statement of theory. His aim for the long term was to set up a system of variables (T. Parsons 1937a: 751). His focus was the dynamic social system in its entirety. But how was the system of concepts, implied throughout *The Structure*, to be formulated in analytical terms?

'Construction' and the residue of idealist methodology

Parsons responded to the interpretative traditions of German social thought in which, for instance, Wilhelm Dilthey had attempted to forge a philosophy of the history of philosophy. Parsons worked on a theory of the development of theory. *The Structure* is a response forged in the context of neo-Kantian approaches to the history of thought. What does this involve?

> Characteristic of the neo-Kantian concept of *Problemgeschichte* was the subordination of historical study to systematic philosophical interests. The history of philosophy, in this view, is the story of the great thinkers' struggle to come to terms with the perennial and immutable systematic problems of philosophy. The contemporary philosopher is intensely interested in this history because he, too, is struggling with these same enduring problems and can expect to gain systematic insight from the giants who have preceded him.   (Wolters 1979: 231)

Nicolai Hartmann subordinated the history of philosophy to systematic philosophical interests (Plantinga 1979), but Parsons' history of theory was subordinated to *theoretical* interests. On this level Parsons' theory shows a clear affinity with that reaction to German Historicism which has been associated with the problem-historical (*Problemgeschichte*) approach. There are similarities between the 'problem-historical' school and the orientation put forward by Bridgman concerning the task of science as the ongoing reformulation of the problems of previous generations of scientists (Bridgman 1955: 149).

Analysing Sombart and Weber, Parsons had referred, following Croce, to the 'story of liberty' in the history of western science (T. Parsons 1928: 646ff.;

ref. Croce 1941). Parsons was seeking for the lines of progress and liberty in theory-building. He 'went beyond' Weber, Rickert and von Schelting to a new formulation of the basic problem for social *science* (T. Parsons 1936d: 678). Not only German-European ideas, but local (Anglo-Saxon) *conditions* were involved, as we have noted above. Parsons' synthesis of idealism and positivism, in his theory-building, was influenced by idealism, but it was not dominated by that trend, as Münch asserts (Münch 1981; 1982). There is an affinity, but rather than seeing himself and his theory in 'problem-historical' terms (i.e. giving contemporary answers to perennial questions common to all theorists) he viewed contemporary theories within the history of science as means to his end – the refinement of a general analytical scheme for the social sciences. Parsons began to construct the theory of action from among the many streams of western science. He charted his course in midstream. But once 'convergence' was established he remained convinced of its validity and sailed with it until the end of his career (T. Parsons 1974).

'Convergence' became the 'relatively constant background of non-change' (T. Parsons 1961a: 220) against which he could chart his own theoretical development. 'Convergence' in his perspective came to represent the intellectual mores of the time, and there was little any one individual could do to change the mores. Parsons had fortuitously discovered 'convergence'; he had stumbled upon an insight which gave him the critical distance he needed to make an important contribution (T. Parsons 1923: 13–14). It is evidence of Parsons having been totally committed to making such a monumental discovery, yet he also located the genius of his work outside himself – in his theory.

Should we not expect that this 'convergence' would be manifest in other fields of human endeavour, theoretical and practical? Even Parsons' running battle with intellectual rigidity (T. Parsons 1959: 5–6, n. 3) did not lead him to develop this concept in its interdisciplinary scope, or even call upon his colleagues to promote it. Of the development of the theory of action he had stated:

> This process may be interpreted to constitute a definite internal breakdown of the positivistic theory of action ... a process in many ways analogous to the recent internal breakdown of the conceptual framework of classical physics.
> (T. Parsons 1937a: 470)

Once he had formulated the concept Parsons was more concerned to specify the *scientific limits* of his discovery rather than seeking its further application in other fields. *The Structure* charted a dramatic change. No longer was he 'on the outside looking in'; he was in the midst of a great intellectual revolution. To be on the frontier of this advance in sociology was also to be at the centre of scientific culture – 'theory' rather than 'raw fact' (or 'dust-bowl empiricism') was the actual cutting edge of this progress.

It is, of course, conceivable that the convergence does not exist at all, but that its appearance in this study is the result of an accumulation of errors of interpretation by the present author. It is also conceivable, though very improbable, that it is the result of an accumulation of random errors on the part of the various theorists themselves. If either of these possibilities is to be considered, it might be instructive to calculate the probabilities that this might occur, considering the number of different elements and their combinations to be taken into account. (ibid.: 722)

Translated, the above statement could mean: 'I am open to the possibility of being wrong, but the chances, on my calculations, are extremely slight.' In such terms Parsons debated with himself about the validity of his 'discovery' for social theory. He seems to have tried to keep an open mind on the subject all his life. Yet he issued a challenge: 'you argue against my theory and you have to argue *against* the weight of tradition which my theory *explains* and *embodies*'. Parsons in his convergence argument was establishing a canon of classics for the social sciences.

'Convergence' was also tactical. Abstract thinking is the heart of theory; theory is the heart of science; science is the means of building a more perfect world. 'Convergence' is a call for professional unity. Parsons' theory, 'a tentative set of working tools', did not exclude other conceptual schemes a priori (T. Parsons 1937b: 13), despite the large claims he had made for it. He was confident that his theory was 'true' and would outlast the others.

Why is 'convergence' so hard to handle? As early as *The Structure* 'the Parsonian theoretical forest', 'vast and tangled, a veritable jungle of fine distinctions and intertwining classifications' (Devereux 1961: 1–2) was present. Was methodological complexity a prerequisite for genuine theoretical development? Parsons' background in German economics made him aware of the ongoing *Methodenstreit* about the *Geisteswissenschaften*, yet though his relativism may have been somewhat existentialist he viewed himself as open-minded, and hence *optimistic* about the long-term future. The entire *construction* of this 'relatively constant background' for theory became, in effect, a bequest which was raised *above* theoretical change. For this reason 'convergence' has been difficult to criticize. It has become a central concept for the modern sociological discipline. It is the capstone of Parsons' philosophy of the history of social theory. It is indicative of his theoretical *Weltanschauung*.

The Structure of Social Action as secondary analysis

Another way of approaching the interpretative problems of 'convergence' is to compare Parsons' method with the *Imitations* of Robert Lowell (1962), the New England poet. This would place Parsons' work in the *cultural* context of American attempts to appropriate the traditions of European excellence, a context wider than academic sociology, and is helpful to highlight aspects of Parsons' project. In his *Imitations* Robert Lowell had presented 'a small anthology of European poetry'. One commentary reads:

As a 'small anthology of European poetry', however, the collection is obviously sparse and crotchety: what is important is the poet's readiness to explore the European intonation, try the agonies and the vagaries of the European subject in a way that his American contemporaries have not, and prove them by translation on his pulses. The effect of his anthology in the long run is to draw the reader's attention constantly to the person of the translator, and away from the ambiance of 'Europe'.   (Belitt 1967: 115)

The parallelism is marked. Lowell's 'small anthology' matches Parsons' study in 'recent European social thought'. Lowell's choice is 'sparse and crotchety' and Parsons' style is by no means 'elegant'. Like Lowell's book, Parsons' study in 'recent European social theory' was based on profound respect. The 'mimicry' was not that of a 'mocking bird in an aviary of European originals' (ibid.: 120), but a composition deeply aware of the style of its own contribution, and of the way in which the American style was viewed in Europe. Both are deferential, but also original. It was Lowell's expectation that all the poetry from Homer to Pasternak and Montale which he 'imitated' could be read 'as a sequence, one voice running through many personalities, contrasts and repetitions' (ibid.: 116). It was written 'as an attempt to write live English and to do what they might have done if they were writing their poems now and in America' (Lowell 1962: xi). Likewise, Parsons had represented the unity of recent social theory, as if his four European writers had all written their theories as contributions to his 'voluntaristic theory of action' anthology.

   The Structure was 'secondary' in two senses. It was an investigation of what some theorists had written, but it was also 'secondary' in a cultural sense. It was an American form of European thought. 'Convergence' is evidence of Parsons, the American critic, incorporating the functions of the theorist and the historian into his secondary account, in a way similar to Lowell's demonstration that his role as poet coincided with his abilities to make a contribution to literary criticism via his poetry. In Parsons' case it was not an example of Parsons the theorist *usurping* the function of the critic, as Bierstedt suggests (Bierstedt 1981: 395), unless we wish to maintain a strict division between the theorist and the historically aware critic of theory. We here recall the argument developed in his Amherst essays concerning the cultural equivalence which pertains between the artist and the art critic (T. Parsons 1923: 12). Parsons was formulating his theory with his theoretical vocation uppermost in his mind. The question of whether Parsons *qua theorist* successfully incorporated the functions of critic and historian into his 'General Theory' can only be answered if we take note of his view of his own 'serendipity' and how that is woven into the theory itself. His assertion that the work is 'theory' rather than 'theories' represents his conviction that 'convergence' has integrity. It was methodologically unified in the empirical sense. The historical function of his 'theory' was of one piece with his task as theorist. Parsons' development should be interpreted in terms of an unwillingness to proceed to a systematic formulation of 'the theory itself' *until* he had proved its utility in empirical analysis. In other words, there is a sense in which *The*

Structure applies the theory he discovered, as well as producing his own 'imitations' for the sociological bookshelf to stand alongside of Weber, Durkheim *et al.*

The Structure, which shaped a generation of secondary accounts in sociological theory, is Parsons' attempt to interpret the 'westward' drift of recent European social thought. He placed himself midstream in that current, yet he was faced with a situation in which scholars young and old had yet to read, let alone understand, his work. 'Convergence' had emerged as his point of departure.

Where, however, was 'diffusion' in relation to Parsons' argument about 'convergence'? In his Amherst Philosophy III essays these two great forces were considered as always working together in cultural development. He viewed himself in terms of both 'convergence' and 'diffusion'. His documentation of 'convergence' in the English language to a predominantly American audience is also evidence of a cultural 'diffusion' whereby European theories had now become available. His 'intellectual opportunism' was interwoven with his belief in his own serendipity; he had discovered a conciliar process which was re-emphasizing the unity of western thought. His theory had emerged for such a time as this.

Parsons the writer of statements and author of theory

How did he receive his own contribution? How did he respond to his own formulations? The 'convergence' concept had first appeared in Parsons' writings in relation to the biogenetic law whereby all species were assumed to go through the same stages of evolution on their way to maturation. In *The Structure* Parsons used this concept in a refined sense. All he saw in Sorokin's *Contemporary Sociological Theories* (1928) was 'diffusion', the corresponding process in evolutionary development to 'convergence'. 'Convergence' arrested the balance. In his empirical study theory and 'convergence' were on the one side; theories and 'diffusion' were implied on the other.

But now how was the theory to be formulated? In *The Structure* the theory was analysed by contrast with its variations. There it was a 'going concern' – a process of convergence on a conceptual scheme. But shortly after its publication he wrote:

> The object of this book was, by a careful and meticulous analysis of the works of four men, to disentangle the outline of the system from the varying approaches, differences in form of statement and in the empirical interests of the different writers, to show its bearings in relation to their empirical problems, and to demonstrate fully the fact of convergence. The accomplishment of these tasks required an extensive and difficult treatment in the course of which it is easy to lose sight of the main logical structure as a whole. Hence there is something to be said for an attempt to outline this structure directly without reference to the critical context which was necessarily so prominent in the book.
>
> (T. Parsons 1939/40: 1)

The broad 'outline' of this conceptual structure is detailed in the following chapter. Here the focus is Parsons' *theory-writing*, one type of which had been set out in *The Structure*. His 'organism' – the theory of action – had been viewed in its environment. Its 'hereditary constitution' had been specified, but what was its 'internal structure'? Unlike the botanist or biologist, Parsons the social theorist was involved subjectively with his 'organism'. The botanist, the biologist, the chemist or the physicist analyses the structure of botanical, biological, chemical or physical systems via a conceptual scheme. In contrast, Parsons' 'organism' *was* his conceptual scheme. Theory-writing was his form of experimentation. Instead of a laboratory and scientific instruments, he used a pen and his yellow writing pad. His writings after 1937 are formulations of the 'internal structure' of the theory of social action. In his writings Parsons was 'doing theory'. His writing was *internal* to his theory. He practised his science *in* his writing. From here we begin our interpretation of his 'social system'. *The Social System* emerged as a primary 'source' for sociological theory-construction, but *The Structure* had been a 'secondary work'.

> In a sense the present work is to be regarded as a secondary study of the work of a group of writers in the field of social theory. But the genus 'secondary study' comprises several species; of these an example of only one, and that perhaps not the best known, is to be found in these pages.   (T. Parsons 1937a: v)

This style was continued in his major works of the period 1937–51. In the essay he wrote with Edward A. Shils, 'Values, Motives and Systems of Action', they noted that the work is not 'scholarship in the traditional sense'. It is an 'essay in theory construction' (T. Parsons and E. A. Shils 1951: 52). The juxtaposition of the two terms 'scholarship in the traditional sense' and 'theory construction' requires elaboration. (1) Parsons acknowledged that his presentation was unconventional. (2) He wrote, as a secondary writer, with a *theoretical* goal. (3) Parsons, the *theory-writer*, documented the process of theory construction. His writing was not the well-constructed prose of 'scholarship'. But *for him theory-writing was the closest he got to theory-in-action.* The 'working out' of a statement of theoretical import required that he work *with*, whilst also refining, a conceptual scheme. This was the 'way of the investigator' (Cannon 1945).

It is also possible that Parsons' 'theory' is his response to his exposure to 'the sociology of knowledge' in his Heidelberg days. The extent of the influence may have been considerable (T. Parsons 1926). Further evidence in this regard is found in the symposium *The Theories of Talcott Parsons* (M. Black 1961), where he indicated a measure of qualified sympathy for those who found the going tough.

> Having reached what I hope is a certain 'age of humility' I am not at all prepared to discount entirely the view that there are peculiar and unnecessary obscurities in my writings. At the same time I can claim to be somewhat sophisticated in the sociology of knowledge and hence in the interpretation of resistances to certain

types of intellectual innovation. In this role I cannot entirely dismiss the possibility
that some of the complaints may be manifestations of such resistances. In any case,
it is not possible for an author to be fully objective about the reception of his work;
any more ultimate judgement will have to be left to the outcome of the process of
natural selection through professional criticism by which scientific reputations
ultimately come to be stabilized.   (T. Parsons 1961b: 320–1)

Parsons' professionalism here is almost equated with his sophistication in 'the
sociology of knowledge', which allowed him to understand his own subjective
and scientific frame of reference. He detected the existence of 'strains of
resistance to innovation', perhaps also in his own thought (note the ambiguous
use of the genetic term 'strain', again in relation to the 'history of ideas'). He
'cannot entirely dismiss the possibility' that complaints about his obscure style
of writing were due to intellectual resistance to intellectual innovation. But we
must ask: was he not equating his writing style with his theory? Does
intellectual innovation *require* clumsy syntax with peculiar and unnecessary
obscurity? Parsons seems to have implied that his writing style was *integral* to
his theory. *And with my interpretation of his theory-writing as his form of experimentation, I have an explanation for the equation. Towards a General Theory of Action* is
better written than *The Social System*, but is *not* easier to understand. The latter
may represent a 'head-long rush' into publication (Gouldner 1971: 204) and
the former may have been constructed with all points logically, sequentially
and parsimoniously covered. But the latter is a better example of Parsons'
theory, because it illustrates Parsons' style of theory-writing, which was *integral*
to his 'general theory of action'.

At the deepest level Parsons seems to have discovered himself by operating
the conceptual frame of reference, then documenting it and developing it
further. His theory can be looked at from two points of view – from the 'central
analytical core' of the formulation or as the process by which the theoretical
logic was derived. As his project unfolded, so these two aspects re-emerged as
the two forms in which Parsons committed his theory to writing. *The Social
System* located the central analytical core of the theory, whilst *The Structure*
charted its progress. Nevertheless both aspects can be seen to be operative in
both forms of theory-construction.

Parsons believed in his own serendipity. He thus took on the serious task of
developing sociology's conceptual scheme. He had analysed the impasse of
rationality. The new view was required; it had to be set out.

In 1951, in the Preface to *The Social System*, he wrote:

The present volume is an attempt to bring together, in systematic and generalized
form, the main outlines of a conceptual scheme for the analysis of the structure and
processes of social systems. In the nature of the case, within the frame of reference
of action, such a conceptual scheme must focus on the delineation of the system of
institutionalized roles and motivational processes organized about them. Because
of this focus and the very elementary treatment of processes of economic exchange
and of the organization of political power, the book should be regarded as a
statement of general sociological theory, since this is here interpreted to be that

part of the theory of the social system which is centred on the phenomena of the institutionalization of patterns of value-orientation in roles.

(T. Parsons 1951: vii)

Careful reading of this explanation is required. The phrase 'a *statement* of general sociological theory' makes the point clear. Comprehensive and general *statement* was the goal of his 1937–51 project in theory-writing. In the unpublished 'Actor, Situation and Normative Pattern' he had begun with a similar observation. There the problematic *method* of *The Structure* was in the background.

> The object of the present essay is to attempt a systematic and generalized statement of the theoretical system without critical references. Like the critical statement in the earlier book it will be confined to a brief statement of the frame of reference, and an outline of the structure of systems. No systematic attention will be paid to the definition of analytical elements or variables. Furthermore attention will be confined to statement. Systematic justification on either methodological or empirical grounds is impossible within the limits of such a brief statement.
>
> (T. Parsons 1939/40: 2)

The work was designed to detail the theory found in *The Structure*, but in the process of writing the statement Parsons seems to have developed a new formulation of his theoretical orientation (T. Parsons 1974: 125). *The Social System* was the culmination of that fourteen-year project. It had begun as an attempt to outline the conceptual scheme implied by 'convergence', in the interests of clearer communication. But it emerged with a new set of difficulties. Another indication of Parsons' aim during these years is found in the introductory statement to the unpublished draft of *The Social System*. This work had the provisional title: *The Social System – Structure and Function* (T. Parsons 1949/50), and comprised in the vicinity of 500 type-written pages.

> The aim of this brief volume is to present for the use and the critical reaction of members of the sociological and related professions an integrated statement, with adequate illustrative material, of a coherent outline of a systematic conceptual scheme for sociological theory, so far as that is possible at this time. The phrase a 'systematic conceptual scheme' is chosen in preference to a 'system of theory' or a 'theoretical system' both because it seems to be a more accurate description of the enterprise and because both of the other phrases are open to misunderstanding in either of two ways. On the one hand they might be held to refer to another attempt at speculative 'system building' of the type which Comte and Spencer have put forth. By contrast with these other conceptual structures the present one is most definitely not meant to be a system of 'principles' in terms of which all social behavior and the processes of social change are claimed to be adequately explicable; it is rather a conceptual framework within which such fragmentary generalized knowledge of this sort as we already possess may be acceptably and conveniently organized and related, and in terms of which research intended to widen and deepen that knowledge in the enormous areas where it is inadequate or non-existent may be guided and coordinated.   (T. Parsons 1949/50: 1)

Overall the aim was to present a way of analysing social systems. Action was its basic idea, and this required considering the established roles and the incentives to perform them, which are part of everyday life. The formulation was limited to a general sociological theory, the theory concerned with the prescription and control of behaviour.

Parsons had assumed the role of author of a theoretical scheme, and had *acted* by committing the theory to statement. When he used the term 'statement' he seems to have been implying that it was up to the reader to judge whether he had performed his role adequately.

A professional audience was in mind. His theory rejected 'system-building' even if the statement used complex sentences and utilized difficult concepts. The project was part of the ongoing evolution of science. Merton's view that Parsons was resurrecting a form of system-building was in the background when this 1949/50 statement was penned. But subsequent professional opinion has not viewed his theory as an alternative to system-building. On the contrary. Parsons' 'general theory' has been taken as the epitome of 'system-building'. Parsons' own use of the terms 'system' and 'systematic', in relation to social theory and society itself, suggests that he was not referring to the systems generated verbally (which Bierstedt criticized (1938, 1981)), but to the theoretical objects of science called systems – real objects of the world.

In *The Structure*, Parsons observed that that work was 'rather empirical' (T. Parsons 1937a: vi). The term 'rather' introduces semantic ambiguity – does 'rather' mean 'on the other hand' or 'to a certain extent'? – but overall it can be read as referring to Parsons' tentativeness. His was an *alternative approach to a certain extent*. The 'gain from serendipity', in this case the emergence of 'convergence', pointed to a significant historical calling. He had steeped himself in the sociological tradition and had come across a totally unplanned result. The subsequent general theoretical statement 'without critical references' attempted to specify the 'theory of action'. The statement was to be made over and over again – the same conceptual scheme was derived from different angles. Parsons remained open to new gains from serendipity as the statement was redrafted, and the meaning of the project unfolded. This again indicates Parsons' evolutionary method. The statement of a theory of systems was one step. The 'statement' was limited because of the underdevelopment of sociology. But things were changing for the better.

[T]he thesis may be advanced that sociology is just in the process of emerging into the status of a mature science. Heretofore it has not enjoyed the kind of integration and directed activity which only the availability and common acceptance and employment of a well-articulated generalized theoretical system can give to a science. The main framework for such a system is, however, now available, though this fact is not as yet very generally appreciated and much in the way of development and refinement remains to be done on the purely theoretical level, as well as its systematic use and revision in actual research. It may therefore be held that we stand on the threshold of a definitely new era in sociology and the neighbouring social science field.   (T. Parsons 1945: 212)

Parsons' own statements of how he viewed his writing show him trying to achieve *realistic* goals.

Even though the definitive solution of most of our theoretical problems is obviously out of the question for many generations, what can be achieved by such an enterprise can be of substantial significance. (T. Parsons 1949/50: 4)

But can Parsons' theory be criticized? Parsons theorized first and *then* in written formulation tried to reflect upon the meaning of his concepts. His method of 'developing' theory was to anticipate criticisms that might highlight 'inconsistency'.

The development of theoretical ideas has been proceeding so rapidly that a difference of a few months or even weeks in time may lead to important changes, so there are some differences . . . taken in the two publications [the reference here is to 'Values, Motives and Systems of Action' and *The Social System*]. Indeed this process of development is such that it inevitably affects the internal consistency of the present book. (T. Parsons 1951: x)

In Parsons' view his formulations needed the criticism of fellow-workers. This was a major requirement if logical integration was ever to be achieved. He was well aware of the possible shortcomings.

Statements like those above may also lead the potentially sympathetic critic to wholesale scepticism (Homans 1983; Gouldner 1971; Mills 1959). The burden of reading the 'theory' has often been too great; it has meant too much trouble. The 'burden of proof', a phrase Parsons used quite often, was unfairly placed upon the reader to 'make sense' of this 'less-than-internally-consistent' theory. Parsons admitted it did not 'hang together' as he would have liked. But simply avoiding his writings does not facilitate any penetrating critique of his theory.

Parsons' view of himself as *writer* of statements and *author* of theory has to be kept in mind, as does his perception of rapid development. Great strides were being made which needed documentation, and *The Social System* was designed to do that. The systematic results which had been achieved on various fronts were uneven.

It is not possible to work intensively on one part without implications of the changes introduced arising for other points; the process of revision thus never fully catches up with itself. (T. Parsons 1951: x)

The urgency to 'press on' seems to have been almost overwhelming. Meanwhile the critical faculties of the reader were prevailed upon to contribute to this 'grand task'.

In general the reader may expect to find some of this less than perfect consistency. I have thought it better to run the risk and get the book published, rather than to work it over and over for too long. It can then get the benefit of critical discussion, and then, within a relatively short time, a revision may be attempted. (ibid.: x)

Parsons had been working on this schema for about fifteen years. It comes as no surprise to learn that he wanted to get it published. The project was in full swing.

PART 4
The theory

7
Conceptualizing *The Social System*

The long-term project

This and the following three chapters are the culminating chapters of this work. In this chapter the theory of action as it was stated in *The Structure* and in the unpublished document 'Actor, Situation and Normative Pattern' is presented. In the next chapter an overview of the development of the theory during the period 1937–51 is given. Chapter 9 looks closely at three formulations which were published during this time. Chapter 10 will provide a detailed statement of principles for the interpretation of *The Social System* by reference to the first two chapters of that work. This will be a critical summary. A full commentary of those chapters is not included here because of space constraint. Though this work is a *critical commentary*, a conventional secondary work, it seems that the 'secondary literature' on Parsons would be considerably strengthened by a line-by-line exegesis of *The Social System* on classical lines.

The conceptual scheme presented in *The Structure* was an outline only – 'not yet worked out in detail'. That task remained. Towards the end of *The Structure* Parsons wrote,

> It has repeatedly been stated that this study has not attempted a systematic treatment of what is, in this sense, the analytical aspect of the theory of action. It has been limited, rather, to working out the structural outline of the generalized systems of action to which such an analytical theory would be applicable.
> (T. Parsons 1937a: 751)

The Structure was thus only a beginning – 'the structural outline of the generalized systems of action'. The focus was 'concrete' (i.e. the writings of his chosen authors), yet there was enough to give the reader some idea of the analytical elements. The kind of work that remained to be done was related to this basic distinction between two approaches to the theory of action.

> The two modes of conceptualization [i.e. the 'structural outline' and the 'analytical theory'] often overlap, however, so there has had to be much talk of variables, of analytical elements. But no attempt has been made to consider the problem of setting up a *system* of variables. (ibid.: 751)

Parsons' long-term aim was to formulate a system of variables for the analysis of action systems. This project was conceived as *analytical* and not *historical*. It was primarily the structural *aspect* of the historically emerging theory that Parsons had traced in *The Structure*. And there would be at least two stages. The first stage had been a difficult undertaking in its own right.

The 'theory' in *The Structure* is found particularly on pp. 43–51 and notes A, B, C and D (pp. 74–86) in Chapter II, 'The Theory of Action'; pp. 697–702 and 719–26 in Chapter XVII, 'Empirically Verified Conclusions' and pp. 727–68 in Chapter XIX, 'Tentative Methodological Implications'. By selective treatment of these passages, an outline of his theory of action as it stood in *The Structure* can be presented. Though Parsons *denied* having set up a fully systematic exposition at this time he yet wrote enough to give the reader a sense of his systematic inclinations. But the outline of the theory does not stand on its own. It exists within the framework of his theory of theory (ibid.: 698). Early on Parsons had announced the essence of his theory.

> The utilitarian branch of positivistic thought has, by virtue of the structure of its theoretical system, been focused upon a given range of definite empirical insights and related theoretical problems. The central fact – a fact beyond all question – is that in certain aspects and to certain degrees, under certain conditions, human action is rational. That is, men adapt themselves to the conditions in which they are placed and adapt means to their ends in such a way as to approach the most efficient manner of achieving these ends. And the relations of these means and conditions to the achievement of their ends are 'known' to be intrinsically verifiable by the methods of empirical science.   (ibid.: 19)

The 'means–end' schema has been a constant theme in western rationality since at least Aristotle's *Politics*. Parsons tried to develop insight into the structure of human action on such a basis. He was trying to 'develop' the various views of his writers in a way parallel to Calvin (as analysed by Weber), who had 'developed' Luther's concept of *Beruf* (calling). It will be noted that in Weber's account Luther had one foot in 'modernity' and one foot in 'mediaeval society'. In Parsons' account Weber was 'read' as having one foot in the 'old form of action theory' and one foot in the 'new'.

The theory in *The Structure*

After *The Structure* how was he to extract his own theoretical frame of reference from his representation of other social theorists? We have seen that he had tried to achieve a differentiation, effecting a break with the 'means–end' schema' of economics, through an evolutionary hermeneutic. The evolutionary 'motor' drove Parsons' theorizing during the period 1937–51 as he tried to locate the 'present position' and 'prospects' of sociological theory.

The Structure set forth the theoretical 'unit' that was required. The next step was to define that unit comprehensively. This was the 'act', and the 'unit act', like the particle in mechanics, had to be defined in terms of its properties. Particles have mass, velocity, location in space and direction of motion.

Parsons' 'unit act' to be so defined had to be related to a set of concepts comprising the action scheme. He listed these in logical order:

> (1) It implies an agent, an 'actor'. (2) For purposes of definition the act must have an 'end', a future state of affairs toward which the process of action is oriented . . . (3) It must be initiated in a 'situation' . . . (4) . . . in the choice of alternative means to the end, in so far as the situation allows alternatives, there is a 'normative orientation' of action . . .   (ibid.: 44)

The 'situation' of action had two basic aspects: 'conditions' over which the actor has no control and 'means' by which he can shape the situation into closer conformity with his own ends. Parsons here implied that the perception of a discrepancy between 'what is' and 'what ought to be' is an essential element of action. Any intention to modify 'the situation' is a manifestation of such perception. This was what he meant by 'normative orientation'. It explains why the subjective point of view of the actor was given a central place in his theory.

> A normative orientation is fundamental to the schema of action in the same sense that space is fundamental to that of the classical mechanics; in terms of the given conceptual scheme there is no such thing as action except as effort to conform with norms just as there is no such thing as motion except as change of location in space.
> (ibid.: 76–7)

In his classification of the various system types in the theory of action Parsons put it in these terms:

> By a theory of action is here meant any theory the empirical reference of which is to a concrete system which may be considered to be composed of the units here referred to as 'unit acts'. In a unit act there are identifiable as minimum characteristics the following: (1) an end, (2) a situation, analyzable in turn into (a) means and (b) conditions, and (3) at least one selective standard in terms of which the end is related to the situation.   (ibid.: 77)

The subjective aspect of the conception was emphasized explicitly thus:

> It is evident that these [i.e. action theory] categories have meaning only in terms which include the subjective point of view, i.e., that of the actor. A theory which, like behaviorism, insists on treating human beings in terms which exclude this subjective aspect, is not a theory of action in the sense of this study.
> (ibid.: 77–8)

Not only had he compared *social science* and *mechanics* in his discussion of 'units' and the construction of conceptual systems, he also considered whether the voluntaristic theory of action might be formulated as a set of simultaneous equations (ibid.: 727, n. 1). In the earlier part of the book, the 'formulae' for the various theories of action were outlined. The most generalized formula for a system of action was defined in these terms:

$$A = S [M \text{ (manifested in T, t, r)} +$$
$$C \text{ (manifested in T, t, r)} +$$
$$ie \text{ (manifested in T, t, r)}]$$
$$+ E$$
$$+ N \text{ [defined in terms of T, t, r, i, or of ie]}$$

+ r [in role other than as manifestation of S, as ir].
Z = (A1 + A2 + A3 ... An) + Rel + RI + Rc
Where A = Unit Act
and Z = a system of Action.

It will be noted that 'a system of action' (Z) is dependent on the definition of the unit act as that is defined by its constituent elements:

S =   a situation
M = means
C = conditions
i =   normative or ideal elements
ie = symbolic expressions of i
E =   an end
N =   a selective standard relating E and S
T =   scientifically valid knowledge
t =   unscientific elements
r =   random elements

Rel =elementary relations of unit acts in a system
RI = relations which are emergent at the level of the individual with no emergent properties deriving from the relations of these individuals to one another
Rc = relations emergent in respect to the relations of individuals as members of social groups.   (ibid.: 78)

This was the basis upon which Parsons developed his theory. Both idealism and positivism had failed (in their respective definitions of 'the situation') to include 'basic elements' constitutive of the unit act. Positivism in general did not deal with symbolic expressions of normative elements, and normative elements were discounted except in a random sense. Idealism, on the other hand, ruled out all mediation by knowledge, scientific and unscientific.

Parsons' general formula for the voluntaristic system presents the most compact statement possible of the theory of action systems.

A = S(T, t, ie, r) + E(T, t, i, r, ie) + N(T, t, ie, i, r)
Z = (A1 + A2 + A3 + ... An) + Rel + RI + Rc [A represents a unit act;
    Z represents a system of action].   (ibid.: 82)

In brief the unit act can be defined by the combination of S ('the situation' which included both limiting conditions (C) and means for facilitating (M)), E (the end in view) and N (the 'selective standards' guiding the selection of means to the end). The system of action (Z) was the set of all the acts and the relations between them at three levels – unit acts, individual actors and collectivities. In contrast to RI and Rc, Rel has no emergent properties. It is assumed that there are certain degrees of complexity in systems of action below which the units have no emergent properties (ibid.: 734). The system so defined provided a means by which observation could be ordered for further scientific investigation. It was indicative of the scientific attitude whereby 'concrete phenomena come to be divided into units or parts' (ibid.: 43). It also provided a theoretical means of controlling the production of concepts which were multiplied through analytical division.

Now in relation to these three levels it is necessary to specify the way in which the 'social system concept' was used in *The Structure*. Parsons' own view was that his 'structural-functional' use of the system-concept first emerged, possibly in 'Actor, Situation and Normative Pattern', when W. B. Cannon's views of homeostasis began to affect his formulation. He had learned the concept from Schumpeter, Henderson and Pareto (T. Parsons 1974: 125–6). But we need to specify its location in *The Structure* if we are to avoid an anachronistic reading of his development.

This also has important consequences for any interpretation of Parsons' development. When his theory in *The Structure* is scrutinized various themes are revealed which have subsequently become identified with Parsons' style of theorizing. To specify four:

1. There is the sense in which *The Structure* was pitched at the level of 'action-theory' and the 'human condition'. Action was his master-concept and action-theory was established, following Freyer, as a *Wirklichkeitwissenschaft* (reality science), alongside of *Logoswissenschaft* (cultural science) and *Naturwissenschaft* (natural science). There are three major categories – nature, action and culture (T. Parsons 1937a: 762, n. 1). When the development of voluntaristic theory, evaluated in terms of the breakdown of positivism, was placed in the context of the 'action' level of analysis, the adjective 'voluntaristic' was explicitly dispensed with. It had served its purpose in showing the development of a new analytical orientation.

2. The social system concept was present in *The Structure*, particularly in relation to Pareto's contribution; but Parsons by no means implied that it was simply an idiosyncratic element of Pareto's conceptual scheme. When it was used he referred to it as a concept in general usage (ibid.: 245, 264).

3. The social system concept was *equated* with 'relations emergent at the level of collectivity' (Rc).

> A sociologistic system is one which besides the emergent relations attributable to the organization of unit acts relative to the same actor, includes further emergent relations attributable to the organization of a plurality of actors *in a social system*, a 'collectivity'.   (ibid.: 80, my italics)

Unlike all other positivistic systems the 'sociologistic' version of positivism included the social system/'collectivity' element Rc (note the printer's error on p. 81, where 'Eel' should read 'Rel'!). Consequently the social system is a constituent part of the general system of action (Z), as 'relations emergent in respect to the relations of individuals as members of social groups', of 'collectivities' (ibid.: 78).

4. Action was the master-concept and the social system was formulated on that basis. In these terms Pareto's contribution, although deficient at the general action level, provided sociological theory with a pertinent impetus.

His work thus provides one of the most promising points of departure for the type of theory in sociology and the related social sciences in which the present study is interested. Progress in this direction lies not in repudiating Pareto, as so many have thought necessary, but in developing what he had begun to a more advanced stage in certain directions.   (ibid.: 460)

The identical sentiment was expressed in the Preface to *The Social System* (T. Parsons 1951: vii).

The 'social system' concept

Having defined all the various elements which make up the formulae for 'the general theory of action', Parsons moved to the next stage, and for him the most promising basis for making any new advance was the *social system* concept. A social system was defined as a plurality of interrelated and interacting human individuals.

Human society has an *organic* character, and the biological *organism* was his 'nearest analogy'. An organism exists in an environment which is, in part, non-organic. A social system exists in a situation which is partly non-social, yet this situation stands in a relation of interdependence with the social system. So there is a system of reciprocity between the non-social 'system' and the social system. Analytical procedure requires the analyst to specify the level of formulation, and the kind of use one envisages, for a 'social system'.

> Actions in turn give rise to social relationships and their differentiation to the structuring of social systems in terms of behavior patterns, statuses and roles. Social relationships, that is, are in fact patterned in such a way that they and their component actions can from several points of view, within certain limitations, be treated as determinately structured. People, that is, do not act at random nor merely 'react' *ad hoc* to the stimuli of immediate situations, but in ways which are distinctively patterned for the specific social system and for the specific status role within it. The patterns which relate to different types of action and different statuses and roles in turn are specifically integrated so as to constitute a more or less coherent system.   (T. Parsons 1938a: 2–3)

Theoretical problems emerge on the different analytical levels. The 'boundaries' of any social system are not as distinct as those of physical and physico-chemical systems. Spatially delimited boundaries are easier to define conceptually than are those which have a 'normative' reference. Often it is a relatively arbitrary choice that determines which sector is under consideration. But the elements that make up a social system are not randomly related.

Via the system-concept Parsons developed his approach to his basic 'units'. Sociological theory, the study of concrete human individuals, their actions, interactions and interdependencies, had to face the fact that every concrete human individual is a physical body and a biological organism. The human individual is a part of physical and biological systems. These are the preconditions of human existence. Parsons focussed upon those categories specific to the orientation of behaviour and to the relations between actors. The actors comprise a system, *belonging together* in what are patterns of reciprocal interdependence. They are socially interrelated, and not simply physical objects with a common spatial association. The everyday experience of all of us gives us 'concrete' concepts of family, community, government, business, property and authority. Such concepts need constant qualification and refinement to 'fit' the various situations and experiences in the human world, but together these 'concrete' terms provide a rudimentary outline of the social system.

In *The Structure* the 'voluntaristic theory of action' was distinguished from positivism and idealism by reference to the 'unit act'. In positivistic theory there are no 'symbolic expressions of normative or ideal elements' (ie). In idealism 'scientifically valid knowledge' (T) has no part of the 'unit act'. Voluntarism incorporates both ie and T. The construction of the 'unit act' determines the composition of the 'system of action'. Any long-term aim to derive the structure of the social system (Rc) would require an inquiry into the functional relations between the constituents of the system of action (that is, between the unit act(s), Rel, RI and Rc). It seems as if this is the way in which Parsons attempted to develop the 'unit act' in 'Actor, Situation and Normative Pattern'. The system-concept was never far away, it seems, and Parsons felt that this concept provided the most fruitful means of further developing his theory. It is very important to underline that he had not equated the social system (Rc) with the system of action (Z).

'Actor, Situation and Normative Pattern'

Introduction

(In the preceding exposition and also in what follows I have had difficulty with tenses – I have, in general, used past tense when referring to Parsons' forming of his theory, and present tense when referring to the contents of the theory itself. But for this discussion I will use the past tense because the work under discussion was never published, since its analytical view was superseded by subsequent developments.)

In the initial chapter of 'Actor, Situation and Normative Pattern' (ASNP), entitled 'Frame of Reference', Parsons related his view of the relationship between what he had achieved and what remained to be done.

> The accomplishment of these tasks required an extensive and difficult treatment in the course of which it is easy to lose sight of the main logical structure as a whole. Hence there is something to be said for an attempt to outline this structure directly without reference to the critical context which was necessarily so prominent in the book. (T. Parsons 1939/40: 1)

This work, a companion piece to *The Structure*, was not intended to be a fully elaborated and empirically justified statement. Setting up the *system* of variables remained the long-term goal (T. Parsons 1937a: 751); even so it is reminiscent of a text-book in mathematical calculus outlining formulae and calculating mathematically precise solutions to elementary problems. The focus was not the writings of others, but the 'theory itself'.

> The object of the present essay is to attempt a systematic and generalized statement of the theoretical system without critical references. Like the critical statement in the earlier book it will be confined to a brief statement of the frame of reference and an outline of the structure of systems.   (T. Parsons 1939/40: 2)

The statement documented requires future intensive consideration. Though never published it was circulated to a circle of fellow-professionals, and illustrates Parsons' theory-construction at an 'intermediate' phase in his programme.

ASNP did not have the critical-historical background in focus. It did not focus on the means–end relation as the special concern of sociology. Its focus was 'action–system' rather than 'means–end'. The formulation of the famous 'pattern-variables' was not a primary concern for this work, and the later 'four-function paradigm' can only be seen, if at all, in embryonic form. (It might, in fact, have been an attempt to work out the various 'combinations' and 'permutations' of Henderson's triangular 'system' (Henderson 1970: 137, 163). We will develop some speculation in this regard below.)

There were *three* basic categories: action, situation and normative pattern. Later in his career Parsons stated his theory in fours: *four* pairs of pattern-variables and *four* basic functions. But here he organized his discussion in *threes*. The ideal of mathematical precision seems to have been *deeply* embedded in Parsons' analytical search. There may be a polemical dimension to Parsons' use of three in this work – contra positivism's law of the three stages and also Sorokin's 1947 work *Society, Culture and Personality*.

There were three aspects, necessary and cumulative phases, of theoretical systems. The first was the 'frame of reference'. This was part of a larger scheme in two respects. It was an aspect of theoretical systems, but it was also related to three other systems – the physical/chemical, the utilitarian and the spiritual.

The second was the 'generalized scheme of the structure of empirical systems'. This was the level at which Parsons was working in ASNP. In his view he was working on a 'structural functional' level, what he would later concede to be a 'second-best' form of analysis. His view of himself working on this 'second-best level' of analysis was established in ASNP.

The third aspect of theoretical systems was the system of interdependent variables. This phase was also the future aspect of Parsons' programme. An important change had occurred. Only economics, of all the social sciences, was anywhere near approaching the formulation of a system of interdependent variables. Pareto's attempts to formulate such a system for sociology was only valid in a broad empirical sense (T. Parsons and F. K. Knight 1930–45, Parsons to Knight, 1 August 1940).

The three basic elements (actor, situation and normative pattern) were articulated with *three* modes of orientation (cognitive, affective and teleological). The situation was analysed as an object in terms of each of these three modes; but Parsons added another dimension to his three basic ones: 'The Situation as Social: The Other Actors' (T. Parsons 1939/40: 11–28).

There were *three* modes of structuralization of social systems, namely, 'status', 'the differentiation of the action system of the individual' and 'the differentiation of social systems'. There were *three* principal modes by which the relations between individual actors in society came to be ordered by status acquisition: 'moral sentiments', 'potential mutual influence' and the 'definition of roles' (ibid.: 127–58).

'Status' had three modalities: an actor's place in the scale of stratification, his relation to the structure of authority and his place with reference to defined roles (ibid.: 130).

There were *three* criteria for defining socially important patterns or institutions: (1) *rules* regulating the status of individuals and the 'forms' of social relationships; (2) the attachment of moral *sanctions* to these patterns; (3) the *expectations* which are built into the social structure (ibid.: 159–61).

There were *three* features which distinguished institutional moral obligations: (1) extensity; (2) intensity; and a third one which was never mentioned in the text! There were *three* main aspects of formal organization: 'its bearing on the constitution of groups, on the exercise of and subjection to authority, and finally, on the *relation* of the individual actor to normative patterns' (ibid.: 164).

There were also three levels of the enforcement of law:

1. In terms of the purely 'subjective' motivation complex of the actor, regardless of any possible 'external' consequences. 2. In terms of those external consequences which arise from the 'spontaneous' unorganized reaction of others to his action, disapproval, withdrawal of hedonic benefits, ostracism etc. with their antithesis on the positive side ... 3. ... Normative patterns become the concern of a functionally differentiated group, those exercising governing authority in the group.
(ibid.: 171–2)

Parsons' attempt to control his discussion seems to involve a superstitious dimension. Why did he prefer the number three? In general it can be expected that when the *system* is studied in *context*, the *relationship* between system and context will provide a third category. Thus there emerge, quite naturally, three possible foci for abstract conceptualization. When these three elements are taken together, as a totality, the functional analysis of their interdependence leads to a 'fourth' emergent element, to which he later applied the term 'superadded' (T. Parsons 1951: 50; Cubbon 1976). Is that all there was to it? Can we simply rest content in the speculation that this was how Parsons' mind worked? It would seem to be a strong indication of Parsons' mathematical *scientism*. A strong commitment to Science was not purely a methodological matter; it had a rhetorical aspect as the Scientist made a public pronouncement about the mathematical precision of his formulations.

Not all listings were in threes. There were *four* types of expressional activities. In the conclusion we learn that 'the structuralization of social systems . . . cut[s] across the functional differentiation both of types of activity and of roles', and the three-fold listing returns with a discussion of 'institutions', 'formal organizations' and 'law' (T. Parsons 1939/40: 159).

We turn from the 'superstitious' dimensions of Parsons' organon to investigate the frame of reference. The analysis of empirical reality involved consideration of a basic unit of reference in its *real* context. The basic unit of reference was a highly complex system; the concept 'system' implied that there exists within reality a real object for analysis comprising a unit, a context and a relationship between unit and context. Such basic units are dependent and independent variables in their own contexts. Consequently they could be analysed in *two* ways: first, by *contrast* with their own situation (the concrete level of analysis); and secondly *in terms of* their own situation and the elements thereof (the analytical level). In this latter case the 'basic units' were not non-changing entities; they were considered as 'going concerns'.

To put it another way: if the basic unit of reference was a highly complex system, then the schema of 'unit–context' must be understood as operative on two levels. Why? Because such a fact implies that theoretical analysis can provide an 'understanding' of the unit by focussing upon the unit *in* its context or by analysing the relationship between the unit and its context *over time.*

Parsons considered temporal duration and temporal sequence as integral to the systemic interdependence of *act* and *situation*. The concept 'time' was basic, if somewhat problematic. It had been in *The Structure* with the concept of 'relations emergent' (T. Parsons 1937a: 78).

The basic scheme for biology was specified as *organism* (unit) and *environment* (context). There the focus was upon the concrete organism and the way in which the organism maintained its characteristics *over time*. When the focus was directed to 'hereditary constitution' the schema did not utilize the *organism* and *environment* schema. The analysis of such a 'going concern' in its environment required a conceptual schema of *heredity* and *environment*. This modification was necessary because, on the analytical level, the concrete organism could be understood as a *product* of environmental influences.

In the same way, Parsons continued, the *actor* (unit) and *situation* (context) can be analysed on two levels:

> On the one hand it is a question of the concrete human individual, so far as he is relevant to the action frame of reference, acting in a concrete situation.
>
> (T. Parsons 1939/40: 3)

This was 'the basic unit of reference'. But the discussion was never in terms of units alone. It involved relations, structures and interdependence. In the search for deeper insight, Parsons delved beneath the concrete level of analysis:

> On the other hand, analysis shows that the concrete 'personality' is in large measure the product of past situational factors, so that on a generalized analytical level methodologically comparable to that of the theory of heredity, the line must be drawn differently.   (ibid.: 3)

BIOLOGICAL SCIENCE	SOCIAL SCIENCE
(i) Organism in environment	(i) Concrete individual in situation
(ii) Organism in relation with the environment	(ii) Concrete individual in relation to situation

Figure 1 The structure of social science compared with biological science

For Parsons, theoretical insight on the sub-human level could be acquired quite adequately *without* adapting the unit/context (organism/environment) schema. But the schema utilized in biology was not a suitable *ideal-type* for theory in sociology. Social theory had to deal with the characteristics of its own 'basic unit': the 'actor'.

> The 'actor' is no longer a concrete unit of an empirical system, even as described within the frame of reference of action, but an analytical abstraction.
>
> (ibid.: 3–4)

But what did he mean by the 'actor' as an 'analytical abstraction'? The human individual acting in a concrete situation can be analysed in terms of many factors. This level of analysis can provide understanding on one level. But when the analysis moved to the analytical level, the concrete 'personality' became a conplex system; this system pertained to a concrete human individual, but it was also a dependent variable, a product of situational factors, past and present.

Parsons continued the comparison between the analysis of the organism and the analysis of the individual.

> In the case of both conceptual schemes, on both levels, it is possible to speak of a certain basic mode of relation between the two main conceptual components.
>
> (ibid.: 4)

We can picture the parallelism as illustrated in Figure 1.

Another important distinction between the two modes of system-theory was also necessary.

> In biology it is a matter of the 'adaptation' of the organism to the environment. In order not to confuse the two frames of reference here the term the 'orientation' of the actor to his situation will be used. (ibid.: 4)

Parsons worked out the implications of these distinctions on the concrete level. The diagrammatic representation of this analytical classification can be developed further, as shown in Figure 2.

In biological theory the organism was described as a 'going concern', manifesting patterns of structure and function through time. These patterns might represent a stage in the life-cycle, or the entirety of the life-cycle, or the

DISCIPLINE	BIOLOGICAL SCIENCE	SOCIAL SCIENCE
FRAME OF REFERENCE	Biological adaptation	Social orientation
UNIT	Organism	Actor
CONTEXT	Environment	Situation
EXPLANATION:		
1. CONCRETE LEVEL	Organism in environment	Actor in situation
2. ANALYTICAL LEVEL	Organism in relation to environment	Actor in relation to situation

Figure 2 Further comparison of social and biological science

focus might involve several generations in a 'species type'. It might even have been an analysis concerned with the changes to species over a much longer period of time. On all these levels the 'going concern' concept presupposed another one: 'a relatively independent "form-pattern" of the organism which is maintained or approximated in its relations to the environment' (ibid.: 4). Presumably, the 'form pattern' allowed consistent reference to the typical species characteristics of the organism under consideration.

That the organism maintained itself as a 'going concern' implied a system of interrelationships with the environment. The environment for the organism was the system of chemical processes enclosed within organic life. These established 'conditions' to which the organism was adapted – 'a continual chemical interchange with the environment is essential to the continuance of life' (ibid.: 5). The organism would, in its environment, meet certain conditions as it maintained an ongoing 'form pattern'. This regularity Parsons defined as adaptive functioning. There would be a continuous interchange between the organism and its environment, a system of interchange with this relatively independent context. When one aspect of this interchange (nutrition, respiration or elimination) was isolated then one of the adaptive functions of the organism had been analytically located.

But functional adaptation in the organism did not only occur 'externally'. Following the insights of Claude Bernard (see Bernard 1957), Parsons wrote:

> But the organism is a complex system. In so far as it has a determinate structure some parts of it will constitute a relatively fixed 'environment' to which the functioning of other parts must be 'adapted'.   (T. Parsons 1939/40: 5)

Thus internal functions of the organism adapted to the 'conditions' imposed by the 'rest'. For Parsons, biological theory involved a variety of *levels* of analysis – 'adaptation' did not refer simply to external relations. Conversely 'environment' could be external or internal. Adaptation was a generalized process which referred to the structuring of organism-in-environment.

In *The Structure* 'the unit act' was set forth as a theoretical alternative to positivistic reductionism (behaviourism) and was formulated as an alternative to idealistic emanationism in which human acts are mere expressions of 'mind'. In ASNP this view was developed considerably by developing the possibility of a 'two-way' interrelation between the actor and its 'environment'.

The *actor*, the 'basic unit of reference', was an abstraction which referred to the individual (a person or a collectivity) in the system of action, in the same way that 'organism' referred to the human individual in the system of theory concerned with human physiology. Parsons eschewed philosophical speculation, and though he admitted that scientific theory (in the meta-system of rational thought) cannot be totally independent of philosophy, his was, in his terms, no 'philosophical anthropology' (T. Parsons 1937a: 76, n. 2).

> The actor is a unit for purpose of description and analysis of systems of action. It is not a physical 'thing' nor an 'organism' since these are units in other frames of reference. (T. Parsons 1939/40: 3, n. 1)

The actor, a complex system, referred to one who 'acts'. Parsons tried to define this 'hard-to-put-your-finger-on' although 'always-within-reach' object. Like the organism the actor could be treated as an independent unit by contrast with its context – its situation. Unlike the organism, its context was viewed as dependent, to some extent, upon its own subjective and active interpretation of its character.

The 'situation' was the context in which the 'system of action' was located. In its simplest sense the 'system of action' comprised the actor's variegated orientation to his situation and its normative patterns. It was the actor's ongoing relationship with the relevant aspects of the 'situation' that was under analysis.

The 'situation' was not simply the context for one single actor. The problematic character of defining social action in terms of the 'situation' was largely due to the fact that it was shared among various actors. Thus the term 'normative pattern' was difficult to specify. 'Going concerns' manifested observable patterns. These patterns were verifiably true to the observer and for the actor. In the biological frame of reference the organism continued to evolve in its continuous chemical interchange. And it was not seen simply as an external relationship. The relationship between organism and environment was fully a part of both organism and environment. This kind of analysis was also applicable in the analysis of action; but the reality of action required a higher level of conceptualization.

> These 'patterns' must . . . be treated on two levels in the theory of action. On the one hand there are certain directly empirically observable tendencies for the actor to maintain a pattern independent of the situation. On the other hand, analytically as seen in terms of the theory of action this involves an 'orientation' to 'normative' patterns. The normative and the empirical patterns are related but by no means identical, since the latter are, analytically considered, resultants of normative and non-normative elements.   (ibid.: 5, n. 1)

Apart from the 'orientation' to 'normative patterns' there was also the aspect of 'character traits', features of human individuality which should not be overlooked.

> As in the case of the organism, there is a complex system of interrelations between this unit, the actor, and his situation. Given what his dominant patterns are, in their maintenance or realization certain conditions are imposed upon him by the features of the situation. Every action-system of an individual will include functionally significant modes of orientation to the features of the situation, which are capable of relatively independent treatment as sub-systems.   (ibid.: 6)

Here Parsons anticipated the functional analysis of actor and situation mediated by 'orientation'. The order which emerged from functional analysis was an analytical order.

> No more than in the biological case will the specific functionally significant modes of action be uniform in all cases or all 'species', but the functional analysis is one way of guiding the search for uniformities in action.   (ibid.: 6)

Though the theory of action was comparable with biology, there were great dissimilarities as well. The observable patterns of action consisted of the actor as a 'going concern', oriented to 'norms'. The theory of action involved 'subjective categories', the 'point of view of the actor' being a primary datum; it involved the 'choice' in conditional and normative aspects. Since 'choice' was integral to action, the focus was upon the elements of interrelation of choosing actors (i.e. not only, or necessarily, choosing individual persons).

Whilst Parsons highlighted the far-reaching logical and theoretical similarities between biology and sociology, he nonetheless insisted that *'the two are analytically distinct conceptual schemes with no presumption of reducibility of either to the other'* (ibid.: 7). He argued for a strict parallelism with the recognition that *action* always presupposed *organic functioning*. The actor was also an organism in an environment – the concrete individual encapsulated a variety of analytical elements, including the 'normative'. What does the concept 'normative' itself refer to? In *The Structure* Parsons had given close attention to this concept.

> The logical starting point for analysis of the role of normative elements in human action is the fact of experience that men not only respond to stimuli but in some sense try to conform their actions to patterns which are, by the actor and other members of the same collectivity, deemed desirable.
>
> (T. Parsons 1937a: 76)

For Parsons the normative dimension was a *real* dimension. 'Norms' and 'normative patterns' were not simply 'epi-phenomena' or psychic reflexes on a large scale. They were real elements of systems of social relations which comprise a plurality of actors. From the *concrete* point of view, the situation included other actors. 'But in the analysis of the social system as a whole this cannot be generalized'. The word 'this' here referred to the concrete analysis of one individual actor. Adapting the Durkheimian notion of society as 'reality sui generis' Parsons drew the *social system* as a functionally adaptive *aspect* of the *actor's* relation to the situation. The 'social system' was part of its own situation. Parsons had derived the peculiar focus for sociological analysis.

> The logic of generalization in this context requires the transfer of certain elements from the situational to the pattern or normative category. In detail the possibilities of error from failing to take proper account of this are numerous and subtle.
>
> (T. Parsons 1939/40: 9)

Parsons viewed reality as dynamic. He accepted that the relations between unit and context, actor and situation, were fluid. Description of the relationship between actor and situation might mean that in some circumstances the 'situation' was interchangeable with the 'normative pattern'. In this sense action can be viewed as oriented 'internally' to the actor's state of mind as situation, although the 'situation' can never be reduced to such a relation. This very complicated aspect of the theory points to the isolated individual as a possible focus for research. Isolated *individuals* are empirical realities, but they are not the basis for the theory of action.

The 'actor' was not the 'isolated individual'. Parsons moved beyond such an equation just as he no longer tied his theory to the means–end schema. In ASNP the means–ends schema was superseded by a discussion of the structure of the 'situation' as object of the three modes of orientation. As theory moved away from its positivist background the means–end schema was transformed.

> The actor ... is defined as an entity oriented to normative patterns and to a situation at the same time. Put somewhat differently, the actor, like the organism, shows a certain independence of his environment or situation. He does not merely 'react' to stimuli, but he 'takes advantage' of the situation to further his goals and normative tendencies. The relation to the situation is a selective one, not merely a dependent one. The actor is 'teleologically' directed, but in terms capable of subjective formulation. It is this subjectivity of the frame of reference of action which makes necessary the distinction, with no biological analogue, between the subjective unit of reference, the 'self' and the relevant normative patterns.
>
> (ibid.: 9–10)

Both normative patterns and situation were 'external' to the unit of reference. The 'externality', however, was not the same for both. The actor was not merely the rational being who followed a purely cognitive process of weighing alternative means for obtaining desired ends. The actor was oriented to his situation in various ways. 'Orientation' in the theory of action was Parsons' analogue to 'adaptation' in biology, but it was also somewhat influenced by psycho-analytic categories.

The three modes of orientation

Orientation was manifested in three basic modes: cognitive, teleological and affectual. The means–end schema was helpful in elucidating the processes of action in relation to orientation, especially in terms of 'teleological directionality'. But 'it does not seem to be sufficiently general to find a place in the most general schema of orientation of action' (ibid.: 21). The theory of action, he had noted, and more particularly the voluntaristic theory of action, was an elaboration and refinement of the basic conceptual scheme of utilitarianism (T. Parsons 1937a: 76, 81–2).

The cognitive mode of orientation was basic and the distinction between cognitive and non-cognitive allowed a break with positivism, a cognitive attitude which would monopolize 'truth' because it 'radically denies the possibility of significant cognitive propositions outside the realm of empirical science' (T. Parsons 1939/40: 31). Utilitarian positivism assumed that a rationalistic rendering of the means–end schema was a sufficient basis for explaining all that could be known about social action. Parsons admitted that he was actively engaged in the cognitive mode of orientation as he analysed the cognitive mode. But science was not an idle curiosity. Professional scientific interest, the pursuit of knowledge 'for its own sake', only emerged under very sophisticated conditions (ibid.: 43). The three modes always act together and concentration on one to the exclusion of the others could only be achieved by abstraction; even then their mutual interrelation was paramount.

> The interrelations of the three basic modes of orientation are so close that it is in a sense 'artificial' to take up any one of them in abstraction from the other two. The limitations of ordinary language in discussing theoretical questions, however, make that type of abstraction necessary.   (ibid.: 51)

Since there were three modes of orientation of the actor to his situation there were at least three ways in which the structure of the situation could be approached. But then the original interrelatedness of these three modes ensured that analysis of one mode involved its relations with other modes.

> But in each case it must be remembered that they always act together, and on every relevant occasion explicit attention will so far as possible be called to the modes of this interaction.   (ibid.: 51)

Chapter III, 'The Structure of the Situation as an Object of the Orientation of Action', was divided into four separate sections. Each of the modes was covered. A fourth section, 'The Situation as Social: The Other Actors', was included. This showed how modal analysis reconstituted the actor's empirical situation: other actors.

The cognitive mode of orientation

Cognition was given priority in the schema (ibid.: 11). Parsons did not assume its total domination over the actor's orientation to the situation.

Many elements essential to the understanding of action are most conveniently thought of as the answers to *questions* on the part of, or from the point of view of, the actor. These answers in the nature of the case are formulated as propositions. Propositions consist of concatenations of linguistic symbols with reference to some 'reality'. (ibid.: 11)

Here cognition was placed alongside asking questions, seeking answers and constructing meaning in lingual form. They are almost indistinguishable. That seems to be Parsons' point. The cognitive orientation in effect defines the 'situation'. But Parsons did not define 'orientation' by exclusive reference to the cognitive art of asking questions and defining answers. That would be too much like reconstructing the actor according to the image of the social scientist. The scientist was one kind of actor. All actors reflect on their situation in cognitive terms. All actors interpret their own actions. The rationalistic bias in social theory had occurred because it was possible to treat the whole of action in terms of cognitive orientation. But 'cognition', as a mode of orientation, was not an equivalent for 'action'. Cognition was always inextricably intertwined with the other modes of orientation.

Teleological directionality

This mode of orientation was not a mode directed to the 'situation' as it was to 'normative patterns'.

From the cognitive point of view situational elements can always be described in terms of existential propositions, even though, in reference to future situations they refer to phenomena not existent at the time the proposition is enunciated. A normative pattern, on the other hand, does not, from the point of view of the actor, 'exist' in the same sense. The propositions involved may, to be sure, describe a 'state of affairs'. But so far as their significance is normative it is not asserted (simply or at all) that this exists or, with a certain degree of probability, will exist, but that it *ought* (or ought not) to exist. The mood is imperative, not indicative. Whether it actually does or will come to exist is indifferent in principle to its normative status. What 'exists' is the normative pattern, an 'ideal' entity, not the state of affairs to which it refers. (ibid.: 14)

Norms and normative patterns were 'external realities'; objects of cognition for the actor. Situational elements could be described by reference to the empirical situation, and in terms of propositions that related to existence 'here and now'. 'Teleological directedness' involved the normative orientation of the actor, the acceptance or rejection of norms and patterns of norms. But there was another dimension of teleological directedness that could not be contained within a discussion of the cognitive apprehension of what ought, or ought not, to exist in the situation.

Seen in its relations to the physical world, to its 'environment', the human organism, like other organisms, is a teleologically directed entity. It is a system which is, within certain limits [here Parsons refers to Cannon 1932 BCW] independent of environmental conditions. It has, then, certain teleological tendencies which are not analytically derivable from the normative patterns to which the actor is oriented. (ibid.: 17)

For Parsons the human person, not the abstracted actor, was the concrete unit of action systems. The human body, with its biologically given 'drives', was an integral element of the person's teleological tendencies. Biology was interwoven with all 'wants', no matter how social or 'normative'. There was a built-in tension between biological wants and normative requirements. 'Wishes' should not be reduced to biological urges. The common conception that the biological element was 'anti-social' was as one-sided as the view that normative patterns totally *transcended* the dimension of biological functioning.

> The subtle interdependence and combination of biological and normative elements exists at many different levels in the complex structure of personality, and it may be said with considerable confidence that in practically all cases of concrete wishes which come into conflict with social norms, analysis will reveal normative pattern elements of crucial importance in the wishes themselves.   (ibid.: 19)

Human 'energy', 'drive' or 'motivation' had often been conceived as having a biological source. Parsons saw no reason to explain the 'energetic' realization of social goals purely by reference to biological functioning.

> Perhaps this tendency of thought derives in part from the conception that all 'energy' is ultimately physico-chemical in nature and that the source of 'motivation' in action must ultimately lie in the physical energy liberated by the processes of oxidation in organic metabolism. But if the biological and the action conceptual schemes are in fact analytically independent in any degree there is no reason on general grounds why the 'driving forces' of concrete action should be of a nature to be exclusively accessible to conceptual formulation in biological terms and in no sense so subject in terms specific to the theory of action. A scientifically cautious student of the theory of action will avoid any gratuitously a priori theorems of this character.
> (ibid.: 19–20. The footnote here reads as follows: 'The Freudian "libido" theory
>   seems to have a large a priori element of this character.')

Parsons was consciously carving out a theoretical perspective which affirmed the human reality of biological functioning. His theory of action rejected reductionistic theories of biology and action. The cognitive mode of orientation involved a self-conscious teleology. But because the means–end schema was not appropriate for all aspects of teleological directionality, a more general term was needed. Parsons considered 'goal' to be the appropriate concept.

Parsons explained why his theory did not imply exclusive reliance upon the means–end schema. Its status varied on different analytical levels.

> On the most concrete level an 'end' is analytically a composite, it formulates both normative and biological elements of teleological directionality in combination with each other and with a cognitive orientation to the relevant situational factors.
>   (ibid.: 21)

Here the important distinction between concrete description and analytical investigation re-entered Parsons' discussion. On the concrete level an actor sought some desirable 'future state of affairs'. On the analytical level the kind of object(s) involved in the attainment of the end was linked with the mode of orientation that must be involved.

> It is only on a more generalized analytical level which regards the biological element as situational that a distinction between biological and normative aspects of teleological directionality becomes feasible or important.   (ibid.: 21)

When this level was reached the teleological content of ends became exclusively normative, leaving in addition only a cognitive grasp of the relevant aspects of the situation.

The way was opened for the normative element to be differentiated from the concrete situation. It could now be analysed as an independent and dependent variable within the situation. The action encompassed biological drives. The teleological dimension of *ends* assumed the combination of biological and normative aspects within the system of action. It thus had an *internal* as well as *external* point of reference.

The affectual mode of orientation

The affectual mode of orientation was a subjective mode concerned with emotions; positive, negative or neutral. Neutrality was conceived as a balanced state between positive and negative attitudes. There were three polarities which were closely intertwined within emotional life: pleasure and pain; moral respect and moral indignation; love and hate. In his discussion of these Parsons referred to the contributions of both Sigmund Freud and W. I. Thomas. Pleasure could have been a manifestation of a biological state. But such subjectivity was never the whole story.

> It may be objected to this view, that many states, and the gratification of many wishes, appear to be pleasurable which are not in any obvious sense biological wishes. This objection seems to be met in part by consideration of the fact that no concrete wish is ever simply biological or wholly unbiological. In addition there is a further consideration. The concrete organism is never wholly the product of what are, analytically considered, biological elements.   (ibid.: 23)

The pleasure–pain principle was fundamental to action because it related to the state of equilibrium in the organism, a pre-requisite for any long-term systematic ordering or systems of action.

The second polarity was that of 'moral respect' and 'moral indignation'. This polarity was parallel to the pleasure–pain one. It indicated a *normative* dimension.

> Moral feelings seem to attach in the first instance to generalized patterns (XX) and to particular persons, objects, etc only in so far as they embody relatively abstract and general principles. Typical objects of moral feelings are such things as 'honesty', 'loyalty', etc. and in justifying a moral judgement of a person we habitually refer to such patterns (XX); we are indignant at him because he has acted 'dishonestly' for instance.
> (ibid.: 24–5; (XX) – the phrase 'matters of "principle" ' is the original term which
>   has been crossed out and replaced by the term 'generalized patterns')

Normative patterns and the affective attitudes of moral respect and indignation were the constitutive elements of what Parsons called the 'value' complex in the theory of action.

> An exceedingly crucial place in the structure of both the individual personality and of social systems is occupied by this complex, or the 'value-orientation' either of a particular actor, or of a plurality of actors in common.   (ibid.: 25)

Morality was a polarity in the affective mode and thus *integral* to the relation between actor and situation. It was not extraneous, as if to be brought in from the 'outside'. Rather it was an internal and external reality. Closely related to 'religious ideas' which manifested the teleological dimension in the affective mode, it involved the cognitive apprehension of non-rational data (ibid.: 25).

The third polarity, love and hate, was not a subjective matter, but pertained to particular persons and things 'as such'. Usually, this mode of orientation was closely integrated with the other two basic affective polarities.

Here we leave Parsons' discussion in ASNP. We have discussed how the basic analytical structure of his theory in *The Structure* was being deepened by an elaboration of its basic elements in relation to the 'three modes of orientation'. It is clear that he was using an evolutionary framework in his theory-building; the comparison with biological science and the use of the system-concept bears this out.

Critical commentary and Parsons' statements

The other 150 pages of this 'experimental' work indicate that Parsons saw 'Actor, Situation and Normative Pattern' as a tentative and provisional statement. He was operating with the same view of the three types of conceptual scheme he had used in the introductory chapter of *The Structure* (T. Parsons 1937a: 27–41). These were:

1. the frame of reference
2. the generalized scheme of the structure of empirical systems, and
3. the system of interdependent variables.

With ASNP Parsons gained confidence that the theory was relatively complete on the first two levels. ASNP, he claimed, made considerable progress towards the construction of the generalized scheme of the structure of systems.

> In short what I think I have been able to do is to proceed systematically from an analysis of the structure of 'action' starting with the most elementary empirical implications of the frame of reference, to a generalized system of social structure on what may be called the 'common sense' level of the social sciences, in which such categories as institutions, associations, state, church, markets, authority, property etc have a rather definite place. I cannot claim that this job has been done so perfectly that the result is 'logically articulated' throughout, but there does seem to be an outline which, however much it is subject to reformulation, is essentially

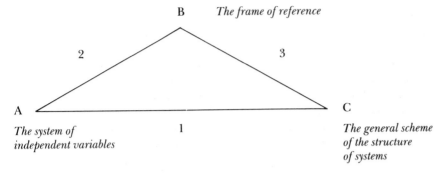

Figure 3 Parsons' theorizing in triangular focus

sound and can serve as a framework for further and further elaboration in various directions.
(T. Parsons and Frank H. Knight 1930–45, Parsons to Knight, 1 August 1940)

Parsons admitted that it was not an original scheme – he was carrying on the work of Max Weber. At that time he did not see his work coming close to the 'third level'. The system of variables, the system of theory, was still a long way off. Here we detect the dynamics of a programme emerging from within a 'triangular system'. The essence of his theorizing was that phenomena should be viewed synoptically. The approach could be pictured as in Figure 3.

Let us develop this 'construction'. Parsons sought to 'complete' the triangle. B had been formulated and he was in the process of developing C. Yet to 'stabilize' the relationship between B & C, the 'connections' AB (2) & AC (1) had to be in place. The only part of the triangle from which to evaluate the connection between B & C is from A. Thus until B & C are stabilized in their relation to each other by reference to A, the relationship between A & C and A & B cannot be determined. In ASNP Parsons evaluated B–C from A, even though he was in no position to define A (from B or C). This is another way of saying that Parsons was defining what he then was not sure about – the system of independent variables. In *The Structure* this was contained under the rubric 'residual categories', and he had observed that 'theory not only formulates what we know it tells us what we want to know' (T. Parsons 1937a: 9). In my view Parsons, via his commitment to Science, completed the triangle 'ficti-tiously'. He placed himself, as scientist, at the point in the triangle of theoretical development where he wanted to be. He assumed the posture of the formulator of a system of independent variables, even though they could not then be formulated, and evaluated the development of the other two elements (i.e. the 'frame of reference' and the 'general scheme') from that point. My interpretation here is, admittedly, hypothetical, but it does help to unravel aspects of Parsons' often difficult-to-fathom procedure and hard-to-follow prose.

A logically articulated theoretical scheme on all three levels as had been

achieved in mechanics was the long-term goal. At this stage his 'structural–
functional' level of analysis was comparable with physiology. There was no
system of variables for a general physiology either. Nevertheless comparison
between 'action theory' and biology provided him with a useful source of
analogies to help with the outlining of his approach.

In ASNP discussion moved from 'basic unit' analysis to the 'common sense'
level of institutions. From the 'frame of reference' he moved to 'the three basic
modes' and to 'the structure of the situation' (in its three basic modes, plus one
other) and to 'some functional needs of social systems'.

The functional needs of social systems are discussed against the background
of the modes of orientation and the diversified discussion of the structure of the
'situation'. In this sense the discussion of 'functional needs' presupposed the
actor's multi-modal orientation to the situation (individually and collectively)
rather than vice versa. Parsons' attempt to build a theory of social action 'from
the ground up' was an attempt to understand how 'consensus' was socially
constructed by social actors – human individuals and groups. The *order* of his
narrative involved a transition from the simplest units of action to the more
subtle and complex dimensions. It is not an evolutionary account of how social
action evolved in the higher primates. It is an attempt to put a statement
together about the structure of systems, from their most elemental particle to
the most concrete level of institutional behaviour.

Diagramatically the development of Parsons' project can be pictured as
shown in Figure 4.

The structure of theory

Parsons' 'theory of theory' was disclosed by ASNP. He had focussed upon the
interdependencies found within social systems. But conceptual dilemmas
remained. Analytical realism was the bridge between idealism and positivism.
In relation to the 'action frame of reference' he had written:

> But in this particular case, unlike that of the physical sciences, the phenomena
> being studied have a scientifically relevant subjective aspect.
>
> (T. Parsons 1937a: 46)

Parsons' investigations of the writings of social theorists had been an investigation of social action. He was seeking to ascertain the 'mind' of these writers.
This was no different from other types of social action analysis.

> That is, while the social scientist is not concerned with studying the content of his
> own mind, he is very much concerned with that of the minds of the persons whose
> action he studies.   (ibid.: 46)

His study had claimed to be a study in social dynamics. But this would seem to
challenge any strict division in our interpretation of the differences between
scientific purpose and the analytically specified 'end' of any action. ASNP was
not a critical work as *The Structure* had been. ASNP was a move away from an

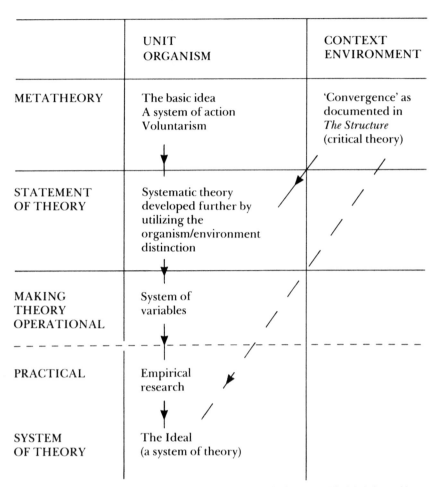

	UNIT ORGANISM	CONTEXT ENVIRONMENT
METATHEORY	The basic idea A system of action Voluntarism	'Convergence' as documented in *The Structure* (critical theory)
STATEMENT OF THEORY	Systematic theory developed further by utilizing the organism/environment distinction	
MAKING THEORY OPERATIONAL	System of variables	
PRACTICAL	Empirical research	
SYSTEM OF THEORY	The Ideal (a system of theory)	

Figure 4 The development of Parsons' programme from *The Structure of Social Action* to 'Actor, Situation and Normative Pattern'

internal or philosophical analysis of the contents of his own mind. He sought to articulate the theory in its own terms. This, of course, was based upon another very important distinction.

> This necessitates the distinction of the objective and the subjective points of view. The distinction and the relation of the two to each other are of great importance. By 'objective' in this context will always be meant 'from the point of view of the scientific observer of action' and by 'subjective', 'from the point of view of the actor'. (ibid.: 46)

This quotation illustrates Parsons' appreciation of Pareto's 'methodological self-consciousness' (ibid.: 454). *Within* the scientific frame of reference *objectivity* must be allowed to transcend *subjectivity*. The *objectivity* of the scientist, whose

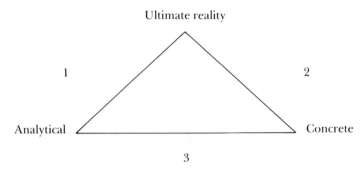

Figure 5 Hypothetical construction of Parsons' view of the three forms of knowledge

goal is analytical and objective explanation, prevailed. The scientist, qua scientific investigator, was defined in terms of a professional need to be objective. Parsons' theoretical orientation was an attempt to live with the difficulties of this philosophical indeterminacy; this was his 'uncertainty principle'.

He put the issue in these words:

> It is a philosophical implication of the position taken here that there is an external world of so-called empirical reality which is not the creation of the individual human mind and is not reducible to terms of an ideal order, in the philosphical sense.   (ibid.: 753)

Parsons did not seek to renovate the philosphical realm of discourse. His sociological theory of action was decidedly non-philosphical, even though philosophical discourse in realms which border his own is not ruled out entirely.

How did Parsons understand the act of theoretical reflection? Scientific theory was not itself an empirical entity but an ideal representation of empirical phenomena or aspects of them (ibid.: 754). According to this view theorizing was the making of 'helpful fictions'.

> But at the same time the fact of verification, that scientific theory 'works', is proof that, though limited, the propositions of human science are not completely arbitrary but are adequately relevant to significant aspects of reality.
> (ibid.: 754)

Theory, for Parsons, was not simply a function of the human ability to engage in logical and abstractive thought. Thought, as action, was involved in a history of cumulative development; 'theory' contributed to the development of science. Analytical theory has its abstractive aspects, but as action it was viewed in various systems of human action through time.

The problem here involved Parsons' three primary categories of thought: 'analytical', 'empirical' and 'ultimate reality'. A triangular conception can also help us to relate these categories to each other (see Figure 5). Parsons' system, though he may have 'inherited' it from Henderson, carried his own idiosyncratic style. Again it is important to stress that this diagram is a hypothetical construction of how Parsons seems to have organized his reflections.

In his theorizing Parsons focussed upon the analytical/concrete distinction and the concrete (i.e. empirical) importance of 'ultimate reality'. He did so from the 'analytical corner'. He did not intend to focus upon the 'ultimate reality of the analytical' or the 'ultimate reality of ultimate reality'. Rather he was concerned with the *analytical* recognition of 'ultimate reality' in its relation with the concrete. He could distinguish 'ultimate' from 'concrete' realities but did not presume to take the 'ultimate reality' corner. To take that approach would involve philosophical speculation.

Of course, it could be asked, 'what is the character of the triangular system?' Analyses directed to the 'analytical' would give rise to many complex problems and difficulties. This kind of speculative approach is not far from Parsons' theory, but he cut short such tendencies with the 'working definition' of the pragmatic goal of science: 'success in explanation' (T. Parsons 1935a: 661).

Thus we can conclude that the 'triangle' is helpful to a point. Parsons, ever seeking the system of theory, did not facilitate the systematization of his thought.

Here the problems of 'translating' Parsons' development and his 'brief statement' into an even briefer outline of his conceptual scheme have been canvassed. Parsons' theory of social action aimed for a fully elaborated system of concepts on all analytical levels. He attempted to encompass the full complexity of social action in an analytical statement. It is very hard to proceed with an immanent critique of his theoretical approach. I have tried to avoid delving deeper, ever deeper, into the logic of each of his various statements to ascertain how each statement related to every other statement. Instead the complexity of his approach has been described by reference to a synoptic triangulation of social theorizing, in some of its phases. This attempt to define the developing theory does have problems. He referred to his theory in terms of three levels, rather than describing his approach from three mutually interacting points of reference. When he later moved to a 'quadrilateral' mode of theorizing the problem of 'developing theory' seems to have been submerged in what was taken as actual development. We shall see how the 'points of reference' in *The Social System* are kept separate from his 'theory of theory'. The *distinction* between theorist and theory seems to have developed into a *separation*. It is not so easy to place him in relation to the *elements* of his theorizing in his later developments.

8
Developing *The Social System*

Background: 1937–51

The aim of this chapter is to trace Parsons' systematic point of view as it unfolded. Whilst I do not want to suppress important aspects of Parsons' biography, it is sufficient to note the problem of keeping exclusively to the theoretical side of things.

Did Vilfredo Pareto's influence upon Parsons progressively diminish during this time? In *The Structure* Parsons had worked with an explanation of his methodological self-consciousness, which he said was derived from Pareto; as he had pointed out it was not a matter of repudiating Pareto, but of building on his conception of the social system (T. Parsons 1937a: 460). Pareto had represented something of a fad at Harvard in the 1930s (T. Parsons and B. Barber 1948: 254), yet when Pareto's system was no longer in vogue Parsons maintained deep respect for his achievement, keeping him in mind when writing the Preface to *The Social System*.

> The title, *The Social System*, goes back more than to any other source, to the insistence of the late Professor L J Henderson on the extreme importance of the concept of system in scientific theory, and his clear realization that the attempt to delineate the social system as a system was the most important contribution of Pareto's great work. This book therefore is an attempt to carry out Pareto's intention, using an approach, the 'structural-functional' level of analysis, which is quite different from that of Pareto ...   (T. Parsons 1951: vii)

Translated into Paretian concepts this indicates that *The Social System* is Parsons' attempt to develop the sociological 'residue' of Pareto's contribution, with a methodologically self-conscious 'derivation' of his own.

In the second edition of 'On Building Social Systems Theory' Parsons added a 1977 footnote, expressing his regret that he had not given Henderson the credit which was his due (T. Parsons 1977: 30–1, n. 21). Parsons' late-in-life reassertion that Pareto and Henderson were influential in his theoretical development, which he had admitted all along, gives support to the view that Pareto's theory of 'residues' was subjectively and methodically applied in his theory-building in more than a merely technical manner. It seems as if Pareto's theory had shaped his entire cognitive orientation. Whether Parsons' theory should properly be interpreted as 'neo-Machiavellian' is an important question which requires further textual and analytical criticism of the relationship between his theory and the orientation of L. J. Henderson.

During this time Parsons, as a professional theorist, gave extended attention to the professions. He commented upon the cultural problems brought on by the ascendency of Nazism and the war in Europe. From 1938 Parsons was publicly advocating that the USA should side with those nations opposed to Hitler, and he warned on various occasions that a new dark age would descend upon the world if the Nazis were allowed to win. His sympathies clearly lay with the British and their allies. (T. Parsons 1938b; 1938c).

Parsons' calling: his sense of duty to the profession

Parsons' theoretical contribution was a consciously professional approach. Other theorists, in his view, are either *allies* or *potential allies*. Convinced that a new 'general theory' was within sight, he very rarely resorted to animus in his writings. The 'enemies', if that is what they were, invariably belonged to past movements in social thought (Hobhouse (T. Parsons 1932: 321–2), Marx, Comte, Spencer (T. Parsons 1945: 219–20), 'English Social Thought' (T. Parsons 1932: 337–8, n. 3), 'German Historical Economics' (1937a: 477), Institutionalism; C. W. Mills being the one notable exception (T. Parsons 1957; 1971a: 116)).

Parsons divined very early the ascendant tendencies in the social sciences and forged his contribution accordingly. His aim in *The Structure*, his aim during the years 1937–51 and his aim in *The Social System* was to 'set the pace'. He would strike a 'third way' in sociology, between 'pure empiricism' and 'pure theory'. 'Analytical realism' in *The Structure* was as much an empirically discovered theory as it was a theory-led empiricism. From his middle ground he would capture both extremes uniting the entire profession around a common 'theoretical' core.

In the mid thirties, when he was articulating his 'aspect' view of the social science encyclopaedia, he explicitly insisted that his concern was limited to 'theoretical re-organization'. But sooner or later theories become embodied in new institutional arrangements. The Department of Social Relations, set up towards the end of the war, was a new initiative for teaching and research in sociology, social anthropology and psychology. In *The Structure* Parsons had favoured an altogether more radical rearrangement of social science encompassing economics, government and history (T. Parsons 1937a: 768–72). But during the 1940s, Parsons' 'general theory' matured as the system of a professional Harvard sociologist. The disciplines closest to sociology in that environment were social anthropology and social psychology.

Developments and underdevelopments

Durkheim's theory became prominent in Parsons' writings when he began referring to himself as a *sociologist*. As a theorist he attempted to articulate his theory of action with all social sciences. But did his 'pragmatism' let him down? As intimated above, 'convergence' became a *means* to a theoretical *end*. The full and integral challenge implicit in *The Structure* became diluted with the 'development' of his theory in the 1940s. If 'convergence' was to be taken seriously it required *extended* application in economics, psychology, anthropology and beyond. 'Convergence' had to be demonstrated for *all* the social sciences.

The 1949 Preface indicates Parsons' change of direction. The inclusion of Freud in the 'convergence' argument was not attempted because it would require very long and arduous labour (T. Parsons 1949b). So Parsons was aware of this anomaly. But could this not indicate that in some important respect the scientific method of *The Structure* was no longer accepted? In the earlier work 'convergence' was put forward as a result, but not an intended one, of a very complex and detailed process. How now could he include Freud *without the empirical demonstration on the level of secondary analysis?* It is to be noted that, despite the co-operative character of his theory-building project, Parsons did not then, or subsequently, call upon other young scholars to test, retest and rework 'convergence'. This seems to indicate that Parsons tended, at times, to view 'convergence' from the viewpoint of one who had proprietorial rights over the 'discovery' – unless, of course, it is now to be read solely as his 'opportunistic' attempt to prove his prowess as a social science professional! In his biography he seems to suggest that *The Structure*, whilst exhibiting 'intellectual opportunism', also carried the marks of the intellectual climate of the time, perhaps making the argument more empiricist than he had intended (T. Parsons 1970: 829–31, 866).

But why confine the 'convergence' discovery to the social sciences? Why not demonstrate the emergence of a single meta-theoretical conception for physics, physiology, economics, sociology, ethics and theology? Parsons placed great store upon Whitehead's *Science in the Modern World* (1925). But did he see his own work as the *extension* of Whitehead's viewpoint? *The Structure* could be read as an attempt to verify empirically the Whiteheadian viewpoint with special reference to social theory. But the failure to continue to demonstrate new convergences in 'recent theory' – 'across the board' – creates the impression that 'convergence' was Parsons' private and idiosyncratic discovery. And Parsons' non-textual approach to Freud's incorporation into his canon of classics increases the doubts here. Perhaps it should be interpreted as Parsons (the theorist) adopting a cavalier approach to himself (the secondary analyst)!

'Convergence' implies the rewriting of the entire history of social thought. The errors of utilitarianism could only be avoided, Parsons insisted in 1932, by a 'thoro' reconstruction of the entire history of socio-economic thought (T. Parsons 1932: 346). The historiography of sociology could not be the same after *The Structure*. But the gargantuan task therein envisaged was not taken up, and has never been attempted subsequently.

Parsons' writings do hint at various kinds of 'convergences'. We should not

criticize him for work he didn't do as for an unsystematic and incomplete out-
working of the basic ideas of his intellectual orientation. For one who
considered *theory* to be the core of scientific endeavour and who considered
himself to be at work in terms of 'the best modern methodology' (T.
Parsons 1935a: 660), he yet showed a peculiar reluctance to develop his 'theory' in this
systematic sense. He was not constructing a complete philosophical system.
But can that serve as a valid excuse for failing to justify the philosophical
foundations of his theoretical orientation? I would suggest that his 'development' has to be judged as a failure in this respect. Like Marshall he seems to
have been evasive. Of Marshall he had written:

> But this study will have served its purpose if it has shown that he cannot be
> interpreted otherwise than as taking a position of the highest importance on the
> fundamental questions he professes to ignore. I am tempted to regard his
> reluctance to recognize that fact as a symptom of a certain evasiveness in
> Marshall's scientific character.   (T. Parsons 1932: 335–6)

Parsons cannot be interpreted otherwise than as taking a position of the
highest importance on the kinds of philosophical issues he professed to pass by.
Taking responsibility for 'a complete philosphical system', once the initial
innocent step in theoretical reasoning had been taken, was a rather terrifying
prospect, he wrote (T. Parsons 1938d: 17). He refuted the empiricist dilemma
concerning theory yet he also sympathetically acknowledged the *terrifying*
character of philosophy. He had been willing to stand alongside the empiricist
whilst also criticizing empiricism. But what was his alternative?

> I do not believe either that scientific theory has no philosophical implications, or
> that it involves no philosophical preconceptions. They cannot, in that sense, be
> radically divorced. But at the same time it does not follow that they are rigidly
> bound together in the sense this dilemma implies.   (ibid.: 17)

Parsons' view of philosophy was directed by his understanding of intellectual
flexibility. But was not his conception of the 'non-rigid' link of philosophy with
theoretical reflection a philosphical conception? Can it be said to be a
theoretical distinction with merely philosophical 'implications'?

Parsons' 'non-rigid bind' between philosophy and theory was counterposed
in this instance to the supposed rigid (and suppressed) connection of the
empiricists. He considered that the empiricist unwillingness to accept philosophical implications inherent in theorizing had led to an anti-theoretical
attitude. Even though he, a non-philosopher, was sympathetic to such fears,
he nevertheless rejected the empiricist dilemma.

For Parsons the anti-theoretical stance of the empiricist was actually a
hidden *philosophical* rigidity. The argument seems to go like this: (1) the
empiricist must be opposed to theory on other than theoretical grounds; (2)
the grounds for opposition must be either theoretical or philosophical; (3)
empiricism must therefore be opposed to 'complete' philosophical systems on
the basis of an *alternative* philosophy.

How did Parsons avoid the philosophical rigidity he perceived in empiricism? His concept of the 'non-rigid boundedness' of philosophy to theoretical reflection was his *theoretical* counterpoint to the empiricist philosophy. But it was also more than that. It was a *theoretical* counterpoint to *all* philosophically based theory. His theory of philosophy would not be rigidly pinned down. Rather than a rigid-boundedness, Parsons' *theoretical* emphasis was indicative of something else. Theory, for him, injected non-rigidity into the theory–philosophy interface. Theory, in other words, provided the framework in which speculation could be directed towards *scientific* ends.

> On the contrary, though they are interdependent in many subtle ways, they [i.e. theory and philosophy] are also independent.   (ibid.: 17)

We recall that in his view theory was 'outward-looking' whilst the philosopher was more concerned with the content of his own mind (T. Parsons 1937a: 46).

The philosophical dogma of theory's autonomy

But had he truly covered all options? What of, for example, the *philosophical* attitude which adhered to the 'non-rigid boundedness' of the relationship between theory and philosophy? That, logically speaking, must have been the philosophical attitude he was after. But it could not function in its dependent and independent character *without the philosophical assumption that within philosophical thought theoretical reflection has to be considered as autonomous and self-defining.* At this point we uncover the hidden *philosophical* dogma basic to Parsons' theory. It was the dialectical character of this philosophical dogma which, in my view, should be viewed as the motor for the theoretical 'efflorescence' during this period. Non-rigid theory had to be allowed to manifest its autonomy.

In his attempts to keep his theory 'open' Parsons derived inspiration from Claude Bernard. It was the concept of system which was important. Bernard had stated:

> One of the greatest obstacles encountered in this general and free progression of human knowledge is the tendency which leads the various forms of knowledge to become individualized into systems . . . Systems tend to enslave the human mind . . . We must try to break the fetters of philosophical and scientific systems . . . Philosophy and science should not be systematic.
>
>   (Bernard in Bergson 1968: 245–6)

Bernard's paradoxical refusal to be systematic meant he aimed to develop a body of knowledge by reference to the *system-concept* which would help in the self-conscious analytical ordering or empirical data. It was to be a central concept to be used, rather than a leading idea which had to be systematically elaborated. The system-concept was, in one respect, an internal guarantee of the theory remaining 'open', but Parsons' theory had more than a merely theoretical character. It was intimately tied to his search for an intellectually independent position in the social sciences. In this sense it also exhibited an historical character and as such also functioned as an appeal to freedom, the freedom of the professional social scientist to chose his own intellectual goals, in his own time. The system-concept was therefore necessary for maintaining theory as an autonomous exercise.

When this is seen alongside of the creative and optimistic theme implicit in Parsons' critique of Weber, we touch on the inner consistency and continuity of his theoretical frame of reference. The philosophical dogma of theory's autonomous character was never proved. It could only be assumed.

Once the theory was given published words it began to take on a formal character, in which it could not avoid being interpreted philosophically. The reader must read it as a definitive form of what Parsons had wanted to say. Despite all the qualifications about its provisionality, the published form must shape the thinking about the theory. The theory was written down. It was committed to paper. For the theory to gain recognition as 'the theory' the reader has to reckon with the fact that Parsons *believed* he was articulating an 'open system', and even though it was now written down and potentially on the way towards being viewed as a system of theory, nevertheless he (i.e. the reader) had to reckon with Parsons' stated conviction that his theory had to be read as 'open' to further development. For Parsons 'general theory' constituted the beginning of a new tradition in western scientific thought.

Another aspect of Parsons' development needs to be noted here. He was at Harvard, working in a North American context. His willingness to give philosophy a place, alongside sociological theory, and the insistence upon the non-rigidity of its influence, also indicate his liberal aversion to taking centre stage. Parsons' approach would not subordinate the social sciences to philosophy. And vice versa. His writings need to be assessed in terms of his cross-disciplinary, inter-disciplinary and multi-disciplinary awareness. But this will also require examination of his performance as a wide-ranging liberal-oriented *administrator*. Our focus here has been upon Parsons-the-theorist.

The development between 1937 and 1951 respecified

As we have noted already, Parsons is best seen as a *writer* of theory, constantly reworking and revisiting previous statements. In a process of human action he derived his statement. The next step was to develop a more adequate statement of a very complex reality. His initial statement, part of his own intellectual reality, was an integral part of the successive formulations. In this way continuity in theoretical development was established. This process is illustrated in Figures 6–8.

The stage after *The Structure* and before *The Social System* is clearly 'Step 3'. But the actual process was not 'linear' as the figure would suggest. The formulations and reformulations were more than a mere elucidation of implications. This process is reminiscent of the 'development' in the pre-1937 phase. It involved constant 'revisiting'. Another series of diagrams may help us here (see Figures 7 and 8).

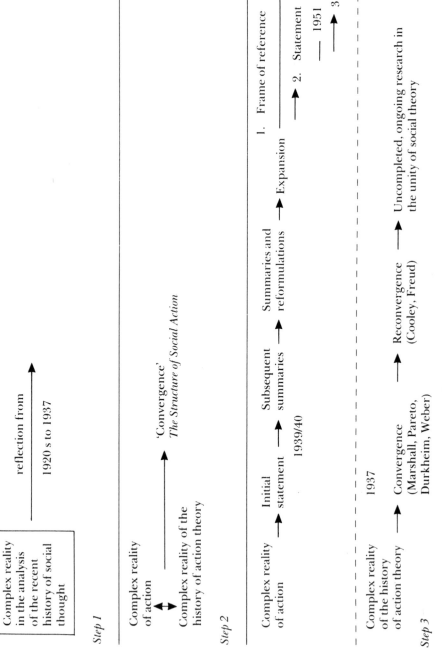

Step 1

Complex reality in the analysis of the recent history of social thought ── reflection from ──▶ 1920 s to 1937

Step 2

Complex reality of action ◀──▶ Complex reality of the history of action theory ──▶ 'Convergence' *The Structure of Social Action*

Complex reality of action ──▶ Initial statement 1939/40 ──▶ Subsequent summaries ──▶ Summaries and reformulations ──▶ Expansion ──▶ 1. Frame of reference / 2. Statement / ── 1951 ── / ▶ 3. System

Step 3

Complex reality of the history of action theory ──▶ Convergence (Marshall, Pareto, Durkheim, Weber) 1937 ──▶ Reconvergence (Cooley, Freud) ──▶ Uncompleted, ongoing research in the unity of social theory

Figure 6 Schematic outline of the unfolding dualistic character of Parsons' scholarship and theoretical development

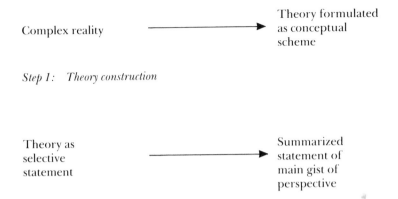

Figure 7 Theory construction and theory development

In Step 1 we note that the 'theoretical perspective', as the point of view of the author, is involved in both elements. In Step 2 the process of respecifying the main gist is not simply by reference to the logical structure of the 'theory as simplified statement'. Consequently a third element is required. 'The picture' needs redrafting. We can usefully employ the 'triangulation method' here again (see Figure 8).

Let us look at some of the major themes of Parsons' writings during this period.

The professions and sociology

In trying to explain *how* he came to formulate the famous system of 'pattern variables', Parsons referred to the time, immediately after 1937, when he began to give the professions his concerted attention. The 1939 essay 'The Professions and Social Structure' was the landmark essay in this process. This essay presented an early formulation of the scheme. There is also the 1937 essay 'Education and the Professions' (T. Parsons 1937c).

In the 1937 essay Parsons commented upon President Hutchins' analysis of utilitarian motives in university administration, teaching and research. The current situation was interpreted as a departure from liberal principles. But these principles had not been superseded. Parsons defended those principles. The current situation 'fails to adequately conform' to these principles.

Parsons formulated his concept of academic *disinterestedness*. The *professions*, through their great traditions, provided a bulwark against the wholesale commercialization of modern social life. Academic disinterestedness implied the love of learning for its own sake. It countered the false conception of utility which reduced everything to the love of money. The 'liberal' and 'learned'

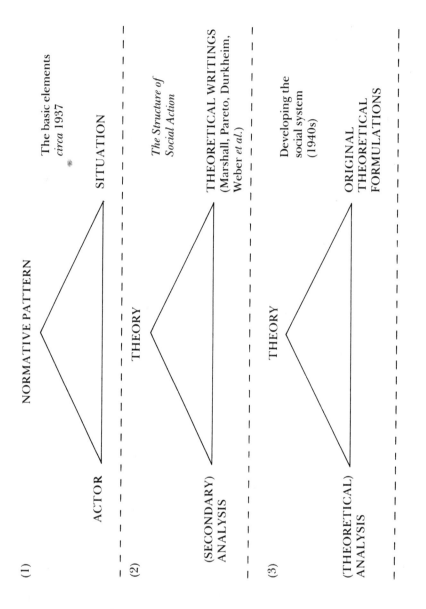

(1)

NORMATIVE PATTERN

ACTOR   SITUATION

The basic elements
circa 1937

(2)

THEORY

(SECONDARY)
ANALYSIS   THEORETICAL WRITINGS
(Marshall, Pareto, Durkheim,
Weber *et al.*)

*The Structure of
Social Action*

(3)

THEORY

(THEORETICAL)
ANALYSIS   ORIGINAL
THEORETICAL
FORMULATIONS

Developing the
social system
(1940s)

Figure 8 How Parsons' project changed between *The Structure* and *The Social System*: theory, analysis and written statements

character of professions provide a stabilizing influence for modern society. The two adjectives refer to interwoven aspects of professionality.

> This ideal of learnedness already contains within itself a component of what may be called 'liberality'. For to master this intellectual content of the professional tradition the liberal spirit is essential. The man who is dominated only by the more sordid motives of gain or even the immediate success of his practical task alone is incapable of it. (T. Parsons 1937c: 366)

Parsons, the professional, subjected himself to the norms of professionality. As part of his professional responsibility he oriented himself to an ideal.

> The valuation of knowledge for its own sake is an integral part of the professional spirit. But at the same time there is another aspect of liberality. The ideal professional man is not only a technical expert in the sense transcending special skills; by virtue of his mastery of a great tradition he is a liberally educated man, that is, a man of general education. (ibid.: 366)

Learning is the nucleus of the professions; the professional dimension of society is centred upon the university. The university is the only professional agency capable of training its own members and the university has an important, if not central, place in the professional training which other professions must give to their own successors.

> Indeed, under modern conditions a group can hardly be accorded full professional status unless an important part of it, which is highly respected by the rest, can become specialized in the teaching and advancement of the professional tradition as an intellectual discipline on the same level as those within the central nucleus of the university. (ibid.: 367)

In other words the modern university was viewed as a central factor in a functional sense, for shaping the professional character of modern society. The place of the professions in society clarified Parsons' view of his role-status, and it raised the spectre of an alternative vision of society to that which operated on the common-sense level.

> In this respect, then, the central university principle ramifies out into the practicing professional groups, instead of there being a rigid line between that which is 'academic' and that which is 'practical'. (ibid.: 367)

He did not say that there was no line at all. Rather, he insisted that drawing the line between the 'academic' and the 'practical' would not lead us to a better understanding of the relationship between professional and non-professional. Parsons was somewhat tentative about the term 'profession'. It had been used very widely and under that term many occupations gained admittance to the university under false pretences. Even if professional training was dominated by pretenders, that should not mean that professional training had no place in the modern university. Parsons' focus was upon 'business', and his analysis was an attempt to 'turn the tables'.

> It is of course true that many, perhaps most, of the traditions of business are not in harmony with professional ideals. And with the advent of business schools in the universities, the tendency has perhaps been more to regard them as schools of the

art of making money than as professional schools in a strict sense. But at the same time it is generally acknowledged that business occupies a key position in contemporary society. The business men are the natural leaders of the community. It may be suggested that if the great cultural tradition is to be perpetuated and developed it is almost necessary that it should come to impregnate the business community. If a business education could be made a true professional education in the sense sketched here, it would be a very large step in the integration of our civilization in the sense in which President Hutchins desires it.   (ibid.: 368–9)

In relation to this problem Parsons divined a task for sociology. The professions should be made aware of their changing place in the structure of contemporary society. Systematic insight into the cultural deposit was required.

Parsons, following Durkheim, placed professions at the centre of modern society. But there was much more to Parsons' approach than simply locating himself and his professional contribution. He was searching for a framework in which, and through which, university-based professional education could continue to pass on its heritage. This, the leaven 'which leavens the lump of the blind struggle for existence and for wealth and power in society', was a respect for 'higher learning', a norm by which his own work could be judged.

It is, indeed, imperative that on the faculty of the university should be many men who, though permeated through and through with the liberal spirit which is alone appropriate to a university, are, at the same time, in the closest everyday touch with the practical life of the world in which the university exists.   (ibid.: 369)

The 'pattern variables' illustrate Parsons desire to contribute to professional-life-in-the-world. The centre-piece of his theoretical programme, they helped to highlight the major structural themes of contemporary society. They were Parsons' attempt to make *theory* useful. It is ironic that it was this part of Parsons' theory which has been criticized for its abstract and idiosyncratic character. The degree to which the pattern-variables have become an exclusive preserve of professional sociology is perhaps indicative of sociology's isolation from the other professions with a clearly articulated theoretical contribution. Sociology, in Parsons' view, was that profession which develops insight about modern professionally oriented society, via *research*. The structure of modern society presupposed that professional contributions could only emerge after hard work.

It is perhaps in relation to the university as a *professional* body that we should interpret Parsons' *failure* to tackle the *departmentalization* in university organization. The division of labour within the university had only emerged after a long and arduous process of many generations. It was Parsons' seeming reluctance to tackle this *in his writings* that indicates, perhaps, an *institutional and self-imposed* impediment to the full disclosure of his theoretical vision.

Parsons' professionalism highlights another aspect of 'convergence', namely his conscious striving for an alternative to academic entrepreneurialism whilst holding on to scholarly freedom. Parsons' theory was his attempt to resist a kind of 'free market' in sociology in which various schools tried to 'sell' their own special European theorist in competition with each other.

Modern institutions

Instead of 'institutionalism' as a frame of reference, Parsons sought to develop a theory of institutions. In the essay 'Professions and Social Structure' together with the exchange with Frank H. Knight, 'The Motivation of Economic Activities' (T. Parsons 1940), Parsons formulated his theory of social institutions. The commonly accepted economic interpretations of social behaviour were replaced by a new paradigm.

Parsons turned his attention in a direction he believed was more fruitful than all hitherto existing general theories (T. Parsons and Frank H. Knight 1930–45, Parsons to Knight, 1 August 1940). His initial point concerned the common-sense contrast between the *acquisitiveness* of modern business and the *altruism* of the professions.

> [T]he business man has been thought of as egoistically pursuing his own self-interest regardless of the interests of others, while the professional man was altruistically serving the interests of others regardless of his own. Seen in this context the professions appear not only as empirically somewhat different from business, but the two fields would seem to exemplify the most radical cleavage conceivable in the field of human behavior.   (T. Parsons 1939: 36)

But Parsons dismissed this vision of social order as too simplistic. There were enough businesses set up by professionals to indicate to him that the distinction between acquisitiveness and professional disinterest refers to institutional patterns rather than personal motivation. Economics, as the theory of market-oriented action, had not differentiated between these institutional patterns. In economics the professional and the businessman showed no great differences in their respective motivations to maximize profit. But there was a definite *structural* difference. In *institutional* terms, the professional and the businessman operated in relation to different expectations.

> The institutional patterns governing the two fields of action are radically different in this respect. Not only are they different; it can be shown conclusively that this difference has very important functional bases.   (ibid.: 46

Parsons came to this conclusion via an analysis of the occupational structure of the contemporary social system. Both professions and businesses operate in terms of 'applied science', the dominant characteristic of which is *rationality*. As part of the institutional structure, scientific-rational norms prevailed which did not allow for *traditionalism* in decision-making. Rationality is thus *institutional*. It is a norm for occupational behaviour in contemporary society. *Traditionalism*, as a way of orienting human behaviour, does not now dominate occupational behaviour in the way that *rationality* does. This is the first major point which Parsons made about contemporary occupational behaviour. He thus included both the professional and the businessman in an analytical frame of reference which related them to each other in terms of factors operative in the same society. They share similar institutional characteristics. Rationality is the norm for both. Traditionalism is, in general, avoided.

Another way in which business is closely allied with professions in contemporary society can be seen in the contrast with kinship relations. Unlike kinship relations, which tend to be 'functionally diffuse', professional and business relations are 'functionally specific'. 'A professional man is held to be "an authority" only in his own field' (ibid.: 38), and 'in the classic type of "contractual relationship", rights and obligations are specifically limited to what are implicitly or explicitly the "terms of the contract"' (ibid.: 39). Parsons analysed professions and business in terms of a shared functional specificity. And in so doing he specified an important dimension of the public/ private dichotomy. There is, he observed, a profound difference between occupational structure and kinship relations. He noted:

> Commercial relations in our society are predominantly functionally specific, kinship relations, functionally diffuse.   (ibid.: 39)

The question of whether there can be any functionally specific relations within the network of kinship other those ones characterised by their commercial and professional aspects was not dealt with. For instance, the sexual bond in marriage could be said to be *structurally* specific and *emotionally* diffuse. Nevertheless functional specificity and functional diffuseness in social relations emerged as another pair of options which seem to be manifest in the pattern of norms for occupational behavior. In contemporary society the occupational pattern tends towards being functionally specific. Here again Parsons was not ruling out the possibility of occupational patterns which, in other societies, at other times, could be functionally diffuse. In *The Social System*, where the pattern-variable scheme was fully elaborated, the Executive and Artisan were so classified (T. Parsons 1951: 86–8), the difference being that in the earlier formulation he had been trying to specify analytically the character of *modern* society. In *The Social System* he was working out the combinations and permutations of social systems *per se*.

Functional diffuseness, as an option, does not exist to any large extent in the normative framework of the contemporary occupational sphere. It can be seen in the kinship sphere and thus seems to have something of a *private* rather than *public* character. Functionally specific relations can be professional, commercial and governmental (administrative) in character. The relationship between two people in the public sphere is specifically tied to the kind of functionally specific relationship involved.

But the differences between occupational relationships and those of kinship were not simply explained by virtue of the distinction between functional specificity and functional diffuseness. Whilst functionally specific relations are segmental (i.e. concerned with a segment, rather than the whole, of social life) not all segmental relations are functionally specific. Parsons used the example of segmental friendship. In a friendship one does not necessarily share all of one's life and interests, but one is involved with a person on a 'total' basis (T. Parsons 1939: 40). In functionally specific occupational relations the involvement is in terms of one partner being treated as a 'client' or 'customer' along with other 'clients' or 'customers'. The person will be responded to not in terms of *who* he is but in terms of universalistic criteria which are applied to all customers and clients. Achievement in the occupational field is judged on the basis of *universalistic* criteria. The other side to *universalism* is *particularism*, which concerns the forming of a relationship on the personal basis of *who* a person is, rather than the technical evaluation of what a person has *achieved*.

> It is one of the most striking features of our occupational system that status in it is to a high degree independent of status in kinship groups, the neighbourhood and the like, in short from what are sometimes called primary group relationships. It may be suggested that one of the main reasons for this lies in the dominant importance of universalistic criteria in the judgement of achievement in the occupational field. Where technical competence, the technical impartiality of administration of an office and the like are of primary functional importance, it is essential that particularistic considerations should not enter into the bases of judgement too much. The institutional insulation from social structures where particularism is dominant is one way in which this can be accomplished.
>
> (ibid.: 42)

In societies such as mid-twentieth-century North America this institutional insulation of the public realm from the influence of particularistic criteria presumably accounted for the 'enlarged' division between the private and the public which we noted above. In this article Parsons demonstrated how the 'self-interest' versus 'altruistic' dichotomy could not, adequately, account for the variation and subtlety within the normative framework of modern society. It also fails to account for a great range of empirically possible societies (ibid.: 42–3). 'Self-interest' had been greatly exaggerated. Instead Parsons identified three elements of the normative framework in which business, professions and government operate – there could well be others (ibid.: 42). He had attempted to specify with analytical precision the place of professions in modern society. It was not merely a categorial scheme; it was a *conceptual* scheme aimed towards the explanation, in theoretical terms, of the character of human society in its manifold diversity.

The administration of modern liberal government

Parsons' view of modern government was outlined in the analysis of 'Professions and Social Structure' (T. Parsons 1939). There are three forms of administration in modern society. The 'professions' and 'business', roughly speaking, are opposites. Yet the polarities of modern society could not be explained by sole reference to the alternative directions they imply for social life. 'Government' was also included. Even though Parsons included 'government administration' in his list of modern forms of administration, he did not then elaborate his view of 'the modern liberal state' (ibid.: 46).

He noted that the universalism and functional specificity of modern governmental administration tied to 'offices' produced tensions and personal conflicts for the administrators of the law.

> The various offices are occupied by concrete individuals with concrete personalities who have particular concrete social relations to other individuals. The institutionally enjoined rigid distinction between the sphere, powers and obligation of office and those which are 'personal' to the particular individuals is difficult to maintain. In fact in every concrete structure of this sort there is to a greater or less degree a system of 'cliques'.   (ibid.: 47)

He outlined his theory of the structural forces which shape governmental policy and administration. Government action is shaped through the formation of 'power blocks'.

> That is, certain groups are more closely solidary than the strict institutional definition of their statuses calls for and correspondingly, as between such groups there is a degree of antagonism which is not institutionally sanctioned.
>   (ibid.: 47)

This is not an endorsement of the 'pressure group' model later propounded by Dahl (Dahl 1961) and others. Whilst not suggesting a strictly elitist model for analysing social policy, as Mills set forth some years later (Mills 1956), Parsons' 'cliques' suggest that the administration of the modern nation-state operates on various levels: psychological/personal, social and cultural.

> The existence of such clique structures places the individual in a conflict situation. He is for instance pulled between the 'impartial', 'objective' loyalty to his superior as the incumbent of an office, and the loyalty to a person whom he likes, who has treated him well, etc.   (ibid.: 47)

In Parsons' view the administration of the State is overshadowed by the intensely *personalistic* character of modern liberal society. He highlighted the importance of the Ideal of Human Personality for modern life. In western society the patterns of personal loyalty and friendship are prominent and deeply ingrained. These considerations can become the main pattern. Obligation to the duties of office, including submission to an authority, can be subverted by loyalty to an individual. A particularistic criterion for judgement in public affairs can replace a universalistic basis (ibid.: 47–8).

The 'Leviathan' of the modern State is continually being reconstructed as the administration adjusts and readjusts to the new constellations of consolidated 'personal forces' that have developed within it. The 'bureaucracy' of the State is not simply the antithesis of 'personal freedom' in some external sense. These tensions are found *within* the administration. It is not simply a tension between bureaucracy and the rest of society. The impersonality of administration and the solidarity of interest-group formation go hand in hand. It is hard to see it in any other way since the administrators function psychologically, culturally and socially within the same social reality. The tensions are not simply a part of the 'external' administration of society; they are indicative of the normative framework of modern society which constrains action from 'within'.

Norms, social order and rationality

The discussion of the common normative elements in the patterning of social order anticipated the development of a general theory of action in at least two respects. (1) Parsons placed professions in relation to business and other parts of the occupational structure such as government and administration. By relating them all to common elements in the normative framework, Parsons developed a general theory of social institutions. Families and friendships were included for comparison. But via these various comparisons the outline of a general theory of American society was foreshadowed. (A major study which was left uncompleted at his death, *The American Societal Community*, was, effectively, begun in these years (i.e. the early 1940s)). (2) Professions were related to the basic elements of the institutionalised normative pattern. Parsons was, in effect, comparing modern society with other societies, ancient and modern, which have different occupational patterns. These other societies have different combinations of the three alternatives mentioned (rational or traditional; functional specificity or functional diffuseness; universalistic or particularistic).

There was perhaps a third sense in which this article anticipated development in general theory-building. The analysis of discrete social institutions can demonstrate the interrelation of all contemporaneous social institutions. In addition comparison with past social institutions can help to specify the 'modern' elements.

We began with Parsons' professional concern to develop a sociological theory. Having derived a sociological theory of the professions we can see how this theory can be applied specifically to sociology. How did Parsons construe the motivation which was presupposed by his own theory? Human motivation had to be seen in terms of the internalization of institutional normative patterns. We have to look at what Parsons wrote about the 'rationality' of science if we are to apply his theory to the sociological profession.

> One of the dominant characteristics of science is its 'rationality' in the sense which is opposed to 'traditionalism'. Scientific investigation, like any other human activity when viewed in terms of the frame of reference of action, is oriented to certain normative standards. One of the principal of these in the case of science is that of 'objective truth'. Whatever else may be said of this methodologically difficult conception, it is quite clear that the mere fact that a proposition has been held to be true in the past is not an argument either for or against it before a scientific forum. The norms of scientific investigation, the standards by which it is judged whether work is of high scientific quality, are essentially independent of traditional judgements. (ibid.: 36–7)

In terms of the rational-versus-traditional option for judgement, science, and hence sociology as a science, must tend to be rational. Sociology, a cognitive endeavour within the modern technological society, is also *rational* by definition. Modern society is *modern* because of the great influence of *scientific* rationality upon the normative framework. Parsons' *bias* was clearly in favour of the rational character of the sociological profession.

A professional science also has to be universalistic. It cannot apply a *particularistic* criterion simply because the question of *who* states a proposition is irrelevant for judgements of scientific value (ibid.: 42).

The relation of science to the functional specificity–functional diffuseness pair is somewhat harder to define. Parsons noted that it is 'only in matters touching his academic specialty that the professor is superior, by virtue of his status, to his student' (ibid.: 38).

> The technical competence which is one of the principal defining characteristics of the professional status and role is always limited to a particular 'field' of knowledge and skill. This specificity is essential to the professional pattern no matter how difficult it may be, in a given case, to draw the exact boundaries of such a field.   (ibid.: 38)

Parsons did not try to *derive* the professional status of sociology. His analysis simply assumed the professional character of his own investigation and the sociological tradition in which he operated. But what kind of professional character? Sociology as a profession had to be concerned with 'understanding' itself ('knowing what it is doing'), but also 'understanding' the professions and social structure in general terms.

9
Formulating *The Social System*

Introduction

Parsons' three major statements about theory in the mid-to-late 1940s show how he then viewed sociological theory and its development. This was a crucial time in the unfolding of his project.

The three statements considered here were all professional statements. 'The Present Position and Prospects of Systematic Theory in Sociology', written in 1945, was his published contribution to the symposium *Twentieth Century Sociology* (Gurvitch and Moore 1945) (T. Parsons 1945). 'The Position of Sociological Theory' was a paper originally read before the American Sociological Society (T. Parsons 1948a). The footnotes included his response to the comments on his paper given by Robert K. Merton and Theodor Newcomb which were appended to the paper. The essay 'The Prospects of Sociological Theory' was Parsons' acceptance speech when he was elected to the position of President of the American Sociological Society in December 1949 (T. Parsons 1950).

'The Present Position and Prospects of Systematic Theory in Sociology'

The development of scientific theory had been defined in terms of three levels: the frame of reference, the descriptive analysis of the structure of systems and the formulation of a set of interdependent variables (T. Parsons 1937a: 27ff.). In that article the first two were singled out as constituting the major framework in which Parsons would formulate his theory (T. Parsons 1945: 214). He acknowledged that in terms of scientific development he was operating on a 'more "primitive" level of systematic theoretical analysis' (ibid.: 216). In physics, mathematics *is* theory; he was searching for 'the nearest possible approach to an *equivalent* of the role of mathematical analysis in physics' (ibid.: 224). Thus whilst seeking an equivalent to mathematics in physics he was seeking structural categories by which he could 'simplify dynamic problems . . . without . . . refined mathematical analysis' (ibid.: 217). He was not ruling out the possibility of a mathematical sociology; but he did not stress its necessity, and in fact minimized its desirability (ibid.: 216). The completion of his theory, on all of its levels, was a future matter. But what did Parsons mean by 'systematic theory'? Science involved theory and 'the most important single index of the state of maturity of a science is the state of its systematic theory' (ibid.: 212). Theory facilitated sytematic description and systematic analysis.

> The two are most intimately connected since it is only when the essential facts about a phenomenon have been described in a carefully systematic and orderly manner that accurate analysis becomes possible at all.   (ibid.: 213)

But how could scientific theory arrive at an adequate *description*? In classical mechanics the frame of reference included three-dimensional rectilinear space, time, mass, location and motion. These constituted the essential conceptual scheme from which the structure of the mechanical system could be built up from its basic unit, the particle. But what about 'structure'?

> The structure of the system consists in the number of particles, their properties, such as mass, and their interrelations, such as relative locations, velocities and directions of motion.   (ibid.: 214)

Dynamic analysis could then proceed. 'Causal explanation' of past events and prediction of future ones and the formulation of 'generalized analytical knowledge' were the result.

> The attainment of the two goals, or aspects of the same goal, go hand in hand. On the one hand specific causal explanation is attainable only through the application of some generalized analytical knowledge; on the other, the extension of analytical generalization is only possible by generalization from empirical cases and verification in terms of them.   (ibid.: 215)

Parsons' theory of general theory was not here preoccupied with 'convergence' among various prominent writers, who may have operated with differing views of causal explanation, the formulation of scientific laws and empirical validation. The systems of differential equations in analytical mechanics were the only case in which the 'ideal' had been attained, at least in the 'formal sense'. The ideal was comprehensive explanation.

> The ideal solution is the possession of a logically complete system of dynamic generalizations, which can state all the elements of reciprocal interdependence between all the variables of the system.   (ibid.: 216)

All scientific disciplines were oriented to this. Sociology should aim at the truth even if the ideal of explaining in full was a very long way off.

> The most essential condition of successful dynamic analysis is continual and systematic reference of every problem to the state of the system as a whole.
> (ibid.: 216)

Dynamic analysis involves relating every problem to the state of the system as a whole. Simplification is necessary because it is not always possible to relate all facts to all other facts within the system.

> If it is not possible to provide for that by explicit inclusion of every relevant fact as

the value of a variable which is included in the dynamic analysis at that point, there must be some method of simplification. (T. Parsons 1945: 216)

Parsons did not exclude the possibility of *full* explanation from his general view of scientific theory. But in the social sciences progress is still slow. Generalized categories have to be isolated so that they can be treated as 'constants'. In mechanics the 'constants' contribute to an explanation of physical systems, as laws 'outside' the system. The laws for social action cannot be formulated in such terms because theoretical explanation of social systems requires that the actor's frame of reference be included.

Parsons introduced 'structural categories' which 'simplify the dynamic problems to the point where they are manageable without the possibility of refined mathematical analysis' (ibid.: 217). The structural categories make analysis manageable. But why did he there use the phrase 'without the possibility of refined mathematical analysis'? The possibility was ruled out on two fronts. In the first place, variables which in any empirical situation could be quantified are not necessarily the most important variables for explaining the structure of the phenomena under consideration. Secondly, meaningful enumeration of these variables does not necessarily lead to a better understanding of their function in a social system.

For Parsons dynamic problems could be analysed without dispensing with any important variables. 'Structural categories' provide a framework within which all problems can be related to the total system under consideration. 'For the structure of a system', Parsons observed, 'as described in the context of a generalized conceptual scheme is a genuinely technical analytical tool' (ibid.: 217).

Parsons developed his concept of 'structure' to fulfil the requirements that it be a 'fact'. Structure, as a fact, is a statement about a phenomenon, rather than the phenomenon itself. Such a concept is of great usefulness to the social analyst.

> It ensures that nothing of vital importance is inadvertently overlooked, and ties in loose ends, giving determinancy to problems and solutions. It minimizes the danger, so serious to common-sense thinking, of filling gaps by resort to uncriticized residual categories. (ibid.: 217)

The structure-concept orders the scientific analysis of systems. Social systems cannot attain the mathematical precision of mechanics. In mechanics 'structure' is not included as a separate theoretical element. It is dissolved into 'process and interdependence'. The simultaneous equations represent the *structuring* between the various elements. But in social systems many variables are non-quantifiable.

> Structure does not refer to any ontological stability in phenomena but only to relative stability – to sufficiently stable uniformities in the results of underlying processes so that their constancy within certain limits is a workable pragmatic assumption. (ibid.: 217)

Parsons juxtaposed 'ontological stability' with 'relative stability'. Logically, he

accepted an 'ontological relative stability'. (This, seemingly, was the equivalent of the non-rigid bind by which he related theory to philosophical
thought.) He proceeded with his scientific account pragmatically. The goal of
success in explanation led him to 'get a handle' on reality without the
presumption of any ontological view of totality. 'Structural categories' have an
empirical reference in a dynamic totality.

> Once resort is made to the structure of a system as a positive constituent of
> dynamic analysis there must be a way of linking these 'static' structural categories
> and their relevant particular statements of fact to the dynamically variable
> elements in the system.   (ibid.: 217)

The 'structural categories' are constituted by *statements* of fact. *These are then
related to the 'variable elements' by way of the concept of function.* What did he mean
by 'function'? Was this being utilized in its mathematical sense? Apparently
not. But it does seem to involve some faint, though definite, association with
the *rigour* of functional analysis in mathematics. Parsons tried to explain
'structure' and 'function' in general terms. The function-concept has its
peculiar application within mechanics, with the corresponding concepts of
'differentiation' and 'integration' in the mathematical calculus. But for his
general purposes, 'function' is explained in these terms:

> Its crucial role is to provide criteria of the *importance* of dynamic factors and
> processes within the system. They are important in so far as they have functional
> significance to the system, and their specific importance is understood in terms of
> the analysis of specific functional relations between the parts of the system and
> between it and its environment.   (ibid.: 217)

'Function' has a concrete point of reference. Analytically, 'function' refers to a
dynamic process of interdependence *between* variables. 'Structure' is a 'function' of the mechanical system, and as such it is capable of being rigorously
explained in mathematical terms.

Parsons painted a different picture in the non-mathematical sciences.
'Dynamic' factors and processes are centrally important and led to a conception 'above' physical systems to 'going concerns'. From this point in his
discussion – i.e. the bottom of p. 217 – Parsons moved *from* a discussion of
mechanical and general systems *to* a further delineation of *living* systems. And
it was here that he achieved what he was looking for: a logical validation of
general theory in sociology which was based upon mathematical canons of
explanation.

> Functional significance in this context is inherently teleological. A process or a set
> of conditions either 'contributes' to the maintenance (or development) of the
> system or it is 'dysfunctional' in that it detracts from the integration, effectiveness,
> etc., of the system.   (ibid.: 217–18)

Functional analysis delineates how units within the system contributed to the
system as a going concern. The purposes of unit and system are mutually
intertwined and it is the unravelling of the *functional* relations between them
that is the central focus of the non-mechanical sciences.

It is thus the functional reference of all particular conditions and processes *to the state of the total system as a going concern* which provides the logical equivalent of simultaneous equations in a fully developed system of analytical theory.

(ibid.: 218)

Next, Parsons criticized the various 'Unsatisfactory types of theory in recent sociology' (pp. 219–24), deriving some general guidelines for developing current theory. Empirical generalizations were often propounded by evolutionists (Tylor and Morgan), but Marx and Veblen also used such a priori points of departure for theoretical analysis (ibid.: 219). This put the cart before the horse. Empirical generalizations *could only come after* the acceptance, refinement and further development of a generalized theoretical system in closest analytical proximity to empirical reality. It was in relation to this that Parsons observed that 'no competent modern sociologist can be a Comtean, a Spencerian, or even a Marxist' (ibid.: 220).

Empirical generalization was valid even if speculative system-building had been discredited. There had also been a swing to the opposite pole.

> While one tendency, it may be said, has sought to create a great building by a sheer act of will without going through the requisite of technical procedures, the other has tried to make a virtue of working with bare hands alone, rejecting all tools and mechanical equipment.   (ibid.: 220)

Another approach had related all of social reality to specially selected 'factors'. This, unfortunately, had led to a war in which each school sought to defend its own factor with as much empirical justification as it could gather. Parsons noted:

> Professional pride and vested interests get bound up with the defense or promotion of one theory against all others and the result is an impasse. In such a situation it is not surprising that theory as such should be discredited and many of the sanest, least obsessive minds become disillusioned with the whole thing and become dogmatic empiricists, denying as a matter of principle that theory can do anything for science. They feel it is, rather, only a matter of speculative construction which leads away from respect for facts, and that thus the progress of science can consist *only* in the accumulation of discrete, unrelated unguided discoveries of fact.
>
> (ibid.: 223–4)

Parsons placed himself squarely on the platform of science. In physics, he reminded his readers, mathematics is theory.

> A science of physics without higher mathematics would be the real equivalent of the empiricists' ideal for social science. This shows quite clearly that what we need is not a science purified of theoretical infection – but one with the nearest possible approach to an *equivalent* of the role of mathematical analysis in physics. The trouble with sociology has not been that it has had too much theory but that it has been plagued with the wrong kinds and what it has had of the right has been insufficiently developed and used to meet the need.   (ibid.: 224)

He worked to head off an empiricist stampede, appealing to empiricists to recognize their own theoretical roots.

The next section ('III: Approaches to a Generalized Social System', pp.

224–7) outlined the current state of affairs in social science with uneven development across the spectrum and isolationism between disciplines. Parsons saw economics, psychoanalysis, psychology and social anthropology as implicated in the developments pioneered by Pareto, Malinowski, Freud, Durkheim and Weber.

Pareto is the single most important theorist to have formulated a general social theory in terms of the 'system' concept. Pareto's background in mathematics and physics led him to systematic theoretical thinking about social systems. But his attempt was a failure. His initial *ad hoc* and flexible attempt to utilize the system-concept suggested a structural–functional approach on all levels. I discuss this in more detail below. Parsons 'corrected' Pareto's over-reliance upon *mechanical* analogies by incorporating physiological analogies into a new formulation.

Part IV (pp. 228–37), 'Outline of a Structural–Functional Theory of Social Systems', summarized 'Actor, Situation and Normative Pattern', the unpublished paper discussed in Chapter 7. By this stage (i.e. 1945), Parsons had psychology included in the general theory.

Parsons emphasized the need to introduce factors which *prevent* direct derivation. It was not a straightforward deduction from simplest unit – act – to the complex analysis of structure and function in social systems.

> In a sense this basic frame of reference consists in the outline of the structural categories of human personality in a psychological sense, in terms of the particular values of which each particular character structure or sequences of action must be described and analyzed. But the structure of social systems cannot be derived directly from the actor–situation frame of reference. It requires functional analysis of the complications introduced by the interaction of a plurality of actors.
>
> (ibid.: 229)

The concept of 'function', and the resultant 'functional analysis', provides the link between the three modes of orientation and the theory of institutions. The framework now insinuated important psychological and psychoanalytical aspects of the actor–situation complex. Parsons was operating with a hierarchy of concepts of increasing complexity:

> From the present point of view, however, a social system is a system of action, i.e., of motivated human behavior, not a system of culture patterns. It articulates with culture patterns in one connection just as it does with physical and biological conditions in another. But a 'system of culture' is a different order of abstraction from a 'social system' though it is to a large degree an abstraction from the same concrete phenomena.
>
> (ibid.: 229)

From this the scale of concepts shown in Figure 9 can be itemized.

But the discussion of the social system cannot stop there. Within social systems the basic elements can be determined. The 'actor', as the basic unit, interacts with other actors and social structure is the patterned system of the social relationships of actors. But in social action the actor is not the part of any

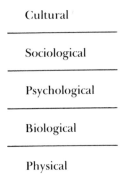

Figure 9 Hierarchy of ontological concepts

particular social whole; rather the actor acted in any particular social situation by and through a 'role'.

> Role is the concept which links the subsystem of the actor as a 'psychological' behaving entity to the distinctively *social* structure.   (ibid.: 230)

Moreover the system of social relationships is a patterned system of actors in these roles. Institutions are systems of patterned role expectations. Institutions are human systems and operate on all levels of reality. Analysis can identify the functional needs of the actor and also of the system.

Parsons' three-fold scheme was very useful (ibid.: 232, n. 14) for the analysis of institutions (i.e. situational, instrumental and integrative). Then he developed his argument schematically in relation to deviance, stratification and social order. He emphasized the central importance of the problem of human motivation for any analysis of the social system whilst arguing for the independence of sociological analysis and its interdependence with psychological explanations.

Yet the same problem emerged here that had dogged him all along. Was sociology the same as the general theory of the social system? This possible interpretation he did not accept. Whereas previously sociology was concerned with 'common value integration' (T. Parsons 1937a: 768), it was now the science of 'institutions' (T. Parsons 1948a: 161–3).

> This would, as here conceived, by no means limit it to purely static structural analysis but could retain a definite focus on problems of structure, including structural change. Dynamic, particularly psychological, problems would enter into sociology in terms of their specific relevance to this context.
>   (T. Parsons 1945: 235)

Thus while psychology and sociology would relate to the theory of social systems in their own way, economics, politics and anthropology, with their special concerns, provided perplexing problems and 'demarcation disputes'. In this essay Parsons did not attempt to resolve the issues, although economics was limited to one particular aspect. Political theory and religion were viewed as independent disciplines applying the theory to their own areas. It was also doubtful whether anthropology, in either its social or cultural guises, constitutes an independent discipline (ibid.: 237).

Parsons aimed to refashion social science, yet his proposals were, increasingly, proposals for sociologists. He aimed to help fellow-sociologists in the inter-disciplinary context; he also encouraged general theory within the discipline.

'The Position of Sociological Theory'

The programmatic character of theory development was emphasized. Parsons wanted a united profession.

> The time when the most important fact about theory in our field was its division into warring schools or the personal systems of individuals is, if not already completely passed, in my opinion, passing.   (T. Parsons 1948a: 157)

Merton expressed complete support for this view. But his agreement was tempered by an acknowledgement of *partial* agreement, then extending the implications of something Parsons had said, and then disagreeing in a profound manner. Looking back on this exchange forty years after, we are surprised by the serious and open difference of orientation. At that time Parsons and Merton expressed whole-hearted agreement about the passing into antiquity of 'warring schools' in sociology. Their names have become inextricably associated with 'structural–functional' theory. This ambiguous relationship was very important for the theoretical enterprise promoted by Parsons. This discussion is kept to the public record of that exchange.

Parsons saw 'theory' as a common task for 'theorists'. Theorists were not, and should not be, an isolated group who simply existed for themselves. They were 'the theoretically interested members' of the professional group of sociologists. The group of theorists to whom he was directing his comments were those interested in theory as a professional task. They were not joined by some esoteric interest in some individual's theory, nor were they joined by some mega-interest in the theories of many different theorists. In accepting theory into the parameters of professional sociology these professionals were attempting to transcend personalism. The basis for this professionalism, as we have noted already, has deep roots in modern scientific consciousness whereby the norms of scientific investigation are judged to be essentially independent of traditional judgements (T. Parsons 1939: 37). Parsons would build a tradition of theory by a professional and rational route.

> We are in a position to agree on certain broad fundamentals of such a character that the large number of people who accept them can be working on common premises and, though their individual interests and contributions will differ and will cover a wide range, there is every prospect that they should converge in the development of a single major conceptual structure. It is as an attempt to assist in the implementation of this prospect that I should like to see this paper considered.
> (T. Parsons 1948a: 157)

This was one of the strangest statements that Parsons ever made. Here he referred to 'convergence' in the *future* tense. He appears to be radically upsetting his own theoretical development. Was he not developing systematic theory *on the basis* of the hitherto historically established convergence of Marshall, Pareto, Durkheim and Weber, on what was, in all essentials, a common conceptual scheme? Is this a point when the entire development threatened to fall apart?

Parsons did not abandon his scientific attempt to establish the historical unity of recent social theory. It was not viewed by him as a mere personal attempt of one investigator to provide a basis for his own theoretic system-building. But why did no one at the time spot the profound ambiguity involved in Parsons' new concept of 'convergence'? The internal logic of Parsons' position seems to be the following: at this point, he was very confident about the possibility of a professionally oriented theory in sociology; he now considered the 'convergence' of Weber, Durkheim and Freud to be an historical anticipation of a *future analytical* convergence; the conceptual scheme would be truly established in sociology by the right use of analytical rationality.

'Convergence' as *hypothesis* had now become 'convergence' as *task*. Convergence-as-analytic-discovery had become convergence-as-ideal. Here Parsons seemingly reverted to Henderson's view of his achievement. He had accepted that there was indeed a commonality between Durkheim, Weber and Pareto, but was not willing to push their agreement too far. The 'convergence' was not something which belonged to them, but to the generation of social theorists who were working on their theories(T. Parsons and L. J. Henderson 1939, Henderson to Parsons, 17 July 1939) 'Convergence' was no longer simply a cultural deposit enabling the theoretically inclined to work together. 'Convergence' had become something which professional theorists would have to make happen. 'Convergence' was not only a guarantee that professional theorists were on the right track; it was something that they now had to *create*. In this sense the ambiguity in Parsons' new concept of 'convergence' was no more and no less ambiguous than the human action he sought to explain via his theory.

Merton took issue with Parsons on two points. The first concerned the distinction between history and theory – Merton sought to extend the implications of Parsons' statement; the second concerned the need for theories rather than Theory. With respect to the first point Merton's statement reads as a 'laid-back' criticism of his teacher's method. We do not get any systematic statement from Merton on the relations between the two issues which he raised. I would like to suggest that here these two leading sociological theorists were talking past each other; when we examine the exchange carefully it is impossible to accept their statements of agreement and disagreement at face value.

The problems in communication arise with Merton's 'extension of the implication' of Parsons' observation about the passing of the state of war between schools and the prospect of a single conceptual scheme emerging. He did not address himself explicitly to Parsons' *professional* desire to build a sociological tradition according to the norms of rationality. There was the inherent ambiguity to explore concerning the *traditional* character of the anticipated theory's *authority* once it had been shown that this single major conceptual scheme had emerged. But Merton moved away from *that* issue into a conceptual distinction of his own. He implied that Parsons, contrary to his claim, did not differ from the 'grand theorists'. Merton did *not* give much credence to Parsons' theoretical account of his divergence on the basis of his professionalism. The a priori distinction between rational and traditional authority, self-consciously applied to the professional task of theory-building, was not examined.

In my view Merton 'fudged' the issue, no doubt with the best intentions. He desired to elevate the discussion about the relationship between theory and the history of theory, but his technique indicates an ambivalence about his teacher's theory; he saw the ambiguity, or privately 'saw through' Parsons' 'system', but since he aimed for 'middle-range' theory, he did not proceed to a *systematic* critique of Parsons' position. After all, such a critique might give the impression that he was propounding an alternative 'system of grand theory'.

> I can only voice strong agreement with the view that the day of rival schools of sociological theory, each purveying its system of doctrine in the marketplace of sociological opinion or engaging in open academic warfare with its enemies, has come to a well-deserved close.   (Merton 1948: 164)

I am inclined to take what Merton and Parsons say here at face value. The common interpretation among the American sociological profession is that they had a formidable, barely repressed, rivalry. In my view this has as much to do with the American way of interpreting public affairs as with what they showed publicly concerning their professional friendship. In my view Merton's comments here do *not* read as an attempt at 'one-upmanship'. He seems to be trying to counter the interpretation that he was motivated by a student's desire to go 'one better' than his teacher. Rather his comments read as a genuine expression of concern, cramped in style because he was very much aware of, if not overly concerned with, the possibility that others would interpret his comments in a personalistic way. From this angle a plausible conjecture emerges. Parsons and Merton were each motivated on this occasion to express total agreement because they considered that the promotion of a common enterprise in sociological theory, whatever else it would do, would also strengthen their relationship internally and thereby offset the environmental interpretation that they were each other's rivals. In this way they worked together in their long-established teacher–student relationship to stop any possibility of war between competing structural–functionalisms.

Merton agreed with Parsons that an era of 'consensus' in sociological theory had arrived. Both 'free enterprise competition' and 'warfare' had been, and had to be, superseded, and any disagreement was now placed in the context of an overall agreement. Competition was to be in the context of mutual professional co-operation. A new atmosphere prevailed in professional sociology requiring a new attitude to theory and theorizing. Merton was, with Parsons, a sociological theorist after a new style. We see them here struggling with the relationship between professionalism and friendship.

> As I shall suggest later, these controversies were in large part a product of the urge to create total systems of sociological thought rather than to create small families of empirically verified theorems.   (ibid.: 164–5)

This creation of 'small families of empirically verified theorems' rather than 'large businesses of grand speculation' was Merton's safeguard against the re-emergence of the previous patterns of academic warfare which stood in the way of the development of sociological theory. The metaphor of 'small families' is significant. 'Getting on' in theory was now a matter of one's own professional efforts, judged by the rational and disinterested criteria of one's professional peers, rather than by association with some greater scheme of things. Merton continued:

> An implication of Mr. Parsons' remark deserves fuller comment. The attractive confusion of sociological theory with the *history* of sociological thought should long since have been dispelled. This is not to deny the great value of steeping oneself in the history of sociological thought. It is only to deny that the history of theory and currently applicable theory are one and the same.   (ibid.: 165)

Now how did this remark connect with the logic of the observation made by Parsons which Merton was using as his 'text'? Was Merton *extending* Parsons' distinction between history and theory as utilized and illustrated in *The Structure*? Or was he using the distinction to criticize Parsons now that he shared with him the same 'firm foundations'? I think it was both; in which case Merton can be read as calling upon Parsons to *resume* that style of sociological theorem verification pioneered by *The Structure*. The phrase 'should long since have been dispelled' implied a criticism of Parsons, but it is not stated exactly by reference to what Parsons actually affirmed. The criticism, or the possibility of criticism, was effectively smothered with Parsons' footnoted reply of 'heartiest agreement' (T. Parsons 1948a: 157). Any 'fundamental' differences were kept within the close confines of this 'professional-familial grouping'. They 'knew' what their disagreement was about; but it is much harder for someone 'outside the family', like the present writer, to figure out precisely what is going on. The further implication of the above statement was that Parsons was seen by Merton as trying to provide a *historical* account of theoretical processes now in train. Merton implied that Parsons' 'convergence' could become an attempt to equate the history of theory with currently applicable theory. Yet Merton pulled back from full critique in this sense. Why? The full reasons for this cannot be found by reference to what was there published. Clearly it had something to do with Merton's subsequent espousal of 'theories of the middle range' (Merton 1957: 5–10). Parsons' reply to Merton is in the footnotes and expresses 'heartiest agreement with his remarks about the relation between theory in contemporary sociology and the history of sociological theories'. The oft-made distinction between 'theory' and 'theories' is repeated. Merton's comments were about 'the relation' between 'theory' and the 'history of theories'. But Merton stated that for him it was rather a matter of making a *strict* distinction between 'the history and systematics of sociological theory'.

Parsons here appeared to view the history of sociological theories as a *classification* based on a backward look. Theory, on the other hand, was to be an action-based *task* looking to the future. Merton saw the 'systematics of sociological theory' in terms of a methodological orientation which looked backwards and forwards and cast its own theories in the middle range of the present. Merton and Parsons diverged quite radically in their views of the sociological discipline.

> To this point, I agree wholly with what I assume to be the implication of Mr. Parsons' statement. But when he suggests that our chief task is to deal with 'theory' rather than 'theories', I must take strong exception.   (Merton 1948: 165)

Where did the dilemma lie? In Merton's terms systematic theory evolved in a particular way. Prior to his statement quoted above he had remarked:

> Current systematic theory represents the selective accumulation of those parts of earlier theory which have survived the test of decades of research. The history of theory includes the large conceptions which were dissipated when confronted with rigorous tests; it also includes the false starts, the archaic doctrines and the plain errors of the past.   (ibid.: 165)

Here Merton was, in effect, calling Parsons *back* to the tentative approach of *The Structure of Social Action*. There, in Merton's terms, 'current systematic theory' represented a selective accumulation of those insights of Weber, Durkheim *et al.* which had stood the test of time, and which had been recognized by a competent theoretical mind. But Merton also argued for the allocation of history and theory 'to distinct and only loosely related spheres' (ibid.: 165).

But did Parsons view the position of sociological theory in terms of Merton's 'survival of the fittest concepts' concept? The answer is found in Parsons' view of the evolution of the theoretical frame of reference, and his view that a *foundation* for sociological theory had emerged. Parsons countered Merton:

> It is my contention that the time has passed when individual theories must be so particularistic that they must lack the common foundations which are necessary to make them building blocks in the same general conceptual structure, so that *theoretically* the development of our science may, to a degree hitherto unknown, become cumulative.   (T. Parsons 1948a: 157, n. 3)

Parsons and Merton thus differed in the interpretation of *The Structure*. For Parsons it was very definitely a 'study in theory rather than theories'. For Merton it would be indicative of a middle-range theory which tested the convergence hypothesis. It was a study not unlike Weber's *Protestant Ethic* or Merton's *Science, Technology and Society in Seventeenth Century England* (Merton 1938/70). Its contribution is its hypothetical positing and testing of a sociological link between phenomena which seemed to be historically separate. The depth of implied difference here may also help to explain Parsons' 'second convergence' as something which the profession, rather than the individual theorist, would establish and confirm. Parsons' seeming 'turn' to Henderson's interpretation of the 'convergence thesis' indicates an anticipated response to the Mertonian critique. Parsons was looking to the future, and turning his attention from the initial 'convergence' to the impending one. Merton, however, was reading Parsons' statement in terms of the development of Parsons' standpoint from his previous articulation in *The Structure*. Parsons' interpretation of *The Structure* diverged from Merton's view, and the *agreement* between the two masked a *deep* difference in orientation.

The above is not to suggest that Parsons should not have used 'convergence' to describe the ongoing task of sociological theory. The fact that he used the term indicated that he was seeking to develop theory in sociology, sensitive to Merton's critique. His own original form of 'convergence' could never rival the 'convergence' in which the sociological heroes of the previous generation had participated. For Parsons professional sociology could be cumulative when the theorists shared a common frame of reference. For Merton the systematics of sociological theory should have been cumulative because the canons of scientific utility prevailed. It was necessary to avoid system-building, and a strict distinction between systematics and the historiography of the discipline would help in this. But for Parsons the ideal of a system of theory was not to be supplanted as a valid goal because of the errors of the past. Parsons was a reformer of social theory; his approach required an ongoing vigilance to guard against 'premature closure'. For Parsons to opt for Merton's view would be tantamount to accepting an individualistic (if not egoistic) interpretation of his own endeavour over the past ten, if not twenty, years. Parsons was asserting that the profession had a current task in theory-building. Merton viewed the individual sociologist as contributing his own 'theories' to the one overall enterprise. For Merton 'Grand Theory' was still far off in the future. He ruled out 'closure' by moving away into theories of the middle range. Parsons ruled out 'premature closure' by dint of analytical and professional vigilance in the grand task of general theory-building.

> The working out of such a framework is itself an essential and fruitful task. But it is quite true that there is a danger of repetition of the old fallacy of premature closure of a theoretical system. Comte and Spencer all over again.
>
> (T. Parsons 1948a: 157, n. 3, col. 2)

Parsons' system remained 'open'. But his system of systems, his commitment to 'convergence', was now a historically established (we could almost say 'closed') datum of a speculative kind. In his anticipation of a single conceptual structure for sociology he would not be swayed. Merton did not confront that issue, which perhaps he of all Parsons' students had come closest to unravelling. This accounts for the fact that even after Merton had expressed his dissent, Parsons accepted his former student's 'theories' as part of the Grand Programme. Parsons' 'General Theory' could not participate in Merton's scheme of things as one theory among many other theories. But Merton's theories could not be excluded from the analytical systematics developed by Parsons. For Parsons the concept of 'system' was central and essential for sociological theory. Theory and programme go together.

> [T]he concept of system functions as a heuristic device to guide the formulation and empirical solution of [theoretical] problems. It is, that is, a necessary basis for the most fruitful program of work in special theories as advocated by Merton.
> (ibid.: 157, n. 3)

The distinction between 'general' and 'special' is crucial. Merton, agnostic about the origins of the ultimate influences upon his theoretical reflection, remained convinced of the validity of tentative middle-range theory.

The relationship between Merton and Parsons is that of a student and teacher, in which the student contributes his 'theories' to the theory-enterprise of his teacher. But Parsons, the self-effacing teacher, seems to relate to his talented student in terms of collegial and professional equality, assuming his ongoing contribution to the professional task he (Parsons) had established.

'The Prospects of Sociological Theory'

Parsons the visionary held general and special dimensions together as two important aspects of one general scheme. His faith in the world-historical character of theory in sociology is announced in his 1949 American Sociological Society presidential speech. There also he stated explicitly that Merton's fear about the revival of speculative systems of the Spencerian type was totally unfounded.

> We have, I think, now progressed to a level of methodological sophistication to protect ourselves against this pitfall.   (T. Parsons 1950: 352)

But what was the 'methodological sophistication' he was referring to? Clearly it had something to do with the new climate of 'theory' that had emerged. For Parsons theoretical and empirical research was converging in one, overall framework. Parsons' promotion of such a convergence was coming to maturity. In his presidential statement all sociology before Durkheim and Max Weber is proto-sociology. He gave Sumner, Park, Cooley and Thomas an important role in the development of theory in America, but they were of lesser stature. He included industrial sociology (Mayo and Roethlisberger) and the Chicago and Cornell Schools, to illustrate developments (ibid.: 349).

We might want to include Alfred Marshall and Vilfredo Pareto, but here he was preoccupied with the prospects of an American initiative in theory-building. The *teaching* of theory in the discipline had evolved so as to enable it to generate its own *theoretical* tradition, '*the* tradition of a working professional group' (ibid.: 350). This change in methodological sophistication would keep the profession from fallacious speculative systems.

> Theory has at least begun no longer to mean mainly a knowledge of 'doctrines', but what matters far more, a set of patterns for habitual thinking.
>
> (ibid.: 350)

In this address we are 'on the verge' of the systematic formulations of *Towards a General Theory of Action* and *The Social System*. Parsons saw a great transformation taking place.

> At any rate, I may presume to suggest that my own election to its presidency by the membership of this society may be interpreted as an act of recognition of this importance of theory, and a vote of confidence in its future development.
>
> (ibid.: 348)

Read out of context of his overriding professional intention this reads as a self-congratulatory pronouncement. Yet this statement indicates a deeply felt professional ethic. This presidential statement identifies his own contribution with the 'theory' that was already of general use in the sociological field. This seems to be a case of his internalization of the external norms that pertain within the arena of professional sociology.

> The basic reason why general theory is so important is that the cumulative development of knowledge in a scientific field is a function of the degree of *generality of implications* by which it is possible to relate findings, interpretations and hypotheses on different levels and in different specific empirical fields to each other.
>
> (ibid.: 352)

General theory is a 'set of patterns for habitual thinking'. It provides the framework for the sociological profession, whereby theory is integrated with empirical research. In the latest 'advances' Freud had joined Durkheim and Max Weber as the principal ground-breaking theorists of the previous generation (ibid.: 353). The various applications of the general theory in sociology, anthropology and psychology had been clarified (ibid.: 357). The general theory encouraged cumulative research (ibid.: 352). It could 'provide a common language to facilitate communication between workers in different branches of the field' (ibid.: 354). General theory was an 'organizing power' which codified and clarified the strengths and weaknesses of existing knowledge.

Parsons conveyed his thoughts about an important 'new development' in which the common ground of sociology, anthropology and psychology had been explored. *General problems* had come into focus (ibid.: 356–7). He saw these 'new developments' in relation to his previous efforts. Hitherto he had analysed social action in terms of *one equation*, following Weber and W. I.

Thomas. There was the actor and the situation. Parsons, following Weber, had tended 'to put "value standards" or "modes of value orientation" into the actor' (ibid.: 357). Now he rejected what he called a 'biological mode of thought' which was central to his earlier draft paper, 'Actor, Situation and Normative Pattern'. But our previous discussion of ASNP (see Chapter 7 above) highlighted the analogical parallels Parsons was developing between action theory and biology 'with no presumption of reducibility of either to the other' (T. Parsons 1939/40: 7). (Parsons here seems to have tried to simplify matters for the sake of clearer communication with his audience – a motive which, he had earlier said, lay behind the ASNP formulation! (ibid.: 1–2)).

It transpired that 'actor' and 'situation' did not really allow for the full analytical discussion of all elements. Consequently he now reformulated his position taking *culture* as a *real* element, an independent system (T. Parsons 1950: 357; see also T. Parsons 1945: 236–7). The three main foci of general theory are *personality*, *culture* and *social structure*, and underlying these three problem areas was 'the fundamental fact that *man is a culture-bearing animal*'. This definition indicates the continued influence of evolutionary, if not strictly biological, concepts in theorizing. The development was analytical – sociology was coming into its own. Parsons was here speaking as a specialist sociologist.

Here he also outlined his 'second theory' of convergence concerning the internalization of value attitudes in Freud, Durkheim, Cooley and Mead (T. Parsons 1950: 353, 359). Here the pattern–variable scheme was also articulated (ibid.: 359–60). But his *vision* of the future of sociology shows how he viewed the entire terrain.

The most important work lay ahead. What are the bases for comparing social structures? That was a central problem (ibid.: 361). It manifests itself on macro- and micro- levels. How does theory come to terms with all the variations *within* and *between* societies? Quite contrary to the stereotype of his theory of the American family as merely a case of 'happy families', Parsons acknowledged a priori the immense variety found within the American middle-class family. He again explained why a 'structural–functional' level of analysis was required.

> In this situation we cannot achieve a high level of dynamic generalization for processes and interdependencies even *within* the same society, unless our ranges of structural variability are really systematized so that when we get a shift from one to another we know *what* has changed, *to what* and *in what degree*.
>
> (ibid.: 364)

Even to say that there is variation from one type to another requires a *general* scheme of structural elements which must function as a 'relative stability' for analysis – 'sufficiently stable uniformities in the results of underlying processes so that their constancy within certain limits is a workable pragmatic assumption' (T. Parsons 1945: 217). But even with 'workable pragmatic assumptions' the implication is that *hard* work is required; 'rigorous theoretical analysis' is needed in a process of continuous checking with 'empirical research'. Parsons set forth his own version of the theoretical task and came close to Merton's approach to 'middle-range theory'.

Theory is limited. Scientific *theory* is one of the ingredients in the 'brew'. It must be articulated with developments in research technique. Statistics, questionnaires, polls and multi-variate analysis had reached such a level of sophistication that the social science of the future would have to consider its methods as much as its theory. A two-fold task was thereby implied.

> I do not think it is fair to say that we are still in the stage of proto-science. But we are unquestionably in that of a distinctly *immature* science. If it is really to grow up and not regress into either of the two futilities of empiricist sterility or empirically irrelevant speculation, the synthesis must take place. In this as in other respects the beginning certainly has already been made but we must be quite clear that it is *only* a beginning. (ibid.: 366–7)

A division of labour required an organic solidarity between all sociologists (theorists, research technicians and field workers), combined in one overall programme. The level of generalization, hitherto very 'broad', had to be supplemented by 'middle theories'. And Parsons saw very good prospects.

But what of the prospects for the entire field? Where was sociology headed? Obviously it was a 'growth area', and in closing this presidential address he anticipated great changes in society. The times were urgent. The demands of the American ethos were plain. Social science had a public responsibility to be practically oriented but not to sacrifice long-term effectiveness in the interests of short-term pragmatism. That long-term professional contribution required that sociology be 'a science, with a highly generalized and integrated body of fundamental knowledge' (ibid.: 368). And general theory had a central role in this advance.

> If the prospects of sociological theory are good, so are, I am convinced, those of sociology as a science, but *only* if the scientifically fundamental work is done. (ibid.: 368)

Theory – the heart of science – was the *raison d'être* of Parsons' contribution, the touchstone of the entire enterprise.

> Let us, by all means, not be stingy with the few golden eggs we now have. But let us also breed a flock of geese of the sort that we can hope will lay many more than we have yet dreamed of. (ibid.: 368)

American culture and sociology, like the Grimm allusions here, had roots deep in Europe. But just as Parsons was wanting to build a *tradition* of theory according to the *modern* norm of rationality, so he wished to develop a universally applicable theory on American soil. If there was to be a critique of Parsons' theorizing based upon its inconsistency then it would have to start here. The anomaly of building a modern tradition of rationality is central. Yet any tension was resolved, apparently, in the overriding American confidence of the project. This optimism reached back to his confrontation with Max Weber in the late 1920s.

Yet I like to think of sociology as in some sense peculiarly an American discipline, or at least an American opportunity. There is no doubt that we have the leadership now. Our very lack of traditionalism perhaps makes it in some ways easier for us than for some others to delve deeply into the mysteries of how human action in society ticks.   (ibid.: 368)

American society, then in its post-war phase, provided a crucible for truly scientific developments. The scientific leadership then emerging would give the necessary direction. This had occurred in a 'non-traditionalistic', and hence potentially scientifically oriented, society. The first-person 'we', 'our' and 'us' make it quite clear that, though this was a sociological association of professional academics, the appeal was also to their common membership in the national community of the United States of America. In such terms Parsons expressed his confidence, in contrast to his early 1930s statement about the unlikelihood of any great American advances in the hedonistic era (T. Parsons 1933: 5–6).

We certainly have all the makings for developing the technical know-how of research. We are good at organization which is coming to play an increasingly indispensable part in research.   (T. Parsons 1950: 368–9)

The immediate goal, via a unity of perspective, was spelled out explicitly:

Can American sociology seize this opportunity? One of our greatest national resources is the capacity to rise to a great challenge once it is put before us.
                                                                    (ibid.: 369)

Recalling Harvard initiatives uniting sociology, psychology and anthropology in one department (ibid.: 356, eight lines from the bottom), as well as the successful Carnegie project (*Towards a General Theory*), Parsons predicted that the historians of American social science would one day evaluate the sociology of the 1940s as a significant configuration of culture growth (ibid.: 369). But how was this challenge going to be met? This most intriguing question will be answered here by reference to what Parsons affirmed in this 'presidential' speech. But when it is read alongside the paper 'Social Science: A Basic National Resource' written shortly before (T. Parsons 1948b), it is possible to reinterpret this challenge as Parsons' call to the social science professions to unite in the face of their exclusion from the National Science Foundation (Klausner and Lidz 1985: xi).

We can do it if we put together the right *combination* of ingredients of the brew. Americans as scientists generally have been exceptionally strong on experimental work and empirical research. I have no doubt whatever of the capacity of American sociologists in this respect.   (ibid.: 369)

How was that combination of theory and research technique to be put together? Would not the sociological profession be swamped by the brew? How could 'rational objectivity' be safeguarded? The right combination of elements was something American sociology could put together as it recognized its derivative status. Standing within the global community of western thought, Parsons placed American sociology on 'the frontier', promoting an ethic of *non-self-centred* service. Here he drew the task for sociology in ways reminiscent of his father's view of the Church's role in society (E. S. Parsons 1904). Sociology must seek a higher, remoter goal to which its instrumentally immediate ends could be related. *Then* it could put together the right combination with scientific objectivity. Like the Church Militant, as E. S. Parsons had depicted it, sociology was 'on the move'. If it stuck to its task it could provide leadership for all the social sciences, such that they would become recognized as 'a basic national resource' (T. Parsons 1946, 1948b).

But how? Parsons' remoter ideal was never totally out of reach, or beyond the grasp of language. The ideal is the *unity* of the western tradition of social theory. Theoretical reason is a unity. In *The Structure* he had observed that 'rational knowledge is a single organic whole' (T. Parsons 1937a: 21). The unity of rationality is a theoretical *task*.

> But as *theorists* Americans have, relative to Europeans, not been so strong – hence the *special* challenge of the theoretical development of our field which justifies the theme of this address. (T. Parsons 1950: 369)

The ideal, respecified for the new era, has an international flavour. Sociology of the American sort must deny itself and strive to be professional. The result would be a theory for comparative analysis and universalistic application on a global scale. *Who* says something is irrelevant as far as the validity of scientific propositions is concerned. This was to be the way in which American sociology could contribute to the development of mankind.

> If we American sociologists can rise to this part of the challenge the job will really get done. We are not in the habit of listening too carefully to the timid souls who say, why try, it can't be done. I think we have already taken up the challenge all along the line. 'The sociology', as my children called it, is not *about* to begin. It has been gathering force for a generation and is now really under way. (ibid.: 369)

Sociological theory was responding to the American challenge throughout the world. Put simply, Parsons challenged the ASS to face the contemporary configuration of world forces which provided a unique challenge. American sociology was ideally placed to fulfil a unique calling because American society would be the focal point for the evolutionary unfolding of world history for some considerable time. American sociology *must* meet its cultural destiny. American sociology *must* be scientific, and take on the role of disinterested observer in the system of modern societies. Sociology must serve the world. Or was it that sociology, in his view, would *save* the world? Parsons' sociology probably involved a measure of sacrificial service with a dose of messianic fervour.

Conclusion

Parsons' admission that sociological theory was not as advanced as physics did *not* mean that he saw his own formulations as unscientific. He viewed his approach to theory-building as logically consistent. His use of 'structural–

functional' theory was, however, indicative of the 'second-best type of theory' which was to be found in sociology (T. Parsons 1951: 20).

> The ideal solution is the possession of a logically complete system of dynamic generalizations which can state all the elements of reciprocal interdependence between all the variables of the system. The ideal has, in the formal sense, been attained only in the systems of differential equations of analytical mechanics. All other sciences are limited to a more 'primitive' level of systematic theoretical analysis.   (T. Parsons 1945: 216)

The Structure had dealt with this issue. That action theory had no mathematical calculus did not mean the abandonment of the study of the functional relations between variables.

> Could it be stated as a system of simultaneous equations, this [i.e. its logically closed character] would be easy to tell. But even though the variables can be satisfactorily defined, it is quite another thing to attempt to state a sufficient number of demonstrated modes of relationship between them to furnish such a test. This study has been confined to certain preliminaries without even attempting such a statement.   (T. Parsons 1937a: 727, n. 1)

During the 1940s the system-concept became his leading idea. It helped him explain the *mathematical* logic of mechanics ('in physics mathematics *is* theory' (T. Parsons 1945: 224)) by reference to a general analytical logic applicable to *all* systems of analytical inquiry.

The structural–functional level of analysis involved a 'functional' analysis as that was understood in mathematics as well as the 'structural' investigations of physics. The essential characteristics of dynamic analysis emerged in the calculus of mechanics, where each variable was assigned its own 'empirical' value. A special kind of technical manipulation 'makes simultaneous dynamic analysis of interdependence of several variables in a complex system possible in a completely rigorous sense' (ibid.: 216).

In this 'ideal' case numerical quantitative values enabled 'complete rigour' to be attained. The ideal of 'comprehensive explanation' had been achieved in mechanics via its theory (i.e. mathematics). By contrast, Parsons' acceptance of a 'second-best', or structural–functional, level for his own theorizing coincides with his attempted application of 'system' to sociological theory. His theoretical system was loosely related to the mathematical ideal; he sought to promote mathematical rigour in social theory. The mathematical-like *quantification* found in the theory of mechanics was not his aim. He may have aimed to formulate social laws with a Newtonian vision of science. But the method he used in his essay-writing seems more akin to quantum mechanics, an attempt to grasp reality on many different levels at once.

Parsons attempted a 'theory of systems' rather than a 'system of theory'. His discussion appears to lack precision. When he discussed functional relations in mechanics as those pertaining 'between the parts of the system and between it and its environment' (T. Parsons 1945: 217), we note the difficulties he had in referring to *all* sciences by means of general concepts like 'system'. How could a *mechanical* system have an 'environment'? The term 'environment' is closer to a biological frame of reference. But is it lack of precision in the use of analogies which is at issue here? Surely Parsons had, to some degree, faced this dilemma when he observed that in mechanics the structure of the system was *not* an element (ibid.: 217). This underlined the special place mathematical systems occupied in Newtonian mechanics. In mechanics the theoretical system of mechanics coincided with the systematic theory (ibid.: 224). Functional analysis in mechanics *is* the mathematical explanation of the structure pertaining *between* particles and their properties. The structure is delineated by a system of simultaneous equations. The equations conceptualize the structure. The structure of the system is the mathematical explanation of the interdependence of its elements.

Now we discern reasons for Parsons' apparently haphazard use of analogies in relation to the social system. Sociology shares this level of theoretical rigour with modern physiology. Perhaps it was when he detected 'homological' parallelism (for his use of the term 'homological' see T. Parsons 1951: 18) between social and physiological theory that he began to explore the usefulness of biological analogies in his theory project. In ASNP the *organism and environment* analogy had been developed. But through the 1940s Parsons progressively isolated what he took to be the *logical equivalent* of mathematics in physics (i.e. his social systems theory). The 'structural–functional' system of analysis, also operative in the biological sciences, requires description of an empirical system to be facilitated by 'generalized categories', which in turn had to be broad enough to include all relevant data within and between phenomena of the same class. Analysis must involve a set of dynamic functional categories which must coincide with the structural categories. The maintenance of the system, together with its changing character and its relations with its environment, had to be capable of explanation through the 'cross-checking' of these two sets of categories – the structural and the functional.

Structural–functional analysis referred to a 'level' of analysis achieved by the non-mechanical sciences. Parsons attempted to develop general social theory which included both mechanical and physiological points of reference. More accurately it utilized the system-concept without exclusive reference to either biological or mechanical points of reference, and hence avoided exclusive reliance upon mechanical or physiological analogies. His view of his theory's place should be understood in terms of elements gleaned from both Bridgman (1927; 1955) and Cannon (1932; 1945). There may be times when the mechanical or the physiological appear to have received priority in his writing. But the aim seems to have been a structural–functional theory which included both.

But if the concept of 'system' in structural–functional sociology includes both biological and mechanical points of reference, what about this form of theorizing in physiology? Could it be said that modern physiological theory itself operated with biological 'points of reference'? This is difficult to answer even though it highlights an aspect which Parsons came to consider fundamental. The theory of physiological systems of Claude Bernard, he claimed, extended its explanatory relevance by developing the concept of 'internal environment' within its conceptual scheme of 'living systems'. The 'system' concept had come into its own as a concept of sufficient generality for biological *systems* to become systems in their own right, rather than be accepted as systems because of their mechanical or even organic character.

The criticism of Parsons' theory solely in terms of its utilization of analogies from one or other of these disciplines misses the point. Just as the human body has both physical *and* biotic structure, so Parsons' general theory of social action developed a structural theory reminiscent of physics *and* biology. It was a functional theory which focussed upon the interdependence of structure and process in social systems.

Perhaps the 'instability' of his theory can be explained by this dualistic analogical reference. He aimed to keep the theory 'open', as in 'living systems' remaining 'sensitive' to environmental stimuli. The long-term ideal involved 'closure' with all elements comprehensively explained, as in the mechanical explanation of physical systems. Parsons' search for 'systems theory' which was neither mechanical nor biotic followed Claude Bernard in this sense. He sought to differentiate social systems, always realizing the continuity between physical, living and specifically human systems (T. Parsons 1970: 830–1). It was a structural–functional theory which used the concept of a social *system* to extend its explanatory relevance. Thus he claimed advance for his theorizing, by referring to his earlier adherence to 'the biological mode of thought' (T. Parsons 1950: 357). Parsons aimed to utilize the system-concept to the full, freeing it from over-reliance upon analogies derived from any one theoretical system. For sociology he wanted the concept of a social system, and following Pareto (and Henderson), he developed his *encyclopaedic* conception by including all aspects of reality.

A critical point should be noted here. Parsons did not explicitly address the philosophical problem concerning the analogical character of theoretical concepts. This philosophical question is not elaborated by his 'system', even if the system-concept itself appears to be a theoretical concept which attempts to account for this philosophical question.

The next chapter is the analysis of *The Social System*. This was the primary statement of Parsons' conceptual scheme for the analysis of the dynamics of the social system. We have already discussed the place of 'statements' and 'theory' in his project. Moreover *The Social System* was a climax in his career of theory-construction. Our aim is to formulate principles for interpreting that work.

My aim in Chapter 10 has been to discover whether, and to what extent, it is possible to consider *The Social System* as an integrated theoretical frame of reference. I outline some important principles that should guide any critical reading of *The Social System*.

10
The Social System

Characteristic transitions in Parsons' theoretical development

In *The Structure* the discovery of convergence had been documented. Parsons had found that all the recent social theories analysed could be cross-matched with each other. The book's construction emphasized the 'empirical conclusions'. *The Social System*, by way of contrast, was constructed along different lines. All the discoveries had been made previously to it. What remained was the task of packing them all into this work: 'his major exposition'.

Sooner or later Parsons would have had to make his definitive formulation of *The Social System*. *The Structure of Social Action* had concluded with the confident proclamation that the foundations for theory-building were soundly laid (T. Parsons 1937a: 775). As we have shown, the primary motivation was *not* simply a search for high social, or even professional, status for himself. It was an attempt to prove that sociological theory should be given a high priority in the social science professions. There would be some residual benefit to himself in becoming known as the discipline's 'incurable theorist', but he had already won a place for himself in the intensely competitive milieu of Harvard and was Chairman of its innovative Department of Social Relations. In the late 1940s he worked to satisfy *himself* that all the effort was worth it.

We have noted that it was in the transition from a logical to a critical (comparative) analysis of Marshall's theory that Parsons began the process of theoretical refinement which resulted in the major sociological theory of twentieth-century American sociology. The transition had conceptual roots in the neo-Kantian vision of the *ideal-type* – a purposely fictitious construction for the analysis of the infinite array of facts (T. Parsons 1929: 31–2) – and was completed in *The Structure of Social Action*. The conflict between the history of theory and the immanent critique of the theoretical logic of various theories, as two distinct tasks, was transcended by Parsons' evolutionary and scientific investigation in Theory. *The Structure* was a secondary analysis.

We have tried here to understand something of the Parsonian process of discovery. In this sense our focus has been upon 'the facts' as Parsons himself defined them – 'the empirically verifiable statement' (T. Parsons 1937a: 41) – rather than the phenomenon of scientific discovery itself. But we have also pointed out that, for Parsons, the process of scientific discovery was very closely intertwined with his method of narrative construction and theory-writing. His 'discovery' of theory was also a *personal* discovery of the analytical elements implicit in his earlier formulations.

The Social System, as the elaboration of the theory of action, involved the *construction* of a deductive framework: a conceptual scheme for the analysis of the social system. The documentation was not so much a *deduction* from 'basic units' as the bringing together of an array of analytical elements to form one conceptual scheme. The resultant *construction* could therefore be interpreted *in toto* by *each* of the respective frames of reference from which it had been derived (T. Parsons 1937a: 682, n. 1). The formulation of *The Social System* was achieved on the basis of a construction of the frame of reference composed of all the analytical elements Parsons had utilized throughout his theoretical odyssey. As we have seen, the process of development between 1937 and 1951 should also be understood in terms of Parsons' incorporation of insights from the 'socio-psychological complex', namely from Freud and the psychoanalytic point of view.

The period 1937–51 was a period of intense analytical development in which Parsons covered all possible areas, but always returned to the issue of 'general theory'. The exact contribution of Harvard's Department of Social Relations to the resultant hegemony of Parsons' theory in the 1950s cannot be fully gauged here, but there is no doubt about its importance.

The development of the social system in the earlier writings of Talcott Parsons

We have traced the development of Parsons' theory from his earliest writings. We have indicated quite strongly that an understanding of his project must include an appreciation of his 'subjective frame of reference' as a theorist. His orientation as an 'incurable theorist' was integral to his theorizing. Just as we can now see *The Social System* as Parsons' 1951 'convergence' in which the theory of action, derived from Weber, Pareto and Durkheim, could also be 'translated' into the terms of Freudian theory without any essential change of meaning, so also *The Structure of Social Action* had been the result of a 'convergence' in which Durkheim's theory had been shown to 'fit' the theoretical schema to which Weber and Pareto (and to a lesser extent, Marshall) had contributed.

But what are we to make of 'Actor, Situation and Normative Pattern'? As an initial attempt after *The Structure* to 'bring it all together', it had not succeeded. The reason that it had failed was not so much a lack of imagination and insight on Parsons' part – it was a failure, primarily, because Parsons judged it to be so. It did not provide the theoretical formulation he was looking for. It may be seen as Parsons' short-lived attempt to distance himself from the 'convergence' methodology of theory construction of *The Structure*.

Under the influence of 'the biological mode of thought' he formulated ASNP, as the attempt to specify his 'organon', in a way somewhat reminiscent of his earliest re-presentation of the sociological theory implicit in Marshall's economics (T. Parsons 1931). In this sense ASNP was Parsons' attempt to formulate his theory so that it *converged* on his own formulation of theory in *The Structure*. It failed to cover the entire field. It had not attained the creative integration of all major currents of social thought. It was a working attempt to *deduce* the overall conceptual framework for the social system, and action in general, which had been intimated in *The Structure* but, as in the initial attempt to work out 'convergence' (T. Parsons 1932), prominent theoretical resources had been left untapped.

The route from ASNP to *The Social System* is indeed complex. It shows Parsons wrestling with the task of formulating his theory over an extended period. If ASNP was formulated in a fit of activism, to prove to himself that his discoveries in *The Structure* were valid, he did not get carried away with his frustration. *The Social System* became his major work not just because it was published and ASNP could not make it to publication. Rather, *The Social System* was the result of his seeking to overcome the inadequacies he sensed in his earlier theoretical formulation.

In various places I have shown that there is a strong continuity between *The Structure of Social Action* and *The Social System*. I have even shown that Parsons' more mature theoretical elaborations have their roots in the earliest phases of his development: at Amherst in his Philosophy III papers; in his doctoral 'Capitalism' articles; and in his critical confrontation with neo-classical and institutional economics. But I have also shown that the process of theoretical development between 1937 and 1951 also has a direct affinity with the kind of development Parsons constructed prior to 1937. *This fact will stand as one of the major findings of this work.* Having followed his writings from 1937 to 1951 I can suggest that 'Actor, Situation and Normative Pattern' stands to *The Social System* in much the same way that 'Economics and Sociology: Marshall in Relation to the Thought of his Time' (T. Parsons 1932) stands to *The Structure of Social Action*. There are some variations, although the pattern is remarkably consistent. Whereas the earliest published article on Marshall (T. Parsons 1931) *was* incorporated unchanged into the text of *The Structure*, it is essentially 'Note B: Schematic Outline of System Types in the Theory of Action' (T. Parsons 1937a: 77–84) which remained a constant conceptual scheme 'in the background' for the articulation of *The Social System*. All elements of the theory of action identified in *The Structure* (ibid.: 78) can be found packed (or repacked) into the theory of the social system.

In *The Structure* the 'voluntaristic' theory of action stands as a *tertium quid* between the two main historical alternatives: positivism and idealism (ibid.: 81–2). And with the 'convergence' came the insight that there are three major systems of reality amenable to scientific and theoretical investigation. The adjective 'voluntaristic', qualifying the theory of action, was explicitly dropped when the system of action was placed alongside the system of nature and the system of culture in 'The Classification of the Sciences of Action', in the final chapter of *The Structure* (ibid.: 762, n. 1). And we would be mistaken if we were to interpret *The Social System* simply as the constructed elaboration of the conceptual scheme to 'cover' the 'action' dimension of reality.

In my opinion the now famous interpretative problems encountered in reading *The Social System* have much to do with the 1937 to 1951 transition. Confusion has often emerged because of a critical *underestimation* of the scope and flexibility of Parsons' range of analytical vision: how, at any particular point, he was widening the scope of his analysis and/or how he was narrowing it. Moreover if Parsons' doctrine about the 'double contingency' factor (T. Parsons 1951: 10) is applied to our understanding of his theory's emergence, the picture becomes much clearer. Parsons' mental set was built up by his 'system of expectations', which along with (i) his confidence that the theory of action identified in *The Structure* had enormous explanatory power and (ii) his aim to make it relevant for theorizing on all levels, also included (iii) his expectation of possible reactions by the community of social science professionals.

Parsons anticipated the emergence of the general theory of action in the social sciences. And whilst the development between 1937 and 1951 shows Parsons' modification of his own theoretical formulations, it also anticipates the formulated and unformulated criticisms of others (possibly in terms of alternative frames of reference). But *The Social System* is *not* the culmination of all this. As a 'major exposition' it is the construction of *one* side of this major 'convergence' in social scientific thought.

The Social System was identified by him as 'a second volume of a systematic treatise' of which 'Values, Motives and Systems of Action' (T. Parsons and E. A. Shils 1951) would be the first, whilst 'two further volumes parallel to . . .' *The Social System* would be required on personality and culture systems respectively (T. Parsons 1951: ix, x). In *The Social System* we can find the peculiarly Parsonian 'convergence' in which he had drawn all the threads of his own theoretical labour together into 'the major exposition of [his] conceptual scheme for the analysis of the dynamics of the social system'. So again Parsons found his way towards his own contribution by a 'middle-brow' focus upon the (analytical) *tertium quid*: the social system.

Now if *The Social System* represents an analysis 'in between' the projected exposition of the cultural and personality systems, and if the General Theory of Action is directed to the 'action' class of the three great theoretical systems (T. Parsons 1937a: 762), we can suggest that some ambiguity pertains to the status of the *cultural* system of action. The *cultural system* is not equivalent with the *cultural sub-system of action*, which is concerned with patterns of value-orientation as these emerge in systems of action. In its most general sense the cultural system is the corollary of action and nature. With the general theory of action the cultural sub-system has a variant status. Indeed, contrary to the dissent of Sheldon in *Towards a General Theory*, 'culture as a system is on a different plane from personalities and social systems' (T. Parsons and E. A. Shils 1951: 7). The study of the culture-system articulates directly with the theory of the social system, which focusses upon 'the phenomena of the institutionalization of patterns of value-orientation' and on motivated changes in them, conformity with them and deviation from them (T. Parsons 1951: 552).

It seems that in Parsons' view, recognition of this variant status (in effect: 'man is a culture-bearing animal' (T. Parsons 1950: 357)) clarified the issue of the analysis of cultural systems in terms of the action-frame-of-reference even if the ultimate meaning of the analysis of action in terms of the culture-frame-of-reference (or *Logoswissenschaft* (T. Parsons 1937a: 762)) remained somewhat undefined.

In effect 'Actor, Situation and Normative Pattern' also functions as Parsons' early formulation of *Towards a General Theory* rather than simply being an embryonic form of *The Social System*. Although it was formulated in a context where he sought, and received, critical comments from his colleagues, it did not attain the inter-disciplinary integration which was foreshadowed in *The Structure*, and which was to be the characteristic of the later Carnegie Project publication. Perhaps some explanation of that project would be helpful here.

The project for general theory thrown wide open

Parsons' preface to *Towards a General Theory of Action* (T. Parsons and E. A. Shils 1951: v-viii) gives his picture of the immediate academic context of his 1951 work. He refers to the history of Harvard social science, and the establishment in 1946 of the Department of Social Relations; Parsons' escape from the unsympathetic former chairman of the Department of Sociology, Sorokin; the salient influence of Paul H. Buck upon Parsons' professional development in the 1940s; his relationship with his students and fellow-academics at Harvard; and his appointment as Chairman of the new and innovative department, a position he held until 1956. The personnel who were involved in *Towards a General Theory* are also indicative of Parsons' 'first main swing' after *The Structure*. The move away from economics and politics towards social and psychological themes had been initially taken up in his study of medical practice 'seen more from the perspective of Freud than of Max Weber or Pareto' (T. Parsons 1970: 837).

From the mid to late 1930s Parsons had known of developments in cultural anthropology through Clyde Kluckhohn. After study in Vienna in the early 1930s, Kluckhohn had advocated the integration of psychoanalytic insights in ethnographic research. The so-called 'Personality and Culture' School was thus represented in the team for *Towards a General Theory* alongside Richard C. Sheldon, a social anthropologist (Parsons' Preface in T. Parsons and E. A. Shils 1951: v), who advocated the rigorous testing of theoretical propositions in scientific research. With Parsons' acquaintance with Malinowski, the field of anthropology (or the cultural system of action) was covered pretty thoroughly. Samuel Stouffer, leading co-author of a celebrated social survey analysis – *The American Soldier* (1949) – was identified with the ideas of W. I. Thomas and Ezra Park and thus could 'represent an almost wholly American influence' (ibid.: vii). Henry A. Murray and Robert R. Sears – two somewhat humanistic behaviourists – with Gordon Allport, a non-behaviourist, represented psychology. The Chicago neo-Gestaltist E. C. Tolman and Edward Shils, representing Chicago sociology, make it plain that Parsons, co-ordinator of the group project, had achieved a comprehensive 'spread'. This gives a good picture of the kind of intellectual environment which he was trying to encourage and control via his general theory.

I would like now to analyse the resultant theory of *The Social System* by reference to the following factors: how Freudian categories became part of the Parsonian 'convergence'; how Parsons avoided the 'biological mode of analysis'; and how he constructed the new formulation of 'convergence'. In *The Social System* Parsons re-articulates the analytical realism which bridged the divide between idealism and positivism. He developed the theory of the social system by distinguishing between motives and values. On the basis of a Freudian conceptualization of ego and alter, as integral to the basic paradigm for social interaction, he articulated a theory of object-relations, and derived therefrom a concept of expectations as an integral element of social systems.

Freud's convergence on the theories of Weber and Durkheim

Parsons, in ASNP, had drawn upon the work of Karen Horney, the Freudian revisionist (T. Parsons 1939/40: 19, 26). His initial attempt to incorporate psychoanalytic categories within the framework of the theory of action was somewhat ambiguous. He asserted that there was a mutual independence of the respective frames of reference for biological and social science (i.e. organism–environment and actor–situation) (ibid.: 7), but looking back upon this attempt he concluded that ASNP was influenced by this 'biological mode of thought' (T. Parsons 1950: 357). Even though he could assert that '*the two are analytically distinct conceptual schemes with no presumption of reducibility of either to the other*' (ibid.: 7 (Parsons' italics)), all conceptual problems were not solved. The strict distinction between the biological and the action conceptual schemes raises the question of the function of the biological organism within action systems and the character of human action oriented to strictly physiological objects. And it was in relation to this conceptual conundrum that Parsons began to make the transition to a psychoanalytic point of view.

Parsons observed that psychoanalysis had demonstrated, beyond any reasonable doubt, that 'there is not a single class of concrete wants or ends, no matter how "high" and apparently removed from the biological level, in which there is not a presumption that biological elements play an important part' (T. Parsons 1939/40: 18). Presumably, the 'biological mode of thought' could concede that there *was* a relationship between the 'cultural' and the 'biological' factors. It then proceeded to construe the relationship in a way which was too heavily dependent upon physiological analogies. Consequently the relationship between the 'cultural' and the 'biological' was only granted from the 'biological' side, with the resultant potential determinism and reductionism. Parsons' diffidence about psychoanalysis concerned the 'lack of clarity' in that frame of reference about the way 'higher factors' influenced the biological satisfaction and wants.

> The correct way to conceive the relation would seem to be not that there are separate biological and 'cultural' wants, but that there are two analytically distinct classes of elements in all concrete wants. Above all the biological element does not define concrete wants at all, but only certain underlying 'vectors' of direction of teleological tendencies. In detail the distinction is always an empirical question to be investigated in terms of the specific facts.   (ibid.: 18)

If psychoanalytic categories were to be used it would have to be via a Freud not wholly compatible with the biological mode of thought. In a way reminiscent of Parsons' earlier rendering of Durkheim in *The Structure*, it was an analytically self-conscious Freud whose theory contributed to the resultant 'general theory of action' rather than the Freud presented, modified, even rejected, in the footnotes of ASNP. It seems as if in ASNP Parsons was trying to utilize psychoanalytic categories but was unsure whether this approach was truly non-reductionistic. Put another way, Parsons had yet to be convinced that Freud had contributed to 'convergence'. The seed of the new convergence between Freud and Durkheim intimated in *The Structure* (T. Parsons 1937a: 386, n. 1; 388), did not germinate as long as Freud's conception of personality remained undifferentiated from that view of culture which derived 'normative patterns' from the interaction between actor and situation.

In ASNP 'normative pattern' was the equivalent term for 'culture' and was absorbed into the relationship between the three modes of orientation and the social situation. The actor, though not simply biological, was nevertheless analysed in terms of a frame of reference derived analogically from biology. Thus the actor–situation frame of reference operated with an actor-and-system interaction as the 'basic paradigm' for social relations. In fact the tendency, though 'biological', was to isolate the human actor so as to establish the basic unit of analysis. But it was not possible to derive 'structures' simply from these 'basic units' without some independent intervening variables which placed human action in its cultural and psychological context. In effect the ego–alter dyad together with the actor–situation system (T. Parsons 1951: 4) became the 'basic interaction paradigm' in *The Social System* – replacing the 'actor', the basic unit of analysis in ASNP.

Consequently, the Freud and the psychoanalytic categories referred to with ambiguity in ASNP are not the same as the Freud and the psychoanalytic categories Parsons built into his argument in *The Social System*. In point of fact

The Social System, which sees Freud converging on Durkheim's conception of normative elements upheld by sanctions, was reaffirming the view of a Freud–Durkheim 'convergence' intimated, but not elaborated, in *The Structure*. Just as it took some time to reassert the view expressed in his Amherst consideration of morals, that Durkheim's theory did imply a psychological aspect of the social-moral order (T. Parsons 1923), so also the full impact of the Durkheim–Freud 'convergence' was only worked out gradually.

In *The Structure* Parsons had stated, *en passant*, that the Durkheimian view of the normative elements, that they are 'internalized' to become 'identified' with the actor, finds a direct correspondence in Freudian terminology concerning the formation of the superego through the process of 'introjection' (T. Parsons 1937a: 385–6; 386, n. 1). A little later he noted that the attitude of moral obligation 'becomes, in the Freudian term, "introjected" to form a constitutive element of the individual personality itself' (ibid.: 388).

The genuinely 'new' factor in *The Social System* is the ego–alter relationship in which both are taken as 'social actors' oriented to a norm or norm-complex. The 'basic interaction paradigm' of *The Social System* is not present in ASNP; nor is the subtlety of exposition whereby three different units of social systems are referable to the individual actor: the social act, the status role and the 'actor himself as a social unit'. Moreover 'the collectivity as actor and as object' is explicitly included. There are two 'cross-cutting modes of organization of social systems' which are articulated by the 'status role' (T. Parsons 1951: 26). There Parsons 're-discovered' the differentiation between Rel (elementary relations), RI (relations emergent on the level of the individual) and RC (relations emergent on the level of collectivity) for the analysis of the social system. These were the various kinds of *relations*, over and above constitutive *actions*, which contributed to all systems of action (Chapter 7 see above, and T. Parsons 1937a: 78).

Without the inclusion of the ego–alter relationship, the analysis of social action in ASNP leaves the individual actor as a sub-system of the social system. We shall return to this point because it is indicative of the 'biological mode of thought' in ASNP. It should suffice to say that the development of Parsons' thought in the 1940s, with the inclusion of Freudian concepts, illustrates his move *away from* the orientation implicit in ASNP – a repudiation of any 'over-socialized conception of man' which can be derived from an unexpanded formulation of action theory in *The Structure*. In other words though the term 'voluntaristic' was already dropped in *The Structure* (ibid.: 762, n. 1), the development between 1937 and 1951 is a move *towards* voluntarism in the sense of wanting to create the analytic safeguards to preserve the recognition of the original freedom of the social actor to choose goals and act accordingly in the social context. Parsons' incorporation of Freud into his 'canon of classics' is, in his view, a move away from a reductionist, and hence deterministic, understanding of the 'socio-psychological complex' (T. Parsons 1970: 837).

Avoiding the biological mode of analysis

Parsons knew the discontinuities in his fourteen-year attempt to formulate the general theory and the theory of the social system. Towards the end of the process he identified the unproductive phase of his post-1937 development with the 'biological mode of thought' (T. Parsons 1950: 357) in which culture was not granted the status of an independent variable (ibid.: 35). The reductionistic tendencies had 'cut both ways'. Either culture was interpreted as a function of social interaction and personality (behaviouristic reductionism) or social structure and personality had been absorbed into culture in an idealistic form of reductionism or 'emanationism'. Both tendencies had, however, been transcended by the discovery that 'man is a culture-bearing animal' (ibid.: 357). Hence man as an indissoluble entity functions equally on all levels; the tendency to reductionism is shortcircuited by reckoning with the independent character of *each* of the systems of action.

But is not ASNP an attempt to show the independent character of action, in which case it is an early form of *Towards a General Theory of Action*? But how did Parsons turn away from the direction implicit in ASNP? It seems that 'the biological mode of thought' had a tendency to identify the 'actor' with the biological–psychological level, the 'situation' with the social situation of interacting actors and the 'normative patterns' with the superadded dimension of culture (see T. Parsons 1951: 50 for *The Social System*'s conceptualization of the 'super-added' dimension contributed by institutionalization; see also the important work by Cubbon 1976). Parsons was then trying to avoid biological reductionism, and was unclear about psychoanalysis, even if he had a well-developed critique of reductionism; he was unclear about psychoanalysis yet had begun to develop his view of the contribution of anthropology to his theory.

There is an ambiguous paragraph in ASNP at the beginning of Chapter V, 'The Integration of Personality and the Relation of Individual Motivation to the Stability of Social Systems', which throws light upon the character of Parsons' formulations in that work and also of his subsequent development.

> Action is always a matter of the behavior of individuals, never of collectivities as a 'unit'; what is usually referred to as the unitary behavior of collectivities is the complex result of the different actions of all the component actors. This remains true, for analytical purposes, no matter how highly integrated or 'well coordinated' these actions may be. (T. Parsons 1939/40: 117)

Here is evidence that the basic interaction paradigm in ASNP, though compatible with the basic elements of the theory of action presented in *The Structure*, nevertheless makes action a function of the actor, and the social system of the actor a function of cumulative actions. There are no mediating elements of a genuinely independent sort. The social system is, in effect, a plurality of personalities, a view explicitly denied later (see, e.g., T. Parsons and E. A. Shils 1951: 7 and T. Parsons 1951: 17–18). The integration of personality is a function of the stability of social systems, and the integration of social systems is a function of the stability of individual motivation. The concept of 'stability' is a direct result of a homeostatic balance between two factors: personality and the social system. In *The Social System* 'symbolic systems' become relevant for the organization of an actor's 'expectation system', 'providing a commonly understood system of cultural symbols' (T. Parsons 1951: 5). But in ASNP there is no intervening factor. It was Parsons' view in ASNP that 'the analysis of the ... stability of social systems ... leads directly to that of the motivation of their component individual actors' (T. Parsons 1939/40: 117). The individual actor 'as a sub-system of the social system of action ... is subject to certain functional necessities which are capable of the same sort of analysis ... which [is] applied to the larger social system' (ibid.: 117).

Now there is a sense in which this view can be deduced from the 'voluntaristic theory of action' if, as Parsons was later to observe, the value standards or modes of value orientation are 'put into the actor' (T. Parsons 1950: 357). For Thomas and Znaniecki it had been a case of putting values into the 'object system' of the 'situation'. Parsons, apparently, had tended to see the relation in the opposite way.

Though the intellectual process by which Parsons resolved this problem is not easy to follow, it is clear that *The Social System* is his resolution of it through the concept of 'orientation' (T. Parsons 1951: 4).

In his 'most generalized formula' the system of action is composed of actions plus the three kinds of relations. Actions and relations are interdependent variables in the analysis of any particular social system of action. The concept of 'orientation' provides the means for deriving the 'underlying vectors' (T. Parsons 1939/40: 18) basic to a social system of action.

In *The Social System* 'orientation' is very prominent. 'The frame of reference concerns the "orientation" of one or more actors ... to a situation.' The relational function of 'orientation' is also made explicit. 'The scheme ... is a *relational* scheme' (Parsons' italics). 'The situation is defined as consisting of objects of orientation, so that the orientation of a given actor is differentiated relative to the different objects ... of which his situation is composed' (T. Parsons 1951: 4).

In ASNP 'orientation' was present – perhaps gaining more prominence from the table of contents than it received in the text of the narrative. But it was almost a residual category, taken for granted in the analysis of the actor's relation to the situation. There was a brief explanation of his use of the term in the initial chapter, 'Frame of Reference'. The place of this concept within the overall framework was almost completely determined by the parallel with biology, and it was in this sense that this 'mode of thought' manifests itself.

> In biology it is a matter of the 'adaptation' of the organism to the environment. In order not to confuse the two frames of reference here the term 'orientation' of the actor to his situation will be used. (T. Parsons 1939/40: 4)

The explanatory context for the term was greatly dependent upon the meaning given to 'adaptation' in biology. Without having defined 'action-orientation', as a concept which articulates with all other dimensions of social action, Parsons, in Chapter II, 'The Three Basic Modes of Orientation', proceeded with his analysis by distinguishing the cognitive, teleological and affectual modes, as I have outlined them above (see Chapter 7). Therefore ASNP became, *in toto*, a residual analysis of 'orientation'. ASNP, in effect, signals the beginning of the incorporation of Freudian categories which led to 'orientation' becoming a 'fundamental' concept for *The Social System* (T. Parsons 1951: 4).

But can the concept be found in the analysis of *The Structure*? It was somewhat inconspicuous in 1937 although it was present in the concept of the 'normative orientation of action'. 'What is essential to the concept of action is that there should be a normative orientation' (T. Parsons 1937a: 45), with the emphasis upon the normative. It was a rather neutral term emphasizing the link between 'an agent, an actor' and 'an "end" . . . toward which the process of action is *oriented*' (ibid.: 44 (my italics)). Again, from Parsons' own statements, it is possible to analyse *The Structure in toto* as an investigation of 'normative orientation' – 'one of the most important questions with which this study will be confronted' (ibid.: 45). If, then, ASNP was the attempted articulation of 'the three modes of orientation', which emerged by implication within the analysis of *The Structure*, it remained incomplete because it was then only an early phase of Parsons' 'swing away' from an analysis of cognitive rationality in the means–end schema of the economic–political complex (T. Parsons 1970: 837). Thus the anticipated convergence of Freud with Durkheim, intimated in *The Structure*, needed full integration with the already-documented convergence before full elaboration in *The Social System* could be achieved. The problem of cognitive rationality needed to be synthesized with the problem of non-rationality.

Reconvergence

Bringing positivism and idealism together

Parsons had already made provision for *all* the developments between 1937 and 1951 in his conception of the combination of positivism and idealism which had led him to his formula for a voluntaristic theory of action (T. Parsons 1937a: 81–2). The situation (S) of action of 1937 'may be subjectively manifested in . . . scientifically valid knowledge' (T) and 'unscientific elements' (t) – from the positivist side (ibid.: 79); but the idealistic factors were also necessary in an adequate theory – the normative factors had empirical relevance, and so the 'selective standard' (N) whereby the situation (S) was organized relative to the end (E) need not be restricted to 'cognitive rationality', as positivism had required. Nor, of course, was idealism's elimination of scientifically valid knowledge (T) or unscientific elements (t) acceptable.

So when we reach the discussion in the early pages of *The Social System* where the focus was upon the differentiation of an actor's orientation to situational objects (as it was in ASNP), it is as if we have travelled a long way from 'convergence' in *The Structure*. But this initial impression is misleading. What we have, in effect, is a re-articulation of Weber's views of the 'Modes of Orientation of Action' reinterpreted in terms of the Durkheim–Freud convergence on the socio-psychological complex. To use the words which Parsons had used to explain the convergence of Weber, Pareto and Durkheim: the conceptual schemes of Weber, Durkheim and Freud can be directly translated in terms of each other without essential change of meaning (ibid.: 682, n. 1).

Parsons' formulation in *The Social System* was his attempt to formulate a conceptual scheme directly translatable, without any essential change of meaning, into the terms set forth by Weber, Durkheim and Freud. This accords with Parsons' view of the way in which social development necessarily involves coming to terms with the mores. Parsons' theory attempted to account for the conservative character of social structure, and also shows a conservative approach to the development of theory.

Motives and values

It is somewhat ironic that Parsons' *use* of Weber's conceptualizations in *The Social System* can be clearly identified when his 1951 discussion of values and motives is compared with his 1937 discussion of Weber's concept of *usage* (as a mode of orientation). In his 1937 discussion he clearly identified his view of the normative aspect implied by Weber's concept of usage (*Brauch*) (ibid.: 650).

In *The Social System* the independent variability of values and motives are modes of orientation. This forms, he writes, 'the logical foundation of the independent significance of the theory of the social system vis-a-vis that of personality on the one hand and of culture on the other' (T. Parsons 1951: 15). This distinction, which Parsons points to in Weber (T. Parsons 1937a: 652, n. 1), concerns 'the fact of *orientation* to a legitimate order and the motives for acting in relation to it' (ibid.: 652, n. 1). The distinction between 'orientation to a legitimate order' (set of values) and 'motives for acting in relation to it' is quite compatible with the distinction made between the value mode and the motivational mode in *The Social System* (T. Parsons 1951: 12–15). There, however, the distinction is articulated in terms of a Freudian understanding of 'object relations' and the conceptualization of both ego and alter as 'social objects'.

Whereas in ASNP 'Action is always a matter of the behavior of individuals, never of collectivities as a "unit"' (T. Parsons 1939/40: 117), in *The Social System* 'a collectivity ... is treated as a unit for purposes of the analysis of orientation' (T. Parsons 1951: 4). This demonstrates that via the concept of 'orientation' *The Social System* established continuity with *The Structure of Social Action* by following a Freud compatible with both Weber and Durkheim. It only remained for Parsons to move from a logical distinction between 'the fact of orientation to a legitimate order' and 'the motives for acting in relation to it' (T. Parsons 1937a: 651–2), to a recognition that motives and values were in fact to be treated as *independent* variables, for the concept of a genuinely *social* system to emerge into view. In the mean time he had to come to terms with the biolo·ical mode of thought as he sought to articulate the relationship between the ac· or, the situation and the normative pattern. In effect, without the distinction between value-orientation and motivational orientation, any articulation of a general theory of action would not be able to articulate the relationships between the personality and culture systems. In ASNP motives and values were mutually *dependent* variables; the truly independent variables were 'actor' and 'situation', so that the analysis of the social system involves 'normative pattern' inserted into the analysis from the actor's side. It was the factor which maintained both the coherence of the analysis and the stability of personalities and societies. But it was not a factor in its own right. ASNP, from the position of *The Social System*, can only be identified as a theoretical elaboration of the social system in an indirect sense.

Objects

In *The Social System* the 'modes of orientation' are no longer put forward as the actor's context for the elaboration of the structure of the situation as in ASNP. Instead they are placed in a framework of 'object relations'. This avoids the possibility of construing the relationship of the individual actor to the cultural system simply in terms of the actor's multi-modal orientation to social objects – another actor (alter) or himself (ego). So an actor's orientations are to the set of social and non-social objects which constitute the 'situation'. In *The Social System* non-social objects are specified as physical and cultural objects (T. Parsons 1951: 4). In this way the three forms of objects can be seen to 'fit' with the 'three great classes' of systems already specified in *The Structure* (T. Parsons 1937a: 762).

Now, what of the place of 'cultural objects'? How are they conceived? It was suggested earlier that there is some ambiguity about the *cultural* system of action. Whereas 'action is non-spatial but temporal', cultural systems are 'non-spatial and a-temporal'. They are '*eternal* objects' in the Whiteheadian sense of not being involved in 'process'. As objects, they are to be found not by external observation, but in their symbolic manifestation.

> Eternal objects constitute the meanings of symbols. As objects they exist only 'in the minds' of individuals . . . [in a footnote he adds:] or 'embodied' in systems of symbols the 'understanding' of which implies a mind.   (ibid.: 763)

We should note Parsons' indebtedness to Whitehead's view of time; suffice it to

say it is a rather important element of his 'conceptual scheme' because it
relates to his concept of theory being somehow 'not involved in "process" '.
Moreover it clarifies why Parsons' theoretical development should be seen as
an attempt to 'solve' the problematic character of culture systems.

Here we note that in *The Social System* 'cultural objects are symbolic elements
of the cultural tradition, ideas or beliefs, expressive symbols or value patterns
so far as they are treated as situational objects by ego and are not "internalized" as constitutive elements of the structure of his personality' (T. Parsons
1951: 4). The question is whether this constitutes a change in emphasis or
whether it is simply an attempt to say the same thing from a different angle.
The 1951 version has a *reduced* emphasis on the 'subjective point of view . . .
of the actor'. The . . . 'mind of the individual' in *The Structure* (T. Parsons
1937a: 763) does not correspond exactly with the 'actor as a point of reference
himself' (T. Parsons 1951: 4). This is a direct result of viewing the actor
as a social object in a classification of object relations. The 'mind', if it is
to be considered, would come into consideration in relation to the personality
system which does not correspond with the emergent RI ('organized units
called individuals') of the 1937 formula (T. Parsons 1937a: 78). Moreover Parsons viewed 'personality psychology' as 'becoming highly oriented
to the actor's relational system . . . his orientation to objects' (T. Parsons
1951: 32), presumably including the actor's relational system to cultural
objects.

The actor's situation in *The Social System* comprises social and non-social
objects. The non-social objects are the cultural and physical objects. We have
seen that this classification (ibid.: 4) corresponds with the three great systems
of *The Structure*. In ASNP normative patterns are distinguished from situational objects because normative patterns are 'external realities' to the actor from
the subjective point of view (T. Parsons 1939/40: 14). In other words their
'externality' is primarily 'internal', and presumably it is in this way that the
'standard' for the evaluation of the act was 'put into' the actor. But when both
alter and ego as actors are taken as social objects, then 'the value standards or
modes of value-orientation [are] treated as a *distinct* range of components of
action' (T. Parsons 1950: 357), and eventually as a separate classification of its
own (cognitive, appreciative and moral), in which '*each* of the three ranges or
sets of modes is classified against *each* of the other two' (ibid.: 358).

Expectations

I have already pointed out that the 'double contingency' factor plays an
important part in the 1951 formulation. This factor refers to the expectations
of the actor. The concept gains its fundamental place in the theory of action
because ego and alter are *both* social objects. Both ego and alter expect each
other to have expectations; in fact the crucial part of ego's expectations is 'the
probable *re*action of alter to ego's possible action' (T. Parsons 1951: 5). But

was this dimension of Parsons' analysis of the social system implicit earlier on, perhaps in an 'undiscovered' guise? François Bourricaud's analysis of this aspect of Parsons' theory ties this to Adam Smith's version of the division of labour, which in fact accords with the one reference to Adam Smith in *The Social System* (Bourricaud 1981: 67). In this sense 'the relational problems enter in when alter becomes significant not only passively as a means or condition of the attainment of ego's goal, but his *reactions* become a constitutive part of the system which includes ego's own goal-striving' (T. Parsons 1951: 70). The double-contingency factor in this sense indicates that for Parsons *The Social System* represents the coming together of the political–economic and the socio-psychological complexes in one generalized frame of reference.

'Expectations' are present in *The Structure*, namely in Parsons' interpretation of Weber's *Zweckrational*-concept. Social action may be determined 'by expectations of the behavior of objects of the external environment and of other persons, and through the use of these expectations as "conditions" or as "means" for rational ends, rationally weighed and pursued' (T. Parsons 1937a: 642). Parsons varies this translation in the 1947 version of Weber's work (M. Weber 1947: 115) by introducing the phrase 'may be classified' instead of 'can be determined', and adding 'according to its mode of orientation' (ibid.: 115).

It was in his 1950 'Prospects of Sociological Theory' (T. Parsons 1950) that he raised the concept by pointing to 'the major axis around which the expectation-system of any personality becomes organized in the process of socialization'. This is 'its *interlocking* with the expectation-systems of others' (ibid.: 359). Here he gives credit to the work of Tolman and Murray, pointing out that in his view Durkheim's theory did not imply the absorption of the personality into the social system.

Parsons was still aware of the need to avoid behaviourism. In *The Structure* he had insisted that that approach had excluded the subjective point of view and could not be accepted as a theory of action (T. Parsons 1937a: 77–8). Behaviourism, in effect, reduced psychology to biological functioning. Having developed his non-behaviouristic viewpoint of 'the personality system' (psychology), Parsons could then utilize the Weberian active–passive dimension (ibid.: 640–4; Weber 1947: 88) to differentiate between *anticipation* and *goal* in the system of expectations (T. Parsons 1951: 8). But what does he there mean by the observation that analytically speaking goal-directedness 'seems to stand on the next level "down" from the concept of expectations because of the logical possibility of passively anticipatory orientation [*sic*]' (ibid.: 8)? It would appear that the concept of 'goal-directedness' is basic to the 'unit act' – this is the 1951 modification of the 1937 'end' – 'a future state of affairs toward which the process of action is oriented' (T. Parsons 1937a: 44) – but 'pushing the analysis to a still more elementary level' (T. Parsons 1951: 8–9, n. 4). Pushing on to a 'more elementary level' simply means that 'no fundamental change has been made'. The analysis 'has simply been carried to a more fundamental level' (ibid.: 8–9, n. 4).

As pointed out above, *The Social System* represents Parsons' attempt to buttress human voluntarism further by seeking to locate all factors inherent on the social-action level, analysing them in terms of social factors, rather than trying to explain them by reducing them to *more basic* elements, as in behaviourism, or viewing human action merely as an 'expression' of the realm of 'ideas'.

The double-contingency factor highlights the need for stability in alter–ego interactions and the development of communication. This cannot be achieved without a symbolic system as an integral and original fact of any 'culture' (ibid.: 5). It is in relation to the symbol-system that Parsons appears to want to iron out the ambiguity in the term 'culture'. Into this discussion he introduces the concept of 'order'. The implication is that actors not only share the symbols; they share communication, which implies the sharing of 'conventions' concerning the meaning of symbols – 'the mutuality of expectations is oriented to the shared *order* of symbolic meanings' (ibid.: 11). This involves a 'conditional standard', 'a normative order' and 'the mutual interlocking of expectations and sanctions' (ibid.: 11).

Here in effect is the formula for the theory of action systems (T. Parsons 1937a: 78, i.e. Z = (A1 + A2 + A3 . . . An) + Rel + RI + Rc) further developed by relating the concept of interlocking expectation systems to *both* actions and relations.

How Parsons develops the argument of *The Social System*

In Chapter 1 Parsons states his perspective. It is an exposition of the purpose stated in the introductory Preface (pp. vii–xii). Though it reads as if he is going over the same ground again, and again, each new step leads on to a slightly more complicated level of analysis. First, he defines a social system of action, then he introduces, as two further aspects of a complete action system, the personality system and the cultural system. He focusses on the elements of action by introducing an analysis of an actor's 'motivational' orientation, and then his 'value' orientation. The concept of 'values' leads on to an exposition of 'culture', and the distinction between its ideal patterns on the one hand and the motivational and situational demands on the other. Social systems in his terms have their own integrity. They cannot be formulated solely in terms of either personality factors or cultural patterns. The theory of the social system is therefore composed of the same basic elements which are found in cultural and personality systems – the elements of the theory of action – but it emerges as a theory in its own right. Culture and personality are subordinate factors in this frame of reference. The structural–functional level of theorizing, appropriate to social system theory, is explained, and the concept of *mechanism*, referring to the 'motivational dynamics' which influence the ongoing existence of a social system, is discussed briefly. This chapter is the initial framework. His desire to pin down his aims and keep his discussion within manageable limits is primary. He stresses factors of 'fundamental' importance.

For Parsons it was 'fundamental' that the basic idea of 1937 was the same as the concept of 1951 (T. Parsons 1951: 8–9, n. 1). Theoretical logic is raised *above* historical reality even though Parsons wanted to affirm that theoretical evolution had taken place. The conceptual scheme had evolved, and the change is not to the concepts *as such* but to the working out of their mutual interrelation in one overall conceptual scheme. This too was fundamental.

Admittedly the 'structural–functional' approach is a 'second-best type of analysis', and human action is so varied and complex that the going is tough. Like other 'fundamentalists' Parsons would call a halt, via the medium of his theory, to the chaos of relativism and random conceptualization. The reality to which the theory is directed is always greater than the reach of human knowledge. That reality, which includes theoretical frames of reference, is capable of being known. And it is with the concept of 'structure' that Parsons maintains developmental order within the evolving theoretical enterprise.

> A particularly important aspect of our system of categories is the 'structural' aspect. We simply are not in a position to 'catch' the uniformities of dynamic process in the social system except here and there.   (T. Parsons 1951: 20–1)

When this structural aspect is seen in the context of his functional analysis we can discern why the concept of system, operative on a variety of levels, is crucial to him. When structural and functional elements are brought together we see Parsons' theoretical system at work. The functioning of this theoretical system has to do with the system-concept itself.

The process of theory is part of the theory. A second-best had to be accepted – a categorial frame of reference would thus be used 'as if' it were a transcendent frame of reference. This is a crucial point for understanding Parsons' alleged conservative bias. The previous quotation continues:

> But in order to give those [uniformities] we can catch a setting and to be in the most advantageous position to extend our dynamic knowledge we must have a 'picture' of the system within which they fit, of the given relationships of its parts in a given state of the system, and, where changes take place, of what changes into what through what order of intermediate stages. The system of structural categories is the conceptual scheme which gives this setting for dynamic analysis. As dynamic knowledge is extended the *independent* explanatory significance of structural categories evaporates. But their scientific function is none the less crucial.   (ibid.: 21)

Parsons was not only making a statement about the necessity of social order but also making a statement about procedure; how the *study* of social order 'gets under way'. The study is always a part of the flux it is itself studying. It can thus become a 'going concern', and as such posits a 'picture' of the *structural categories* in terms of which the social processes can be analysed. Ten years later he wrote the same thing:

> The specificities of significant change could not even be identified if there were no *relative* background of non-change to relate them to ... To me the concept of structure is simply a shorthand statement of this basic point ... descriptions of structure constitute the primary reference base for describing and analyzing processes.   (T. Parsons 1961a: 220–1)

In the background, as we have noted, is his interpretation of the classical physics, a system of well-established scientific theory. Parsons would learn from the way 'structural concepts' are in general use in the sciences – 'in some parts of physics and chemistry it is possible to extend the empirical coverage of such a deductive system quite widely' (T. Parsons 1951: 20). He would apply the concept in the analysis of social systems. The 'social system' is the concept which allows for the spelling out of the fundamental pre-requisites of social order, the fundamentally different aspects of human motivation and social equilibrium, the fundamental limits that are placed upon the actor in his situation.

The Social System is Parsons' book on fundamentals. Like *Towards a General Theory of Action* it is a work *in* theory, not a work of scholarship 'in the conventional sense'. The outline of his own organon will provide the necessary foundation upon which to promote further deductive rigour in the study of society.

With the documentation of the 'pattern variables' at the end of Chapter II, Parsons had opened up another analytical area for his investigation: the structure of the social system. These three chapters (II, IV and V) culminate in the documentation of the 'Principal Types of Social Structure', as four distinct patterns. The patterns, derived from 'The Pattern Alternatives of Value Orientation' (the pattern-variables), provide a framework for the systematic comparison between and within empirical societies (T. Parsons 1951: 200). The full implications are not spelled out in *The Social System*, but Parsons claims that it is a beginning which seems to overcome the failures of 'the older evolutionary sociology' (ibid.: 182). It is a schematic, introductory sketch.

Clearly Chapters I to V present a new analytical integration, but they also demonstrate a clear continuity in intention with his previous writings. He had been aiming towards a general theoretical framework for the analysis and comparison of societies and social processes. Having set out the framework, he needed to spell out the implications. Chapter VI ('The Learning of Social Role-Expectations and the Mechanisms of Socialization of Motivation'), Chapter VII ('Deviant Behavior and the Mechanisms of Social Control'), Chapter VIII ('Belief Systems and the Social System: The Problem of the "Role of Ideas" ') and Chapter IX ('Expressive Symbols and the Social System: The Communication of Affect'), should be seen as refined applications in specialist areas of the theoretical organon with which he worked between 1937 and 1951. There is an important sense in which Parsons' empirically oriented theorizing always led him to test the general theory in specialist application; he also used the specialist application to develop the general level of analysis further. The sociological analyses of socialization, religion, knowledge and science, deviance and social control, art and culture, and sexuality are all developed in terms spelled out in the 'analytical' chapters. The culmination in *The Social System* is the *integration* of a frame of reference from which all these 'specialist' areas can begin to generate their own analytical precision.

Chapter XI on 'The Processes of Change in Social Systems' is a respecification of Parsons' opting for a structural–functional level of analysis of human action. The specification of the relatively constant background of non-change must precede the theoretical explanation of social change.

Finally, Chapter XII rounds out the formulation of the sociological organon by placing sociological theory among the sciences of action. Whereas, in *The Structure*, the encyclopaedia of the social sciences had been envisaged with political science and economics as potential contributors to the theory of action on a common level with sociology, the priority in *The Social System* points to sociology, cultural anthropology and social psychology as constituting an 'inner core' of action disciplines. This, no doubt, relates to the reorganization among the social sciences at Harvard in the early 1940s. It also highlights a specific instance where Parsons' theoretical development was closely tied into that temporal system of human action known as university organization.

The specialist sociological applications of the general theory had occupied him all along. His 'incurable theorizing' was motivated, in large part, by the incredible and immense diversity of human reality; the application was held 'in limbo' until he was satisfied that the theoretical tools had been fashioned to do what was required. *The Social System* signalled the point at which the peak of this confidence was reached. But in this transition 'General Theory' also became his *specialist* concern. The empirical character of theory in *The Structure* had reached its culmination in the arrival of a specialist general theory of the social system. What he had left to 'another time' in his Amherst essays of 1922/3 had, finally, come into its own.

Conclusion

The difficulties encountered in reading *The Social System* can in large measure be attributed to Parsons' synoptic vision of action – his ability to articulate the theory from the respective standpoints of personality, society and culture. *The Social System* is an analytical and interdisciplinary approach to the general theory of sociology. Parsons' works in the 1940s demonstrate his attempts to argue the theory from all sides, and to learn from all possible approaches.

No doubt the exercise was laced with a degree of frustration. 'Actor, Situation and Normative Pattern', as an initial attempt to 'bring it all together', had not succeeded. It remained uncompleted, and lacked the sustained theoretical and analytical overview which had been envisaged in *The Structure*. But it had begun the process.

The incorporation of Freud into his canon of classics (T. Parsons 1949b) became coincidental with his own wrestling with psychoanalysis. His introduction to psychoanalysis was intertwined with 'some personal reasons for seeking psychotherapeutic help' (T. Parsons 1970: 840). It is indicative of the analytical single-mindedness of this 'incurable theorist' that he could not separate himself from the *analytical residues* that accrued in that clinical experience.

'Actor, Situation and Normative Pattern' (1939/40) and *The Social System: Structure and Function* (1949/50), as early drafts of the definitive work, give hints of the breadth and depth of analytical detail which were part of Parsons' vision for general theory.

Parsons was eager to contribute to the social science professions. In simple terms he wanted to help. And *The Social System* as a course of rational action in which ego anticipates alter's reaction to ego's possible action embodies Parsons' response to the anticipated reaction of the professional community to his work. As an answer to the questions which would be raised about it, *The Social System* was also an attempt to recast the basic question of sociology. In this sense it was both a defence and an attack. *The Social System* was Parsons' sociological Question, the documentation of his long-term goal.

When he traced the emergence of the theory of action, theory itself had become an evolving 'organism' which was subject to its own evolutionary god: Science (T. Parsons 1937a: 41). But the *analytical* formulation of this 'organism' could not be achieved whilst the theory of theory was formulated solely in terms of developmental/physiological analogies. The formulation of the general theory had to be analytically separated from its historical evolution in the history of social thought. In his writing he progressively 'disengaged' his theory from any historicist interpretation which could result if *The Structure* were viewed as the end of the matter. In this sense the documented discoveries of *The Structure of Social Action* came to be interpreted by Parsons as his attempt to prepare social science community for the fully elaborated organon. His 'Empirically Verified Conclusions' in Chapter XVIII of *The Structure* were his experimental results – the discovery of a *non-empiricist* approach. The format for *The Structure* accommodated his theory to the empiricist standards which were then acceptable to the scientific community (T. Parsons 1970: 829–31).

The question which emerges about ASNP concerns his use of the organism–environment analogy to order his explanation of the theory of action. It seems as if, on the one hand, Parsons were trying to convey the complexity of his great idea by using a simple analogy pragmatically for pedagogical purposes. On the other hand, there is the sense in which he was wrestling with the character of theory itself.

The self-conscious use of the organism–environment analogy in ASNP derived from a desire to keep the seamless web of theory integrated, in its subjective and conceptual aspects. The theory of theory and the theory of action, both discussed in terms of this analogy, could be viewed as of one piece. But the breadth and depth of social reality could not be incorporated into such a scheme as it was. In *The Social System* the dimension of methodological self-consciousness is not as explicit. But the first two chapters can without any distortion be read as a commentary on Parsons' own process of rational action in the 1940s as he laboured on his statement. It was not until he had clearly made the transition to the concept of the analytical system, which reaffirmed his commitment to the autonomy of theoretical thought, that he was able to formulate his 'engine of analysis' (T. Parsons 1929: 33–4; see also 1928: 643–4) in a way that he considered satisfactory.

We can conclude that the twelve chapters of *The Social System* are organized so as to illustrate Parsons' overall approach. The first five develop the conceptual scheme for the analysis of social structure, the next six are concerned with social process, and the final chapter demonstrates the conti-nuity of Parsons' work in the theory of action. The last chapter recalls the last chapter of *The Structure*, where he had alerted the professional audience to 'convergence' and the tasks which lay ahead. He concludes the book by quoting the final paragraph of the 1937 work.

> 'It is not, therefore, possible to concur in the prevailing pessimistic judgement of the social sciences, particularly sociology ... Notable progress on both empirical and theoretical levels has been made in the short space of a generation. We have sound theoretical foundations on which to build.'
>
> This statement seems to have been amply justified by the event. Further empirical progress has certainly been made in the intervening years with many students contributing to it. Similarly on the theoretical side, which has been our concern in the present book. *The Structure of Social Action* proved, as it was hoped that it would be, only a beginning. If the theory of the social system had not advanced notably since it was written, the present book would not have been possible. By the same token, the present effort is only a link in a much longer chain. We can have full confidence that many further links will be forged, and soon.
>
> (T. Parsons 1951: 555)

Whilst *The Social System* is throughout 'a theoretical work in a strict sense' (ibid.: 3), the first 'structural' half stands to the 'process' half in a way reminiscent of 'theory's' orientation to 'practice'. 'The descriptive level' of social action is illustrated by the 'process' chapters (Chapters 6–11). The 'descriptive level' is present in the first half of the book in the 'Principal Types of Social Structure'. This involves the analysis of the 'empirical differentiation' in the structure of societies. In both halves the theoretical slant of the book shows that Parsons had, during the 1940s, incorporated much by way of empirical sociological research findings into his ongoing project of theory-building. In that sense he sought to build a general theory of action systems which was 'open' to new developments. This 'openness' led him, as in the final statement quoted above, to profess bold confidence in the future of his work.

PART 5
Parsons' theory as it stood at 1951

11
Conclusion

Interpretative difficulties and theoretical problems

A detailed exegesis of Parsons' theory in *The Social System* could have provided the content for the previous chapter. The detailed exegesis of what Parsons wrote was vital for writing this book. I found that I could not come to terms with *The Social System* in the way Parsons seems to have wanted it to be read, *without writing down my own response to his work as I read it*. And this 'discovery' confirmed my view of that work as an experimental record – an account of Parsons' 'thinking in progress'. *The Social System* in this sense is a consistent development of 'The Theory of Human Behavior in its Individual and Social Aspects' (T. Parsons 1922). And having established that essential continuity I could then read his 'major exposition' in terms of what had preceded it.

This chapter and the previous one have been the most difficult to write. The previous chapter, no doubt, is very difficult to read. Seen only in terms of its 'development', against the background of earlier statements, *The Social System* appears to be little more than a laborious commentary on how Parsons 'tuned up' for new major works. For Parsons, publication of his 'thinking in progress' was a convenient analytical sign-post. But *The Social System* established his pre-eminence in twentieth-century sociology. As such it needs to be treated as a work in its own terms and not simply as a 'development'.

Parsons' theory in *The Social System* will appear 'flat' until it is realized that it was the documentation of the basic idea that had been guiding his theorizing all along, or at least since the discovery of 'convergence'. It was also his attempt to *develop* that idea in interaction with the thought of his time – pre-eminently the anticipated and actual responses of his fellow social science professionals. The initial discovery had been synthesized in the crucible of recent European thought. Everything after that was a matter of formulation, 'revisiting' and then extension.

The analysis that I have set forth has shown how *The Social System* was anticipated by his early writings. His thirty years' work culminated in this most famous publication, and in turn became the springboard for another twenty-eight years' work on theory, the system of modern societies and the human condition.

The Social System became identified with that mode of sociological theory known as structural functionalism. What prior to 1951 was the *end* for which he had been striving for so long became, after its publication, another *means* to a yet greater and more comprehensive end. It raised new theoretical problems which required new avenues of investigation. Parsons himself did not consider his work to be finished. It was not formulated along conventional lines. His writings were not scholarship in the traditional sense, but set forth for 'the use and critical reaction of members of the sociological and related professions' (T. Parsons 1949/50: 1).

In taking a chronological approach to Parsons' theory I have attempted to reconstruct the process by which the major components of his theory came together. In that sense the sequence of development which I have outlined sometimes seems to cut across the logical sequence which Parsons had devised for the exposition of the theory. Parsons' theory has been read as a process of action and its development analysed in terms of its sequential disclosure *over time*. I took this approach specifically for the purpose of developing an immanent critique of the theory of this 'incurable theorist' of action. But this could only be done if I doubted Parsons' theoretical view of the relationship between theory, action and time.

> A scientific problem is one of bringing into coherent relations data, all observed *in the past* by the scientist. But an end of action is not to the actor something observed as having happened. It is the anticipation of a future state of affairs. While a scientific theory (not necessarily the phenomena it explains) is timeless, a course of rational action is by its very essence something spread over time. Hence any theory of action which squeezes out this time element is fundamentally objectionable. It can only be done by somehow denaturing the factor of ends. This is generally done by trying to assimilate them to the category of 'given data', as seen by the actor.
>
> (T. Parsons 1934a: 514)

Theory, for Parsons, somehow transcends time whereas action does not. The timelessness of scientific theory contrasts with the time-boundedness of a course of rational action. But this may, in fact, place theory in a special relationship to culture systems, which, as he pointed out in *The Structure*, were distinguished from action- and physical-systems by their 'non-temporality' since they were 'not involved in process'. They exist in the minds of individuals or are '"embodied" in systems of symbols the "understanding" of which implies a mind' (T. Parsons 1937a: 763, n. 2). But what of that rational action he engaged upon as his life's work: scientific theorizing about action? Would not any theory of the action of theorizing which 'squeezes out this time element' be objectionable? In other words, when Parsons' theory is applied to his theory we encounter antinomy. I have postulated in my analysis of his writings in the 1940s that the transition from a biological to a systems mode of thought became possible because of the undisclosed influence of the dogma of the autonomy of theoretical thought. In *The Structure* scientific theory 'is not only a dependent but an independent variable in the development of science'

	TEMPORALITY		ETERNALITY
1.	Process	and	structure
2.	Activity	and	passivity
3.	Time-boundedness	and	timelessness
4.	Means	and	ends
5.	Action	and	theory
6.	Rationality	and	science
7.	Work (secular)	and	vocation (sacred)
8.	Writer of statments	and	author of theory
9.	Theory of systems	and	system of theory

Figure 10 The temporal and non-temporal dimensions of Parsons' theory according to the principles set out in his writings

(T. Parsons 1937a: 6). The 'independence of theory' came to be given priority over the 'dependence of theory' in his project; it was this transition which constituted the major change in his pre-1951 thought. The analytical coherence of his argument in *The Social System* cannot be understood without appreciating this transition. His theory, as a human artifact, makes no sense if we do not appreciate the progressive power which this viewpoint had upon his formulations.

How can the critic incorporate Parsons' view of the timelessness of theory into the representation of Parsons' theory? Parsons' taken-for-granted secular view of the relationship between the *temporal* and *eternal* realms is, no doubt, closely related to the perspective of Alfred North Whitehead. At this point we can detect a dualistic picture of theory's place in the cosmos.

When Parsons' theory of action is read as a theory of time we encounter his theory of theory in the distinction between activity and passivity, process and structure (T. Parsons 1951: 8, 48–9). *Structure* is the constellation of elements which is maintained through time. *Process* refers to the dynamism within reality which is indicated by the changing relationship of elements. Parsons locates *theory* on the *structural* side (i.e. relatively static, timeless constellation of elements) *as if* the structuring of elements in reality is the 'relatively timeless' structure of reality. We are bordering on the complex issues of Parsons' cosmology – this would be a worthy focus for future debate. In the mean time let us describe this fundamental dualism by listing various dichotomies that are evident in his theoretical *Weltanschauung* (see Figure 10).

The 'temporal' elements refer to a process, whilst the structural scheme is alluded to by the 'eternal' elements on the right. The temporal, as elements of human action, cannot be understood without the context provided by the elements of 'timelessness'. The left-hand side refers, in general, to the realm of human action, but the right-hand side is no less human. In this sense Parsons' world-view is somewhat mediaeval, seeking to follow a high (sacred) calling in his (secular) work. In terms of post-Reformation scholasticism he sought his vocation from within 'nature'; theory is sought from within the realm of action. For this reason his 'incurable theorizing' always 'returned' to the mundane world of action, the world of work and action. His theorizing had an ultra-mundane character.

This is not to say that his work, as a unified project, was without contradictions. It seems fair to say that he worked with these internal contradictions in the hope of resolving them in a yet greater framework in which they made sense. Though rationality and tradition are opposites, he yet envisaged *The Social System* as an encouragement to a renewed tradition of rationality. Though theory is 'timeless', he yet adjusted his formulations to accommodate the anticipated reactions of his fellow-scientists. Though science is separate from religion and philosophy, he yet based his theoretical vocation upon an unproven philosophical dogma concerning theory's self-sufficiency. Though theory is both a dependent and an independent variable in the development of science, he yet gave priority to its independence. Though science is essentially universalistic so that the value of a statement is independent of the status of the scientist (T. Parsons 1939: 42), yet it was very important in a personal sense for Parsons to formulate his conceptual scheme in its definitive form.

There are good reasons for interpreting *The Social System* as a mundane account. It is wholly indicative of Parsons' post-puritan worldly asceticism. It is not all that different from what he had written before. It is another statement, containing statements which Parsons had been formulating for many years. Yet it is his attempt to formulate, within time-bound reality, the timelessness of his theoretical idea. It is his 1951 attempt to chart the logical progress in theorizing about human action and social reality. It is not a system of theory, having reached the point where closure would be possible, but a genuine theory of systems (T. Parsons 1951: 536–7).

The formulation *is* conceived as a 'system' – it is open to new empirical *inputs* and has not specified all possible analytical *outputs*. There is an important ambiguity which Parsons shared with Claude Bernard. The conceptual scheme for the analysis of the social system is a system, but is *not* systematic in the sense of providing a system of theory (T. Parsons 1951: 537; see also Bernard quoted in Bergson 1968: 245–7).

As an American cultural artifact *The Social System* could now be presented in terms of both American and European antecedents. In his work the impetus was not only that dedication required to establish himself as a prominent theorist. It was also a matter of seeking to demonstrate that a new kind of sociological theory had emerged.

These factors have to be kept in mind when reading the text of *The Social System*. They are just as important as the ultra-mundane analytical details which Parsons worked into his narrative.

The Social System as culmination

I have tried to show that Talcott Parsons belongs to that part of the sociological tradition which is reformist, working in the Western European tradition of science. He sought to extend the scientific revolution of the sixteenth and seventeenth centuries by promoting a realistic social science for the twentieth century. His general theory of social action affirmed the importance of working within the cultural context in which sociology had emerged. As a reformer of sociological theory he was by no means an uncritical admirer of those European social theorists he preferred.

The Social System signals Parsons' emergence as the pre-eminent American sociological theorist for the twentieth century. Since 1951 sociology throughout the world has been labouring with the impact of his intellectual formulations. *The Social System* is a consistent elaboration of the various aspects of his project which since the 1920s had come to expression in his writings. Let us delineate them in turn. There are fourteen points listed here which, separately and together, illustrate how *The Social System* functioned as the culmination of Parsons' project to that stage.

The Social System as world-view

The Social System is Parsons' articulated response to the liberal-Christian world-view in which he had been raised (Chapters 2 and 3 above).

The Social System as completion of Amherst Project

The Social System is the culmination of a project anticipated in his 1923 undergraduate paper, 'A Behavioristic Conception of the Nature of Morals' (1923). It is a fully elaborated scheme for the analysis of the moral order.

The Social System as a theory of capitalism

The Social System is Parsons' scientific and analytic response to capitalism. It is his attempted ideal-type formulation of human society in its entirety, constructing the general theory which he could not find in Weber's work (1927–30).

The Social System as organon

The Social System is Parsons' fully developed conceptual scheme which rejected Marshall's intellectual evasiveness outright. It is his response to orthodox economics (1931–2), but it is also the systematic elaboration of a way of intellectual endeavour he had gleaned from the Institutionalists, Ayres and Hamilton.

The Social System as elaboration of the system-concept

The debt to Pareto (with Schumpeter and Henderson) is acknowledged explicitly in his work. They had pointed the way towards a more effective utilization of the system-concept; but it was not only the system-concept which provided the momentum for formulating *The Social System*. The system-concept was present in Parsons' earliest publications on capitalism (T. Parsons 1928: 641–5), and in that sense the Pareto–Henderson influence led to the reconstruction of the concept in his thought. With the concept of 'pure theory', a theory of systems could be accepted as a self-generating system, at once a dependent and independent variable in the development of science. This methodological a priori in *The Structure* later emerged as an indispensable, but untested, assumption of the autonomy of theory for the entire project as a whole.

The Social System as professional 'conscience collective'

The Social System is Parsons' attempt to formulate the set of patterns for habitual thinking by professionally trained sociologists. He achieved this by transforming Durkheim's concept, creating social theory as a *reality sui generis*.

The Social System as formulation of alter–ego microcosm

During the 1940s Parsons progressively incorporated the insights of Sigmund Freud into his evolving theory, and in so doing included Freud among the pantheon of his sociological heroes. *The Social System* is the formal declaration of a 'convergence' between Freud, Durkheim and Weber.

The Social System as experimental results

Parsons 'wrote out' his theory to clarify the new conceptual developments which were breaking in upon his consciousness. Writing, as an empirical result of human action, became his analytical equivalent to laboratory experiments. *The Social System*, like all of his earlier works, was inherently provisional. Moreover it was the formulation of one who had gone on from being a critic of theories to a formulator of Theory, in the sense in which he had analysed Veblen's understanding of 'workmanship'.

The Social System as personal record of analytical odyssey

In his writing Parsons conveyed an appreciation for himself as a writer. He saw his theory-writing as his own way of acting upon the world, albeit in an analytical manner. There is a constant teleology in his formulations looking forward to the time when all elements would come together in one general conceptual scheme. *The Social System* completed the task which had been left unfinished by the Amherst disruption of 1923. *The Social System* elaborates the basic idea which had also guided the construction of *The Structure*. In *The Social System* an orientation to the general level of analysis is maintained: the system of theory had *not* been contained in the theory of the system. The full reality was to a great extent beyond the grasp of theorizing. *The Social System* indicates Parsons' piety – his devotion to Science. This piety helped him overcome the charge of Grand Theory implicit in Merton's critique – he happily extended the structural–functional theory project to include and accommodate Merton's emphasis on 'theories of the middle range'.

The Social System as project for further development

The formulation, though provisional, represents analytical progress *towards* a system of theory anticipating further professional and practical research on the whole range of issues. It was also the outline of a programme for future action.

The Social System as statement about rationality

Rather than utilizing a traditional rationality, Parsons considered his task to lie in developing a rational tradition. His theory, as he saw it, was for the utilization of the social scientific profession. He aimed towards the breakdown of any disciplinary rigidity by promoting the development of an integral approach to the study of human action. Although rational authority and traditional dogma are presented as polar opposites, he yet opted for a reform of the tradition of rationality in a way reminiscent of his commitment to the timelessness of theory. The general theory of action couched in rational terms is not simply a theoretical explanation of modernity. The general theory provides guidelines for the internal analysis of discrete societies and for the comparison between differing societies, at different times and places. In this sense it transcends the problematic application of the *ideal-type* in Weber's work which had prevented him from developing a systematic general theory.

The Social System as critical theory

The Social System is, in its intention, and in basic conception, an attempt to offset reductionism of any sort in the human sciences. Behaviourism since his earliest Amherst essays had been a primary foil in his writings. Moreover positivism would explain science purely in terms of methods applicable to the natural sciences, and was thus incapable of resisting the analytical tendency of reductionism. Parsons saw himself as a consistent opponent of positivism.

The Social System as action theory

The basic concept of *The Social System* is action. Parsons derived the unit-act initially from Max Weber's analyses. It is a central building block of his entire conceptual scheme. *The Social System* was also the result of Parsons' action; theory had become fact. In its 'methodological self-consciousness' it would be fair to say that the Paretian 'stream of consciousness' of *The Structure* has, in *The Social System*, been transformed into the Freudian concentration on the relation of ego to alter. Convergence as 'residue' in *The Structure* coincides roughly with Parsons' response to the anticipated reaction of the sociological profession in *The Social System*.

The Social System as fact

Consistently developed throughout his writings is Parsons' view of himself as a theorist of action. He was a reforming liberal who saw his contribution to human society in terms of a 'calling' to do theory. This orientation, though secularized in its basis, led Parsons to view himself in terms of his Christian-Liberal background. His commitment to 'theory' was radically oriented to this world. In terms of his liberal education at Amherst his endeavour can be viewed as his attempt to provide an integral overview of the human realm. The claim of *The Social System* is that that had been achieved. There can be a unified interpretation of the human condition when human action is viewed in terms of the social system. More generally, human action in the social system can be placed in perspective when seen in terms of the general theory of action. All aspects of reality (physical, psychological, social and cultural) could find a place in relation to each other by means of the system-concept.

Parsons had succeeded in formulating his Question. Here was the articulation of the basic parameters of his *own* frame of reference. It embodied his optimistic belief in the creative freedom of theory. In this sense Parsons was truly an Enlightenment thinker (Seidman 1983).

The Social System is now a fact. This means, in Parsons' terms, that it is not itself a phenomenon but a proposition *about* one or more phenomena (T. Parsons 1937a: 41). What is the phenomenon which *The Social System* represents? It has been my aim here to answer that question. It can be done now in simple terms: *The Social System* represents Parsons' view of the fact of theory. In that sense his theory, as fact, stands for Talcott Parsons' relentless analytical confrontation with the world.

The challenges for those who study Parsons are manifold – we need to find a form of theoretical argument which will

(i) critically and textually set Parsons in the history of theory without simply placing him according to his own account of that history; his 'convergence' argument was his innovative contribution to the history of theory – what are its antecedents? Is anything like it to be found in Weber, Pareto and Durkheim? Does anyone construct 'convergence' nowadays?

(ii) promote the disciplined theoretical study of human society without the explicit or implicit dogma that human life has first to be reconstructed according to an abstract scheme;

(iii) promote the disciplined theoretical study of human society without reducing this study to the critical examination of the theories promulgated by its prominent theorists;

(iv) promote the disciplined study of social theories without reducing critical appreciation for the social theorist to mere critical understanding of the theory;

(v) find a way to respect humbly our own calling in theoretical scholarship without any mindless adulation of, or uncritical rejection of, the theoretical work that has preceded us.

This book has only begun to address these issues.

Some recent publishing on Talcott Parsons' theory: a bibliographical essay

Who now reads Talcott Parsons? Recent publishing on Parsons indicates that the former seer of Harvard is maintaining his influence within sociology and throughout the social sciences. It is but ten years since his death at the age of 77 in Munich. The collection compiled by W. Schluchter, *Verhalten, Handeln und System: Talcott Parsons Beitrag zur Entwicklung der Sozialwissenschaften* (Suhrkamp, 1980) contains Parsons' last public lecture, plus important comments and critical re-examination by Schluchter, Graumann, Luhmann and Habermas. Parsons is still being taken seriously by circles of scholars in the social sciences and related disciplines throughout the world. It is none other than Jurgen Habermas who has stated that 'any theoretical work in sociology today that failed to take account of Talcott Parsons could not be taken seriously' (*Sociological Inquiry*, 51: 3/4 (1981), 174; see further discussion below).

Parsons set forth his own sociological contribution with a clearly formulated distinction between 'theory' and philosophical–historical analysis. But 'action theory' is now being subjected to philosophical and historical criticism and the *Corpus Parsonium* is being rediscovered as an important perspective on a number of fronts.

The path-breaking analysis of Parsons' theory was that of Harold J. Bershady, *Ideology and Social Knowledge* (Blackwell, 1973). This was new and innovative within the North American sociological discipline because it treated the Parsons *oeuvre* as a body of literature with its own character and integrity. Theoretical criticism became something more than intra-disciplinary bewilderment feeding off an *ad hominem* polemic against Parsons. This style of Parsons-criticism (still very powerful in some introductory text-books) had been pioneered by C. W. Mills' *The Sociological Imagination* (Oxford University Press, 1959). It was then canonized by Alvin W. Gouldner's contra-systematic *The Coming Crisis in Western Sociology* (Heinemann, 1971). Of course, the Max Black symposium *The Social Theories of Talcott Parsons* (Prentice-Hall, 1961) had performed a most important critical task, but it was only after Bershady's volume appeared that Parsons-studies began to place his theory squarely within the context of the philosphy of history, the Kantian heritage and the cultural matrix of the North American scientific community's appropriation of European thought. After Bershady, students in sociology no longer felt compelled to go 'outside' the discipline to engage in a critical confrontation with the writings of sociology's theoretical achiever.

The emergence of a self-consciously philosophical analysis of Parsons' writings had a lot to do with the way Parsons responded to Bershady's work. It is almost as if he refused to be his own philosopher, waiting until a line of philosophical critique emerged with which he could engage as theorist. Parsons' review of Bershady's book is found in *Sociological Inquiry*, 44: 3 (Fall 1974), and this is reprinted in Parsons' *Social Systems and the Evolution of Action Theory* (Free Press, 1977), together with Bershady's reply (also a reprint from *Sociological Inquiry*, 44: 4 (Winter 1974)). This exchange coincided with Parsons' energetic work on 'the human condition' in the last years of his life – chapter 15 of *Action Theory and the Human Condition* (Free Press, 1978). Reference should also be made here to Parsons' essay 'Karl Jaspers' in the *Biographical Supplement* to the *International Encyclopaedia of the Social Sciences* (Macmillan, 1979).

The Bershady–Parsons exchange was the beginning of a fundamental reinvigoration of the sociological tradition of theorizing which Parsons had begun back in the 1930s. The *philosophical* reconsideration of Parsons' theory drew attention to, and sometimes drew upon, those principles which Parsons had laid down for the interpretation of his work in *The Structure of Social Action* (McGraw-Hill, 1937). Attempts to reinterpret Parsons' theory critically and build his concepts into the imposing edifices of new theoretical systems have now been forced to reconsider Parsons' methodological ground-work. The tradition of sociological theorizing initiated by Parsons makes it difficult to sustain a theoretical critique without recourse to Parsonian insight somewhere along the line. It is difficult to contribute critical observations without seeming to develop Parsons' 'system' beyond the limits he had already set for his enterprise. Thomas Burger's 'Talcott Parsons, the Problem of Order in Society, and the Program of an Analytic Sociology' (*American Journal of Sociology* 83:2 (September 1977), 320–34) retraced Parsons' attempt to solve the 'Hobbesian problem', and Parsons gave his reply to this immediately after (335–40). And so the philosophical reconsideration of Parsons was underway.

Both Alexander's *Theoretical Logic in Sociology* (4 vols, Routledge & Kegan Paul, 1982–) and Habermas' *The Theory of Communicative Action* (Beacon, 1983–) enshrine the neo-Kantian formulae, particularly when it comes to their consideration of Talcott Parsons: 'To understand ... means to go beyond' (Windelband) and 'The way to honor a great man is to endeavour to make his labours one's own and develop further the lines of his ideas' (Jaspers). In this sense, both Alexander and Habermas have explicitly affirmed that they are seeking to honour and go further than Talcott Parsons. Together they have 'set the scene' for the analysis of Parsons' work for some time to come.

Another substantial work is the Kantian interpretation of Richard Münch, 'Talcott Parsons and the Theory of Action I: The Structure of the Kantian Core' (*American Journal of Sociology*, 86: 4 (1981), 709–39) and 'Talcott Parsons and the Theory of Action II: The Continuity of Development' (*American Journal of Sociology*, 87: 4 (1982), 771–826). It is worth noting that in contrast to my work in this volume Münch's attempt to explain the Kantianism implicit in Parsons' *method* in *The Structure of Social Action* does not pay much attention to any *inner* connection between Parsons' leading ideas and his method of narrative construction. But to give Münch his due, the unravelling of the various philosophical strands, including neo-Kantian influences, from the complex interweaving of Parsons' theory proves to be extraordinarily difficult.

Works like those of Alexander, Habermas and Münch surely set the tone for the scholarly appraisal of Parsons. Stephen P. Savage, *The Theories of Talcott Parsons* (Macmillan, 1981), Guy Rocher, *Talcott Parsons and American Sociology* (Nelson, 1975) and Adrian Hayes, *Talcott Parsons and the Theory of Action* (Polity Press, 1986), to name but three, are indicative of work on Parsons in English-speaking countries outside the USA.

Jeffrey Alexander's monumental *Theoretical Logic in Sociology* is a work which seeks to revive the tradition of self-conscious and self-critical theory-building which Parsons began. Despite Alexander's detractors this four-volume work follows and refines Parsons' philosophy of social science as that was outlined in *The Structure of Social Action*

(1937). The difference is that whereas Parsons incorporated and modified the Whitehead–Henderson philosophy of science into his investigation of recent social theories, Alexander builds the perspective of T. S. Kuhn *The Structure of Scientific Revolutions* (University of Chicago Press, 1962) into his exposition of the evolving structure of theory in the sociological discipline. Bernard Barber, 'Theory and Fact in the Work of Talcott Parsons' (in S. Z. Klausner and V. M. Lidz, *The Nationalization of the Social Sciences* (University of Pennsylvania Press, 1986), pp. 123–30) provides a succinct and critical summary of the basic ideas in Parsons' 'theory of theory'. Parsons *had* tried to do this himself in *The Structure of Social Action*, and Barber's article points this out whilst also providing a useful explanation of the contours of Parsons' theory.

An almost totally neglected review by Gert Müller of one of Parsons' famous and important 'later' works, *Societies: Evolutionary and Comparative Perspectives* (Prentice-Hall, 1966) is to be found in *History and Theory*, VIII: 1 (1969), 145–56. This review fêtes the work as one of the most stimulating historiographical monographs of recent time. This evaluation draws attention to the transition which Antoni had charted in *From History to Sociology* (Merlin,1962) and which H. Stuart Hughes had elaborated in *Consciousness and Society* (Vintage, 1958). Bershady was not unaware of this persistently underdeveloped historiographical dimension in the examination of Parsons' contribution, and commenced his study in *Ideology and Social Knowledge* from just this point. The Müller review is also indicative of an ongoing review, appropriation and criticism in 'applied' fields (law, health care, religion, education, science) beyond the domains of professional social science and sociology. I will not include discussion of these works here; it is appropriate to mention them in passing to indicate the wide-ranging influence that Parsons' theory has had.

By the time Parsons wrote 'Revisiting the Classics Throughout a Long Career' (published posthumously in 1981 in Buford Rhea (ed.), *The Future of the Sociological Classics* (Allen & Unwin)) it was becoming clear to many scholars of the sociological tradition that Parsons' technique of 'revisiting' was not just an idiosyncratic side-issue. It was an attempt to build theory whilst keeping in closest possible contact with the classics. It was this which had lain dormant at the heart of Merton's disagreement with Parsons all those years; see R. K. Merton, 'Comment', in *American Sociological Review*, 13 (1948), 164–8 in response to Parsons' 'The Position of Sociological Theory', *American Sociological Review*, 13 (1948), 156–64, and also Merton's more elaborated article 'On the History and Systematics of Sociological Theory', in R. K. Merton, *On Theoretical Sociology* (Free Press, 1967, pp. 1–38).

Human Studies, 3:4 (October 1980) focusses upon Parsons' contribution to and involvement with the phenomenological tradition of social philosophy. The volume arose after the publication of the Parsons–Schutz correspondence in the Richard Grathoff volume *The Theory of Social Action* (Indiana University Press, 1978). This exchange from the 1940s was arranged originally with the help of Eric Vögelin after Schutz, a newly arrived émigré from Germany, had contacted Parsons about his critical review of *The Structure of Social Action*. (Schütz had suggested that Parsons should head up a Max Weber Society in the USA. Such an organization, Schutz had thought, would attract and co-ordinate the work among the increasing numbers of German social science refugees.) The exchange is supplemented with a Foreword by Maurice Natanson and also contains Parsons' 1974 'Retrospective Viewpoint'. Helmut Wagner gives his comments on this in the *Human Studies* volume, pp. 387–402.

Mention should be made here of the 1976 *Explorations in General Theory in Social Science*, a two-volume collection of essays in honour of Parsons edited by Jan J. Loubser *et al.* (Free Press). The essays are in the Parsonian style. There are important reconsiderations of the philosophical and methodological underpinnings of his approach; notable among them are: Enno Schwanenberg ('On the Meaning of the Theory of Action', pp. 35–45), who muses on the convergence between Parsons and Heisenberg; Loubser, who in his General Introduction (pp. 1–25) elaborates Parsons' General Theory; Thomas J. Fararo (pp. 90–122), who compares Whitehead and Parsons; and John O'Neill, who gives his view of 'The Hobbesian Problem in Marx and Parsons' (pp. 295–308).

Sociological Inquiry, 51: 3/4 (1981) is a volume about Parsons' contribution to the sociological discipline. The volume contains four parts: I, 'Collaboration with Parsons'; II, 'Questions about Action Theory'; III, 'Some Empirical Aspects of Action Theory' and IV, 'Extensions of Action Theory'. Habermas sees a fundamental discontinuity in Parsons' theoretical development ('Talcott Parsons: Problem of Theory Construction', pp. 173–96), a view which he shares with Ken Menzies, *Talcott Parsons and the Social Image of Man* (Routledge & Kegan Paul, 1976). Habermas and Menzies consider that the later 'system' paradigm is in conflict with the earlier 'action paradigm'. Whereas Münch had posited an ongoing elaboration of Kantian categories as the *leitmotif* of Parsons' entire development, Habermas saw ambivalence and inconsistency between the earlier and later stages of his thought.

Increasingly, writers who are critical and sympathetic have attempted to render accounts of Parsons' theoretical development which show the *integral* connection between the leading ideas of his theoretical system and the way he shaped his theory's development. In my own 'Talcott Parsons' Appraisal and Critique of Alfred Marshall' (*Social Research*, 48 (Winter 1981), 816–51) I have attempted to draw attention to the way in which Marshall, Pareto and even Sombart were incorporated into Parsons' evolving 'organon'. Attention is drawn to how their respective contributions were translated into the final form of *The Structure of Social Action*.

Hans P. Adriaansen's *Talcott Parsons and the Conceptual Dilemma* (Routledge & Kegan Paul, 1980) attempts to introduce some precision into what he sees as an extremely complex programme. Adriaansen's interpretation of Parsons' development between 1937 and 1951 underestimates the restoration of continuity between *The Structure* and *The Social System* which had been somewhat threatened by an over-dependence upon biological analogies, of which Parsons himself became aware after struggling with the formulation of 'Actor, Situation and Normative Pattern' (1939/40). Perhaps its publication will provide much more, by way of clarification, than I could hope to achieve in this book through my extensive reference to its opening pages. The exact contours of Parsons' development through the 1940s needs to be closely examined. It is a key phase in his career and open to much misunderstanding.

An underestimation of Parsons' involvement in economics has tended to emerge in the secondary literature; perhaps this has been a result of Parsons' own movement away from economics. In his own intellectual autobiography, 'On Building Social Systems Theory: A Personal History' (*Daedalus* (Winter 1970), 826–81), he admitted that it was not until the early 1950s that he read John Maynard Keynes' *General Theory of Employment, Interest and Money* (Macmillan, 1936) for the first time (845). In Alexander's fourth and culminating volume, *The Modern Reconstruction of Classical Thought – Talcott Parsons* (Routledge & Kegan Paul, 1984) (the fourth volume of *Theoretical Logic in Sociology* (1982–4)), there is not one reference to Alfred Marshall – Keynes' predecessor at Cambridge – or Vilfredo Pareto.

But François Bourricaud's *The Sociology of Talcott Parsons* (Chicago University Press, 1981) has subtly shown (p. 67, n. 16) how Parsons' important and strategic doctrine of the 'double contingency' in the ego–alter dyad has its roots firmly established in the social perspective derived from Adam Smith. His analysis is admirable in many ways, not least because it identifies in a systematic fashion the various phases of Parsons' endeavour. Parsons is viewed as a sociologist from the standpoint he had achieved in *The Structure*. The various dimensions of his sociology are then explored as an elaboration of this. But Parsons' *initial* identification of himself as a sociologist was in the late 1920s or early 1930s, when sociology in the American academy was inextricably interwoven with ethics, institutional economics and the wider encyclopaedic context thereby implied. At Harvard it was seen as an 'interstitial' general social science, a discipline concerned with matters which 'overlapped' several social sciences or which couldn't be exclusively classified by reference to one or other science. It should be stated in this context that, sadly, Parsons' Amherst essays and his initial (German) draft of his Dr. phil from Heidelberg, 'Kapitalismus bei Sombart und Max Weber', remain unpublished; a most important part of Parsons' *oeuvre* remains beyond the reach of serious scholarly criticism. This present work can try to fill a gap, and it is likely that the Heritage of Sociology Series (University of Chicago Press) will publish a volume including all of Parsons' pre-1937 published articles. That work, compiled by Charles Camic, coincides with Camic's provocative analysis of the methodological principles of *The Structure of Social Action*. It argues that Parsons got the shape of a basic methodology from neo-classical economics. He then reshaped it to suit the rising star of this 'low-status' discipline. 'The Making of a Method: A Historical Reinterpretation of the Early Parsons' is found in the *American Sociological Review*, 52 (August 1987), 421–39. Recognizing that Parsons' development is tied to economics is clearly an important insight, but perhaps no more 'new' than Bernard Barber's 'Biographical Sketch' to supplement the 1949 volume of Parsons' *Essays in Sociological Theory: Pure and Applied*. Camic works with Parsons' *published* writings, and there is a good case for arguing that Parsons constructed his own theoretical development by building upon his own published works. Camic starts with the 1928/9 dissertation articles on capitalism, and does not give any attention to the non-published documents that are available in the Parsons Collection in the Harvard University Archives. Camic argues *empirically*, by reference to what Parsons had argued in print, and succeeds in giving a picture of the 'making of the method' in terms of what it was when it initially became public, not in terms of what it became later on.

William Buxton's *Talcott Parsons and the Capitalist Nation-State: Political Sociology as a Strategic Vocation* (University of Toronto Press, 1985) makes a most important contribution to understanding the complex fabric of Parsons' contribution to American political science. He rightly points out that an accurate assessment of Parsons' work can hardly escape from Parsons' attempt to assess the vocational concepts inherent in the polity of the West. Parsons has to be understood as an activist and reformer; as a Harvard academic he may have tried to mute his personal values, in the interests of the ethic of scientific disinterest, but world-changing aspirations were a central part of his vocational self-concept.

Barry Johnston has made a most useful study, 'Sorokin and Parsons at Harvard', in the *Journal of the History of the Behavioral Sciences*, 22 (April 1986), 107–27. Peter Hamilton's *Talcott Parsons*, in the Key Sociologists series (Chichester, Ellis Horwood, 1983) divides the Parsons corpus into three distinct phases and thereby succeeds in giving a brief and comprehensive overview of Parsons' contribution in terms of what he achieved via publication. This is an introductory rather than a critical volume.

Some other recent works need to be noted here: firstly *Neo-Functionalism* (Sage, 1985), edited by Jeffrey C. Alexander. Alexander's rationale for this book derives from his desire to trace the re-emergence, or rebirth, of the theoretical perspective fathered by

Talcott Parsons. It also coincides with the rise and fall of neo-Marxism. In this volume the contribution by Sciulli, 'The Practical Groundwork of Critical Theory: Bringing Parsons to Habermas (and vice versa)' (pp. 21–50) is notable for its contribution to the long line of works which would see a new paradigm emerging from a synthesis of Parsons' theory with that of another prominent contemporary.

Robert J. Holton and Bryan S. Turner have brought together an interesting and unusual collection: *Talcott Parsons on Economy and Society* (Routledge & Kegan Paul, 1986). The essays by Holton and Turner, 'Reading Talcott Parsons: Introductory Remarks' and 'Against Nostalgia: Talcott Parsons and a Sociology for the Modern World', are worthy of note because they focus upon Parsons' *experimental style of writing*, highlighting the fact that he was also a *distinctly modern thinker*.

The names of Jeffrey Alexander, Anthony Giddens and Richard Münch reappear in relation to the revival of interest in Talcott Parsons. Together these three, representing the USA, the UK and Germany have done much to revive what Alexander has dubbed the tired discipline of sociology; interest in Parsons shows no signs of abating. In Anthony Giddens and Jonathan H. Turner, *Social Theory Today* (Polity Press, 1987), Münch has contributed 'Parsonian Theory Today: In Search of a New Synthesis' (pp. 116–55), indicating perhaps that for Münch the future lines of development in sociological theory lie in the direction which Parsons pioneered. Alexander's 'The Centrality of the Classics' (pp. 11–57) re-emphasizes the Parsonian view that progress in theory must be in line with what has been achieved hitherto. Again these essays draw attention to the historiography of the sociological discipline, and the principles which should guide the construction of sociology's story.

Alexander's contributions cover a very wide canvas, usually with his multi-dimensional theoretical paradigm in view. In *Twenty Lectures: Sociological Theory Since World War 2* (Columbia University Press, 1987), there is a strong emphasis on the way in which Parsons laid the foundations for his sociological enterprise in the construction of *The Structure of Social Action* (1937). In this way Alexander rightly shows how American sociology was built on Parsons' attempt to work with the classics, whilst also deriving his own contemporary theory. Alexander has also given an over-view of 'The Parsons Revival in German Sociology Today' in *Sociological Theory*, 2 (1984), 394–412. Here English-speaking readers are given some idea of how and why Parsons has become so attractive to German social theorists after the demise of neo-Marxism. Alexander here opens a discussion which Geoffrey Hawthorn had briefly touched upon in *Enlightenment and Despair* (Cambridge University Press, 1976). Commenting upon the American 'revolt against formalism' which saw Parsons' influence begin to wane, Hawthorn added an ironic touch when he wrote: 'But meanwhile some Europeans had been beginning to rediscover themselves in *The Structure of Social Action*' (p. 216). So it is clear that not only is the concern for the classics which Parsons had emphasized being rekindled, but Parsons' 'construction' of their ongoing significance for theory-building is still highly regarded.

Leon Mayhew has written an extensive introduction to the Heritage of Sociology volume *Talcott Parsons on Institutions and Social Evolution* (University of Chicago Press, 1982) from the standpoint that 'it is questionable that his most original ideas have ever been warmly accepted in the sociological community' (pp. 2–3). In the main, Mayhew has selected post-1937 writings, but he does succeed in showing Parsons' organon as a dynamic, evolving set of concepts, which also has pre-1937 forms.

Parsons' unpublished paper from 1948, 'Social Science: A Basic National Resource', is now available in a volume entitled *The Nationalization of the Social Sciences*, a collection of essays edited by Samuel Z. Klausner and Victor M. Lidz (University of Pennsylvania Press, 1986). Apart from the important statement by Parsons, there are important secondary studies. Part 2, 'Cambridge: Parsons and Empirical Research', contains three essays which add considerably to our understanding of the context in which Parsons was building his theory in the 1940s. Bernard Barber's 'Theory and Fact in the Work of Talcott Parsons' has been referred to above; Benton and Miriam M. Johnson give a view of the Department of Social Relations at Harvard, highlighting the contribution it made to 'The Integrating of the Social Sciences' (pp. 131–40). They emphasize the internal dynamics of this change in terms of a theoretical commitment for the restoration of empirical research. Victor M. Lidz in his idiosyncratic and impressionistic collage 'Parsons and Empirical Sociology' (pp. 141–82) reinforces the Johnsons' viewpoint, stressing the ultra-worldly, empirical orientation of the 'incurable theorist'. Says Lidz: Parsons could claim to be renovating the empirical attitude because he was neither idealistic nor empiricistic.

Finally Martin Martel's 1979 entry in the *Biographical Supplement* of the *International Encyclopaedia of the Social Sciences*, vol. 18, together with the 1980 Memorial Volume of *The American Sociologist*, provides the scholarly community with some pertinent personal reflections about Parsons' career, cultural roots, life-style and world-view. They are very useful because they give us an 'insider's view' of a man who from his prose appears very forbidding because it is so hard to fathom, but in his person was single-minded in his commitment to theorizing.

References

This list of References contains simply those works referred to in the text. Readers who would seek a more comprehensive listing of the works of Talcott Parsons, together with the secondary literature, are referred to the volumes cited in the Appendix above. Talcott Parsons' own bibliography of his writings is found in the work referred to under T. Parsons 1977 below.

Note: I have included Parsons' works within the alphabetical listing of other works referred to in the text. Whenever possible I have designated the year of first publication of the book or article in question. Hence, e.g., (T. Parsons (1939): 460) is to be found in T. Parsons (1954) at p. 460. I have chosen to do this because the sequential character of Parsons' theoretical development has been a major concern in my analysis, and I felt that such referencing would reduce possible anachronistic impressions.

* indicates unpublished material from the holding of Talcott Parsons' papers and documents in the Harvard University Archives. With such entries a General Title and a Classification Designation (HUG(FP) ... Box ...) is included. This refers to the various sections into which the Parsons Collection has been divided in the Harvard University Archives, as well as the shelf number of the boxes in which the documents are to be found. In this regard special thanks are due to Mr Clark Elliott of the Archives, whose advice has been of tremendous benefit. I must also again thank Mrs Helen Parsons and Professor Charles Parsons for permission to read and consult the Parsons Papers.

Alexander, J. C., 1982. *Theoretical Logic in Sociology*, Vol. I, *Positivism, Presuppositions and Current Controversies*. London, Routledge & Kegan Paul
  1984. *Theoretical Logic in Sociology*, Vol. 4, *The Modern Reconstruction of Classical Thought – Talcott Parsons*. London, Routledge & Kegan Paul
Amherst College, 1818. *Constitution*
  1923. *Some Addresses Delivered at Amherst College – Commencement Time 1923*
  1924. *Programme for Graduation* – Amherst College, May 1924
Antoni, C. 1962. *From History to Sociology: The Transition in German Historical Thinking*, trans. H. V. White; Foreword by B. Croce. London, Merlin
Armstrong, W. H. 1983. Correspondence
Arnold, T. 1968. Walton H. Hamilton. In *International Encyclopaedia of the Social Sciences*, ed. David L. Sills, Vol. 6, New York, Macmillan, pp. 315–16
Belitt, B. 1967. *Imitations*: Translation as Personal Mode. In Michael London and Robert Boyers, *Robert Lowell: A Portrait of the Artist in his Time*. New York, David Lewis, 1970, pp. 115–29

Bergson, H. 1968. The Philosophy of Claude Bernard. In H. Bergson, *The Creative Mind*, trans. M. L. Andison. New York, Greenwood Press, pp. 238–47

Bernard, C. 1957. *An Introduction to the Study of Experimental Medicine*, trans. H. C. Greene. New York, Dover

Bershady, H. J. 1973. *Ideology and Social Knowledge*. Oxford, Basil Blackwell

Bierstedt, R. 1938. Is Homo Sapient? (Review of T. Parsons 1937a) in *The Saturday Review of Literature*, 12 March 1938, 18–19

1981. *American Sociological Theory: A Critical History*. New York, Academic Press

Black, M. (ed.). 1961. *The Social Theories of Talcott Parsons*. Englewood Cliffs, NJ, Prentice-Hall

Blaug, M. 1968. *Economic Theory in Retrospect*, 2nd edn. London, Heinemann

Bourricaud, F. 1981. *The Sociology of Talcott Parsons*, trans. Arthur Goldhammer; Foreword by H. M. Johnson. Chicago, Chicago University Press

Breit, W. and Culbertson, W. P., Jnr. 1976. Clarence Edwin Ayres: An Intellectual Portrait. In Breit and Culbertson (eds.), *Science and Ceremony*. Austin, University of Texas Press, pp. 3–22

Bridgman, P. W. 1927. *The Logic of Modern Physics*. New York, Macmillan

1955. *Reflections of a Physicist*. New York, Macmillan

Buck, P. (ed.). 1965. *Social Science at Harvard 1860–1920: From Inculcation to the Open Mind*. Cambridge, Mass., Harvard University Press

Camic, C. 1987. The Making of a Method: A Historical Reinterpretation of the Early Parsons. *American Sociological Review*, 52, August 1987, 421–39

Cannon, W. B. 1932. *The Wisdom of the Body*. New York, Norton

1945. *The Way of the Investigator*. New York, Norton

Coats, A. W. 1976. Clarence Ayre's Place in the History of American Economics: An Interim Assessment. In W. Breit and W. P. Culbertson (eds.), *Science and Ceremony*. Austin, University of Texas Press, pp. 23–48

Cooley, C. H. 1902. *Human Nature and the Social Order*. Introduction by Philip Rieff; Foreword by G. H. Mead. New York, Schocken Books, 1964

Croce, B. 1914/66. *Historical Materialism and the Economics of Karl Marx*. London, Frank Cass & Co. (reprint)

1941. *History as the Story of Liberty*, trans. Sylvia Sprigg. London, Allen & Unwin

Cubbon, H. A. 1976. The Social System and the Superadded. La Trobe Sociology Papers. La Trobe University, February 1976

Dahl, R. 1961. *Who Governs? Democracy and Power in an American City*. New Haven, Conn., Yale University Press

Devereux, E. C. 1961. Parsons' Sociological Theory. In Max Black (ed.), *The Social Theories of Talcott Parsons*. Englewood Cliffs, NJ, Prentice-Hall, pp. 1–61

Dooyeweerd, H. 1953. *A New Critique of Theoretical Thought*, Vol. 2, *The General Theory of the Modal Spheres*. Amsterdam, H. J. Paris

Feuss, C. M. 1935. *Amherst: A Story of a New England College*. Boston, Mass., Little, Brown

Fischoff, E. 1964. Translator's Preface, Max Weber, *The Sociology of Religion*, Boston, Mass., Beacon Press, pp. ix–xvii

Freud, S. 1963. *An Autobiographical Study*. Authorized translation by James Strachey. New York, Norton

Galbraith, J. K. 1981. *A Life in Our Times*. Boston, Houghton Mifflin

Gaus, J. M. 1923. Initiation by the Professors. *The New Student*, 2: 8, 13 January 1923, 7

Gouldner, A. W. 1971. *The Coming Crisis in Western Sociology*. London, Heinemann

Gurvitch, G. and Moore, W. E. (eds.) 1945. *Twentieth Century Sociology: A Symposium*.

New York, Philosophical Library

Habermas, J. 1981. Talcott Parsons: Problems of Theory Construction. *Sociological Inquiry*, 51 (3–4), 173–96

Hamilton, W. H. 1923. Freedom and Learning (29 May 1923). In Amherst College 1923, pp. 4–14

1932. Institution. In *Encyclopaedia of the Social Sciences*, Vol. 8, ed. E. R. A. Seligman. New York, Macmillan, pp. 84–9

Harvard University, 1930– . *Annual Catalogue: Faculty of Arts and Sciences*. Cambridge, Mass., Harvard University Press

Henderson, L. J. 1970. *L. J. Henderson On The Social System*. Selected writings, edited and with an Introduction by Bernard Barber. Chicago, University of Chicago Press

Homan, P. T. 1933. The Institutional School. In *Encyclopaedia of the Social Sciences*, ed. E. R. A. Seligman. Vol. 3, New York, Macmillan, 387–92, 395

Homans, G. C. 1983. Steps to a Theory of Social Behavior: An Autobiographical Account. *Theory and Society*, 12, 1–45

Horace Mann Records. 1919–20

Iggers, Georg C. 1968. *The German Conception of History: The National Tradition of Historical Thought from Herder to the Present*. Middletown, Connecticut, Wesleyan University Press (revised edn, 1983)

Jaspers, K. 1965. *Leonardo, Descartes, Max Weber, Three Essays*, trans. Ralph Manheim, London, Routledge & Kegan Paul

Keynes, J. M. 1936. *The General Theory of Employment, Interest and Money*. London, Macmillan

Klausner, S. Z. and Lidz, V. M. (eds.). 1986. *The Nationalization of the Social Sciences*. Philadelphia, University of Pennsylvania Press

Knight, F. H. 1940. Professor Parsons on Economic Motivation (reply to T. Parsons 1940). *Canadian Journal of Economics and Political Science*, 6: 3, August 1940, 460–5

Lowell, R. 1962. *Imitations*. London, Faber & Faber

Martel, M. 1979. Talcott Parsons. In *International Encyclopaedia of the Social Sciences*, ed. David Sills, Vol. 18. *Biographical Supplement*, pp. 609–30

Meiklejohn, A. 1923a. Is Our World Christian? Sermon, Amherst College, Sunday 17 June 1923. In Amherst College 1923, 20–32

1923b. Address to Amherst Alumni Dinner, 20 June 1923. In Amherst College 1923, 48–58

Merton, R. K. 1938/70. *Science, Technology and Society in Seventeenth Century England*. New York, Howard Fertig

1948. Comment. *American Sociological Review*, 13, 164–8

1957. *Social Theory and Social Structure*, 2nd edn. New York, Free Press

Meyer, D. 1964. The Dissolution of Calvinism. In A. M. Schlesinger, Jnr and Morton White (eds.), *Paths of American Thought*. London, Chatto & Windus, pp. 71–85

Mills, C. W. 1956. *The Power Elite*. New York, Oxford University Press

1959. *The Sociological Imagination*, New York, Oxford University Press

Morison, S. E. 1936. Harvard's Past (address, 18 September 1936). In *The Tercentenary of Harvard College; A Chronicle of the Tercentenary Year 1935–1936*. Cambridge, Mass., Harvard University Press, 1937, pp. 47–62

Müller, G. 1969. Review of Talcott Parsons, *Societies: Evolutionary and Comparative Perspectives* 1966. *History and Theory*, VIII: 1, 145–56

Münch, R. 1981. Talcott Parsons and the Theory of Action I: The Structure of the Kantian Core. *American Journal of Sociology*, 86: 4, 709–39

1982. Talcott Parsons and the Theory of Action II: The Continuity of Development. *American Journal of Sociology*, 87: 4, 771–826

Nelson, B. 1974. Max Weber's "Author's Introduction" (1920): A Master Clue to His Main Aims. *Sociological Inquiry*, 44: 4, 269–78

Niebuhr, H. R. 1951. *Christ and Culture*. New York, Harper & Row

Parsons, E. S. 1889. A Christian Critique of Socialism. *Andover Review*, June, XI (1889), 597–611

1903. The Earliest Life of Milton. *Colorado College Studies*, X, March 1903. Colorado Springs, Colorado College, 1–5

1904. The Church and Education. Colorado College Series, General Studies, No. 37 (1904), Language Series, Vol II. Nos. 20, 21, 85–97

1912. *The Social Message of Jesus*. A Course of Twelve Lessons. New York, National Board YWCA

Parsons, T. 1922*. The Theory of Human Behavior in its Individual and Social Aspects. Philosophy III Essay, Amherst College, 19 December 1922 (23 typed pages). Miscellaneous Correspondence and Papers 1923–40 (HUG(FP)–42.8.2 Box 2)

1923*. A Behavioristic Conception of the Nature of Morals. Philosophy III Essay, Amherst College, 27 March 1923 (24 typed pages). Miscellaneous Correspondence and Papers 1923–40 (HUG(FP)–42.8.2 Box 2)

1925*. Parsons' copy of *Heidelberg Catalogue*, 1925–6. Miscellaneous Correspondence and Papers 1923–40 (HUG(FP)–42.8.2 Box 2)

1926*. Die soziologischen Schulen in Deutschland und ihr Verhaltnis zum Modernen Kapitalismus (4 typed pages). Miscellaneous Correspondence and Papers 1923–40 (HUG(FP)–42.8.2 Box 1)

1927*. Der Kapitalismus bei Sombart und Max Weber. Inaugural-Dissertation zur Erlangung der Doktorwuerde, einer hohen philosophischen Fakultaet der Ruperto-Carola Universitaet zu Heidelberg (114 typed pages – less one (113)). Miscellaneous Correspondence and Papers 1923–40 (HUG(FP)–42.8.2 Box 1)

1928. 'Capitalism' in Recent German Literature: Sombart and Max Weber I. *Journal of Political Economy*, 36: 6, 641–61

1929. 'Capitalism' in Recent German Literature: Sombart and Max Weber II. *Journal of Political Economy*, 37: 1, 31–51

1930. Translator's Preface to Max Weber 1930, pp. ix–xi

1931. Wants and Activities in Marshall. *Quarterly Journal of Economics*, 46: 101–40

1932. Economics and Sociology: Marshall in Relation to the Thought of his Time. *Quarterly Journal of Economics*, 46, 316–47

1933*. Lecture outline. 3 May 1933. 7 pages (typed notes). Course material: lecture notes, outlines, reading lists etc. 1930s–1960s (HUG(FP)–15.65 Box 1)

1934. Some Reflections on 'The Nature and Significance of Economics'. *Quarterly Journal of Economics*, 48, 511–45

1934b. Thrift. *Encyclopaedia of the Social Sciences (ESS)*, ed. E. R. A. Seligman, Vol. 14, New York, Macmillan, pp. 623–6

1934c. Sociological Elements in Economic Thought I. *Quarterly Journal of Economics*, 49, 414–53

1935a. Sociological Elements in Economic Thought II. *Quarterly Journal of Economics*, 49, 646–67

1935b. H. M. Robertson on Max Weber and his School. *Quarterly Journal of Economics*, 43, 688–96

1935c. Ultimate Values in Sociological Theory. *Ethics*, 45, 282–316

1935d. Review of Pareto, *The Mind and Society* (1935) and L. J. Henderson, *Pareto's General Sociology: a Physiologist's Interpretation* (1935). *American Economic Review*, 25: 502–6

1935e*. The Significance of the 'Elementary Forms' in Durkheim's Theoretical Development. Mimeo, 6 pages. Unpublished manuscripts *c.* 1929–67 (HUG(FP)–42.41 Box 1)

1936a. On Certain Sociological Elements in Professor Taussig's Thought. In J. Viner (ed.), *Explorations in Economics: Notes and Essays in Honor of F. W. Taussig*. New York, Howard Fertig, pp. 359–79

1936b. Review of V. Pareto, *The Mind and Society*. *American Sociological Review*, 1, 139–48

1936c. Pareto's General Analytical Scheme. *Journal of Social Philosophy*, 1, 244–62

1936d. Review of A. von Schelting, *Max Weber's Wissenschaftslehre* (1935). *American Sociological Review*, 1, 675–81

1937a. *The Structure of Social Action: A Study in Social Theory with Special Reference to a Group of Recent European Writers*. New York, McGraw-Hill

1937b*. The Unity of Contemporary Social Theory. Lecture notes, 25 August 1937 (13 typed pages). Unpublished manuscripts c. 1929–67 (HUG(FP)–42.41 Box 2)

1937c. Education and the Professions. *Ethics*, 47, 365–9

1937d. Georg Simmel and Ferdinand Tonnies: Social Relationships and the Elements of Action. Unpublished draft, Chapter XVIII, for T. Parsons 1937a (28 typed pages). Unpublished manuscripts *c.* 1929–67 (HUG(FP)–42.41 Box 2)

1938a*. Untitled typed manuscript beginning: 'The most promising basis for the systematization of social theory seems to be …' (date approximate; 3 typed pages). Unpublished manuscripts *c.* 1929–67 (HUG(FP)–42.41 Boxes 1–2) or Manuscripts of articles and essays 1937–*c.* 1970 (HUG(FP)–42.45.4 Box 1)

1938b. Nazis Destroy Learning; Challenge Religion. *The Radcliffe News*, 23 November 1938

1938c. New Dark Ages Seen if Nazis Should Win. *Boston Evening Transcript*, 28 September 1938

1938d. The Role of Theory in Social Research. *American Sociological Review*, 3: 1, 13–20

1939. The Professions and Social Structure. In T. Parsons (1954), 34–49

1939/40*. Actor, Situation and Normative Pattern (date approximate, 175 typed pages). Manuscripts of articles and essays 1937–*c.* 1970 (HUG(FP)–42.45.4 Box 1) (German translation by Harold Wenzel published by Suhrkamp Verlag, 1986)

1940. The Motivation of Economic Activities. In T. Parsons 1954, 50–68 (see F. H. Knight 1940 and Parsons' reply to Knight in *Canadian Journal of Economics and Political Science*, 6: 3, August 1940, 466–72)

1945. The Present Position and Prospects of Systematic Theory in Sociology. In T. Parsons 1954, 212–37

1946. The Science Legislation and the Role of the Social Sciences. *American Sociological Review*, xi, 6 December 1946, 653–66

1948a. The Position of Sociological Theory. Paper read before the annual meeting of the American Sociological Society, New York City, 28–30 December 1947. *American Sociological Review*, 13, 156–71

1948b. Social Science: A Basic National Resource. Paper submitted to the Social Science Research Council, 1948. In S. Z. Klausner and V. M. Lidz (eds.), *The Nationalization of the Social Sciences*. University of Pennsylvania Press, 1986

1949a. Preface to Second Edition of *The Structure of Social Action* (1949), pp. A–F

1949b. The Rise and Decline of Economic Man. *Journal of General Education*, 1949: 4, 47–53

1949/50*. The Social System: Structure and Function (date approximate) – an extensive draft, 500+ pp. Manuscripts of articles and essays 1937–*c*. 1970 (HUG(FP)–42.45.4 Box 3)

1950. The Prospects of Sociological Theory. Presidential address read before the meeting of the American Sociological Society in New York City, December 1949. In T. Parsons 1954, 348–69 (first published in *American Sociological Review*, 15, 1950, 3–16)

1951. *The Social System*. New York, Free Press

1954. *Essays in Sociological Theory*, revised edn. New York, Free Press

1957. The Distribution of Power in American Society. Reprinted in T. Parsons, *Politics and Social Structure*, New York, Free Press, 1969, pp. 185–203

1959. A Short Account of my Intellectual Development. *Alpha Kappa Deltan*, 29, Winter 1959, 3–12

1961a. Some Considerations Towards a Theory of Social Change. *Rural Sociology*, 26: 3, 219–39

1961b. The Point of View of the Author. In Max Black (ed.), *The Social Theories of Talcott Parsons*. Englewood Cliffs, NJ, Prentice-Hall, 311–63

1961c. Introduction to Herbert Spencer, *The Study of Society*. Ann Arbor Paperbacks, University of Michigan, pp. v–x

1970. On Building Social Systems Theory: A Personal History. *Daedalus*, Winter 1970, 826–81

1971. *The System of Modern Societies*. Englewood Cliffs, NJ, Prentice-Hall

1973. *The American University*, with Gerald M. Platt. Cambridge, Mass., Harvard University Press

1974. Review of H. J. Bershady, *Ideology and Social Knowledge*. In T. Parsons 1977b, 122–34

1977. On Building Social Systems Theory: A Personal History (revised). In Talcott Parsons, *Social Systems and the Evolution of Action Theory*. New York, Free Press, pp. 22–76

1978. *Action Theory and the Human Condition*. New York, Free Press

1979. Karl Jaspers. In *Biographical Supplement to the International Encyclopaedia of the Social Sciences*, ed. David L. Sills. New York, Macmillan, pp. 341–5

1981. Revisiting the Classics Throughout a Long Career. In B. Rhea (ed.), *The Future of the Sociological Classics*. London, Allen & Unwin, pp. 183–94

Parsons, T. and Barber, B. 1948. Sociology 1941–1948. *American Journal of Sociology*, 52, January 1948: 4, pp. 245–57

Parsons, T. and Cutler, A. T. 1923. A Word from Amherst Students. The New Student, 3: 3, 20 October 1923, 6–7

Parsons, T. and Henderson, L. J. 1939*. Miscellaneous correspondence and papers 1923–40 (HUG(FP)–42.8.2 Box 2)

Parsons, T. and Homan, P. T. 1932*. Miscellaneous correspondence and papers 1923–40 (HUG(FP)–42.8.2 Box 2)

Parsons, T. and Knight, Frank H. 1930–45*. Miscellaneous correspondence and papers 1923–40 (HUG(FP)–42.8.2 Box 2)

Parsons, T. and Manthey-Zorn, O. 1925/6*. Miscellaneous correspondence and papers 1923–40 (HUG(FP)–42.8.2 Box 2)

Parsons, T. and Shils, E. A. 1951. Values, Motives and Systems of Action. In Parsons and Shils 1951, 45–275

Parsons, T. and Shils, E. A. (eds.). 1951. *Towards a General Theory of Action.* New York, Harper & Row

Parsons, T. and Vogelin, E. 1941*. Correspondence and related papers *c.* 1930–59 (HUG(FP)–15.2 Box 23)

Persons, S. 1963. Introduction to William Graham Sumner, *Social Darwinism: Selected Essays.* Englewood Cliffs, NJ, Prentice-Hall

Plantinga, T. 1979. Dilthey's Philosophy of the History of Philosophy. In J. Kraay and A. Tol (eds.), *Hearing and Doing.* St Catherines, Ontario, Paideia, pp. 199–214

Prettyman, V. 1915. Ideals of the Horace Mann School for Boys. *Teacher's College Record,* XVI, 107ff.

Ringer, F. K. 1969. *The Decline of the German Mandarins: The German Academic Community 1890–1933.* Cambridge, Mass., Harvard University Press

Robertson, H. M. 1933. *Aspects of the Rise of Economic Individualism – a Criticism of Max Weber and his School.* Cambridge, Cambridge University Press

Salin, E. *Geschichte der Volkswirtschaftslehre.* Berlin, 1932

Schluchter, W. 1980. Statt einer Einleitung – Ansprache zur Eroffnung des wissenschaftlichen Kolloquiums zu ehren von Talcott Parsons. In W. Schluchter (ed.), *Verhalten, Handeln und System: Talcott Parsons Beitrag zur Entwicklung der Sozialwissenschaften.* Frankfurt am Main, Suhrkamp, pp. 9–15

Seckler, D. 1975. *Thorstein Veblen and the Institutionalists – a Study in the Social Philosophy of Economics.* Foreword by Lord Robbins. London, Macmillan

Seidman, S. 1983. *Liberalism and the Origins of European Social Theory.* Berkeley, University of California Press

Skinner, B. F. 1976. *Particulars of My Life.* New York, Knopf

Smith, A. 1793. Of the Principle Which Gives Occasion to the Division of Labour. In T. Parsons, E. A. Shils, K. Naegele and J. Pitts (eds.), *Theories of Society: Foundations of Modern Sociological Theory,* one-volume edn. New York, Macmillan, 1965, pp. 104–5

Sorokin, P. A. 1928. *Contemporary Sociological Theories.* New York, Harper & Row

1963. *A Long Journey.* New Haven, Conn., College and University Press

Spengler, O. 1918. *Der Untergang des Abendlandes.* Munich, C. H. Beck'sche Verlag

Stouffer, S. S. et al. 1949. *The American Soldier,* Vol. 1. Princeton, Princeton University Press

Sumner, W. G. 1906. On the Mores. In T. Parsons, E. A. Shils, K. Naegele and J. Pitts (eds.), *Theories of Society: Foundations of Modern Sociological Theory,* one-volume edn. New York, Macmillan, 1965, pp. 1037–46

Wearne, B. C. 1978. *The Development of The Structure of Social Action in the Early Writings of Talcott Parsons.* M. Soc. Sc. thesis, University of Waikato. Hamilton, NZ

1981. Talcott Parsons' Appraisal and Critique of Alfred Marshall. *Social Research,* 48, Winter 1981, 816–51

Weber, M. 1904/5. Die protestantische Ethik und der Geist des Kapitalismus. *Archiv fur Sozialwissenschaft und Sozialpolitik,* 1904 (1–54); 1905 (1–109)

1922. *Gesammelte Aufsatze zur Religionssoziologie* J. C. B. Mohr, (Paul Siebeck), Tübingen

1930. *The Protestant Ethic and the Spirit of Capitalism.* Foreword by R. H. Tawney; trans. Talcott Parsons. London, Allen & Unwin

1946. *From Max Weber: Essays in Sociology.* Translated and edited by H. H. Gerth and C. W. Mills. New York, Oxford University Press

1947. *The Theory of Social and Economic Organization.* Translated by A. M. Henderson and Talcott Parsons; edited with an introduction by Talcott Parsons. New York, Oxford University Press

Weisskopf, V. 1984. Niels Bohr, the Quantum and the World. *Social Research*, 51, 3, Autumn 1984, 583–608

Whitehead, A. N. 1925. *Science and the Modern World*. New York, Macmillan

Wolters, A. M. 1979. On Vollenhoven's Problem-Historical Method. In J. Kraay and A. Tol (eds.), *Hearing and Doing: Philosophical Essays Dedicated to H. Evan Runner*. St Catherine's, Ont., Paideia, pp. 231–62

Index of names

Index of Parsonian concepts

The various terms in this index are conceptual; they are meant to be indicative rather than exhaustive. The aim here is to allow the reader to trace the important Parsonian concepts from their earliest formulations.